C IS FOR COLORED

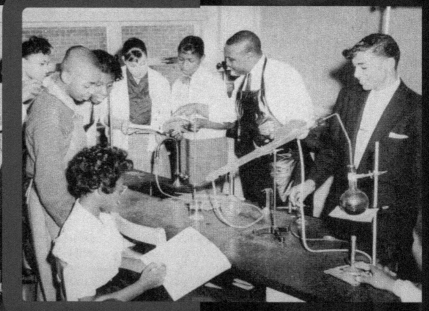

LARRY J. FORD, M.D.

Library of Congress Control Number: 2022916811
ISBN-13:   Paperback: 978-1-64749-830-6
             Hardcover   978-1-64749-832-0
             ePub: 978-1-64749-831-3

Printed in the United States of America

GoToPublish LLC
1-888-337-1724
www.gotopublish.com
info@gotopublish.com

This book is dedicated to the memory of Mercy D. Robinson Griffin, my mother; to Miss Isabel, Mister Elias and Miss Karina; and to the wonderful teachers of the Havre de Grace Colored and Consolidated Schools.

And a special thank you to the science mavens of The National Institutes of Health.

ACKNOWLEDGMENTS:

The heroic women in my life: from family members, teachers, to family and personal friends, they have influenced or provided my perspective on most things of importance and substance. They showed me that I have a foundation, why it was built, and what it is for.

Mom: for being you, which was more than enough, and smarter than I could ever be.

Patricia: for being the consummate scholar, protective big sister, and academic beacon

Mrs. Addie Lee Haley: my grandmother and spiritual center of our family

Mrs. Susie Dean Haley: my great grandmother, for the Cherokee handy fearlessness and guile.

Mrs. Margaret Cason: my official other Mom, and brilliant mathematician next door.

Miss Carrie McWhite: my 1st grade teacher, who taught me personal responsibility and shoeing.

Miss Cora Fleming: my 2nd grade teacher and family friend for decades.

Miss Martha McWhite: for teaching kindness, humanity and preparing me for better days.

Mrs. Elizabeth Davage: for showing me how a difficult environment looked and how to survive it.

Miss Marie McGreevy: drama coach and teacher, who wanted to cast me as God in the play "J.B."

Mrs. Arlene Golbin Burns: one of a kind friend, conversationalist and life saver without peer.

ACKNOWLEDGMENTS:

National Institutes of Health: this book would not have been finished without the medical and spiritual assistance given by these extraordinary people. From remembering the expectant joy on their faces, behind their masks, before the first bone marrow biopsy, to their utter delight and surprise when they saw what their treatment had allowed me to write, and now share. You were my family during some very dark days, and you remain so, in these much lighter times.

Mrs Mabel Hart: for making me bring my "A" game always and getting me started with a solid understanding of the people around the times of the book. You are everybody's favorite 2nd grade teacher, whether we were actually in in your class or not

Havre de Grace Colored High School Museum Foundation: for being the keeper of the flame of the history and the academic foundation and anchor for an entire community, now spanning five generations of Old School and Consolidated families.

Patrick Spicer, Esq: the former counsel for the Harford County Board of Education, who wrote the eloquent and piercing history of segregated education in the Harford Historical Bulletin, numbers 105 and 107. The work provided a scholarly assessment of the period and confirmed the assumptions many in the Black community had concerning the Board of Education and Dr. Charles Willis.

Mrs. Gladys Allison: for assuring that the work of my beloved Consolidated School teachers was not in vain. And, for being on Gilman Quad on college graduation day.

CONTENTS

BOOK I

The Harford County Board of Education, politicians, and White citizens of the county had never supported adequate elementary or secondary education for Negro students, despite claims to the contrary. It was difficult, frustrating, and time consuming to receive consistent support, or money, for "colored schools" in the county. The first Harford County Colored School was built in 1930 in Havre de Grace, after many years of battle between the Negro PTA association and the Board of Education and the conservative citizens it served. Before 1930, if a Negro student wanted to go to high school, he would have to go out of the county to a place that would accept students of his race. Students would have to go to school in Baltimore, Wilmington, or, curiously, Cecil County, a train ride across the Susquehanna River from Havre de Grace. A few Negro students, determined to get an education, undertook the daily train ride to obtain it.

Mr. Leon S. Roye was the first principal of the new, small Colored School in the city, and it was the only high school for Negroes in the entire rural county of Harford. This was a situation that had been in place comfortably for decades. When the Colored School was built, the courses taught were limited, and no academic diplomas were awarded to its graduates. In fact, the Board of Education explicitly prohibited the teaching of algebra, geometry, and other academic courses, but Mr. Roye did teach it anyway. The legendary Dr. Percy Williams took the daily 20-mile train ride to Cecil County to Elkton Colored High School. Education for Negro children stopped at age 13 in Harford County, until 1930.

After his secondary education, Dr. Williams went to college at Bowie Teachers College, a state school for Negroes in Maryland, and graduate school at both Temple and New York University. Since the state of Maryland did not admit in-state, or out-of-state Negro students to the University of Maryland, the state paid the tuition of the students to graduate school in other states. Dr. Williams returned to Harford County after obtaining his doctorate and became an essential person in the battle against school segregation. It was how things were done in the state in the early and mid-1900s. In those times, equality was not openly considered, or accepted as a debatable issue.

The Board of Education had only one county Colored High School until 1952 when Central and Havre de Grace Consolidated were both suddenly built. The years of efforts by Negro citizens to soften the thick, historical White opposition, and lack of concern about Negro education, were largely unsuccessful. But something else happened to alert them to the scary, changing times ahead. If it wasn't the hand of God that moved White people to build the "new Colored Schools," they so triumphantly touted, then it may have been a federal court case that came out of Westminster, California, in 1946.

The case of Mendez vs. the City of Westminster was sending an alert in certain political circles and setting the table for the landmark Brown vs the Topeka Board Of Education case, the 1954 Supreme Court ruling that outlawed public school segregation by race. The Mendez case affirmed that denying Mexican children the same education as White children, in the same school, was unconstitutional and detrimental to minority children. Not by accident, the young attorney for the plaintiff, Sylvia Mendez, was Thurgood Marshall. The God-fearing Christian White people of the county seemed to find more reasons to build the new Colored Schools after the Mendez court ruling, than from what they had heard in their churches before it. Sometimes, fears move things when faith won't. Harford County would meet and face Thurgood Marshall in court, in the coming years.

The powers in Harford County didn't want to integrate, and they thought the two new schools would give them a little breathing room, and some cover, in the coming conflict, to continue and prolong segregation in schools. The Board argued they should have local control over the schools, and they should be free to use the desires of White county citizens to decide how to proceed, despite the Supreme Court ruling. They argued this in court, over and over again, in lawsuits, with considerable success in delaying the integration process. In 1956, a local newspaper editorial proclaimed that since a few Negro students already had been admitted to white schools, "segregation is no longer the problem," and they were concentrating on continuing the process in their own way.

Before I started school in 1957, that was the state of play, in what truly was a game of control to limit the expectations, and aspirations, of Negro students in the Harford County schools. The county was willing to use extraordinary arguments in court, and display beliefs bordering on racial delusions, to keep things the same in the schools, for as long as possible. But the pliant little colored boy the Board of Education had planned and hoped for never showed up. Instead, they got me and my family, which was a problem for them.

Artist's aerial view of Havre de Grace Consolidated School in 1957. It replaced the original Havre de Grace
Colored School in 1952.
(From the 1959 Havre de Grace Consolidated School,
Eagle Yearbook)

Image: Courtesy of Harford County Board of Education

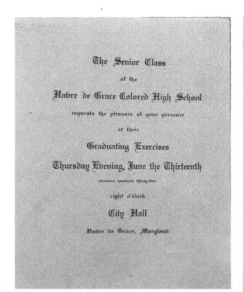

The Senior Class

of the

Havre de Grace Colored High School

requests the pleasure of your presence

at their

Graduating Exercises

Thursday Evening, June the Thirteenth

nineteen hundred thirty-five

eight o'clock

City Hall

Havre de Grace, Maryland

Class Roll

WALTER GEORGE BANKS
GRACE WATSEKA BARNES
LAURA HAZEL CHRISTY
RUTH MORELAND HALL
EUGENE HILL
GEORGE LEHMAN
WILLIAM HENRY MERCHANT
WILLIAM CARROLL RICE
JAMES RALPH WEBSTER
BLANCHE MARIE WHYTE
GLADYS IRENE WILLIAMS
GRAYSON PERRY WILLIAMS

Sermon to graduates Sunday, June 9th, at eleven o'clock at
Union M. E. Church, Swan Creek, Md.

This is a copy of the 1938 Colored School Commencement Program,
which was held at Havre de Grace City Hall.

Image: Courtesy of HDG Colored School Museum collection.

The Class Of 1932 had 12 graduates. Mr. Roye is seen standing center of the back row.

Courtesy of HDG Colored School Museum collection.

CHAPTER 1

The World After Brown

It was 1958, four years after the Supreme Court ruled, in the Brown vs Topeka Board of Education, that education based on race in the United States was illegal. Very little had changed in Maryland since that time in regard to advancing school integration. We were beginning to see how slow the "all deliberate speed," prescribed by the Court, was going to be in reality. The South was being rocked by forced integration and forced busing, with poor results so far. It seemed that Harford County, and much of Maryland, were in no hurry to comply with the federal courts or the Supreme Court, and no one seemed urgently interested in forcing their compliance. Baltimore City had integrated their schools in 1952, but advancement in Maryland school integration stopped there. In Harford County, it seemed like it was still 1952.

In Maryland, there had been no federal troops in the streets, or schools, holding bayoneted rifles, like in Little Rock. There were no irate White parents standing along the path to school, throwing objects at Black school students protected by United States Marshals, like in New Orleans. The fears and hopes were present in equal amounts in much of the country, as it once more fought against doing the right thing on race. That was the state of play across much of the country, as I started elementary school, at the Havre de Grace Consolidated School. It was referred to as the "Colored School" by the school board and many White people of the county, but we seldom used the term. A consolidated school contained grades 1 through 12, and they had not been used for White students since the 1930s.

The Board of Education had been locked in a series of legal disputes and lawsuits with the NAACP as to what "all deliberate speed" actually meant in regard to the integration of public schools. The school superintendent, Dr. Charles Willis, was dearly loved by many White citizens, and he was equally despised by Negroes, for his unyielding and unapologetic racist bent on things. He could never imagine Black and White students sitting together in the same classroom in Harford County. His plan for integration was to delay it as long as possible, sandbagging the federal courts with the old Okie-doke for as long as Judge Thomsen would let them.

My big sister, Patricia, who we all called Pat, would have to shove me into the door of my first grade classroom every day for the first month of school. I had always been her shadow, but I couldn't follow her around all day like I wanted. I missed my very first day of public education in September 1957. Mom was talked into letting me stay home with her one more day, as I pretended not to feel well, with some imaginary, minor ailment. Besides, if I had been born a day later on September 2nd, and not on September 1st, I couldn't have gone to school until the following year, 1958. It seemed like delaying going to school by an extra day wouldn't hurt anybody, especially myself.

Pat liked school, and she always had. She went to a private kindergarten when we lived in Georgia. She was ahead before starting her first day of school in Albany. She was in school in Georgia for only the first-grade. Then we moved to Aberdeen, Maryland, just below the Mason-Dixon line. There was no kindergarten program for Negro children in the state of Maryland. Starting school was to be my first exposure to formal education and forced socialization.

Every morning was a challenge for me to find enough enthusiasm and courage to survive another day and to suppress my fears of the tough boys from the Hamilton Court projects. My greatest concern was getting on the wrong bus going home and ending up there, in the projects, with no idea of how to get back to my family. It was another day to practice containment of numerous fears, real and imagined, and focus on learning how to be around other people, and getting used to the idea of eating food prepared by complete strangers. While still in bed, I could smell the cafeteria food already, like stewed tomatoes, beets, kale, and stuffed peppers every single day. I never had these foods at home or in Georgia. It was difficult to completely awaken, and then hurry to get ready to catch the bus for school. Many times I would be in bed, already thinking about school, having heard the morning sounds of the crowing roosters and the irritable, clucking brown hens next door in Miss Leona's yard. They announced that another unsettling day was here.

Our old two-story, red shingle house was drafty and without a source of heat upstairs, making the winter mornings particularly uninviting. I would get out of bed and scurry down the creaking, old narrow stairs to the bathroom, and wash up as quickly as possible, with the tepid water from the spigot. I would then greet my Mom, eat a little cereal, and try to soak up the heat from the ancient, groaning black kitchen stove, full of dangerous glowing coals. I would get my book bag, full lunch box, and head for the back door, right behind Pat.

We would walk down the narrow, pocked street that ran through our neighborhood of small bungalow houses. Only Negro families resided in our neighborhood, and the housing pattern was similar to other areas across the country, where Negroes lived in proximity to White people. It was the natural order of things at that time, just like graveyards being segregated by custom, if not by law. It seemed everything was, or could be, segregated by the law, short of reinstating slavery.

The school bus stop was only a quarter mile away. Depending on the season, the short walk might greet you with a bracing, windy slap in the face, or a soul-numbing, cold, drenching rain. Later in the year, the oppressive Maryland heat, and the unforgiving humidity of late spring, may make you yearn briefly for winter. If the weather was especially inclement, wet, freezing, or snowy, Pat and I would leave home a little early, and go to Miss Lily's house, right across the street from the bus stop, at Bill Harris' beer garden.

Miss Lily was always glad to see Pat and me. She welcomed us to enjoy the warmth of her little home and get out of the damp. She had a soft and soothing voice, with a light, pleasing touch in her hands that made you feel special, even if you were not her kin. She reminded me a lot of my grandmother, Addie, in Georgia. Pat and I would warm away our chill, watch TV for a little while and talk to Miss Lily about school. She liked watching Dave Garroway, and various baby animals that would show up on the Today Show from time to time. Or, sometimes, we would just watch the news out of Baltimore.

Miss Lily had a teenage son, Larry. He went to a Catholic school all the way in Wilmington, Delaware, and not with the other neighborhood children. I always thought he must be very smart to go to a Catholic school completely in another state, with White kids too. We hardly ever saw him, except on holidays and in the summertime. It must have been a very different experience to legally go to school with White children, but you had to leave the state of Maryland to do it. Larry was in a short historical line of other Negro students who had to leave the county, or the state, to get an education. The state of Maryland loved the principle of segregation so much that they paid for Dr. Percy Williams, the principal of Central Consolidated School, and several other teachers to go out of the state for graduate education, including Ph.Ds. Graduate degrees were not available at the state's Negro colleges, and the University of Maryland, generally, did not accept Negro students, even from their own state.

When Pat saw the bus out of Miss Lily's frosty front window, we would dash out the door into the cold, across Edmund Street to the bus stop. I would always hope that the driver wasn't the predictably unpleasant White man we had sometimes, Mr. Foote. We called him "Foots," and nobody liked him. He was big with a scruffy, stubble face and a foul attitude to go with it, so early in the morning. He clearly didn't like his job. And, I was pretty sure he didn't like any Negroes who were unfortunate enough to cross paths with him. He would just sit there in the driver's seat and glare at us boarding his bus. When he got tired of that, he'd stare out the side window until the bus was fully loaded.

One of the big high school boys wrote in ink on the back of a seat, "Foots is a Dog!" He was usually the only actual White person I had contact with all day. You could always tell when it was going to be Foots driving us because it wouldn't be a regular yellow school bus pulling into the stop. Instead, it would be the old-fashioned bus coming to pick us up. It looked like it was straight out of the 1940s like you might see in the "Fun with Dick and Jane" books. It was streamlined, silver in color, and with a torpedo back, shaped like an old man's fat stogie. It was the kind of bus you might take on a summer trip to Hershey Park, but not to regular school. The front of the bus seemed to be leaning forward, and it's diverging lines made the old heap look like it was speeding, even at a dead stop. The bus was definitely long in miles, and smelled well used inside, with a musty, dank organic note.

Our regular bus was a standard issue Yellow Bluebird. When the White kids had a bus out of service, this one was most likely resurrected for the day and given to us. It was always hard to tell what White people thought about Negroes. In their minds, maybe they thought we were used to things being in disrepair, spoiled or well used. They couldn't expect their White kids to ride in this antiquated spore and mole preserve.

Foots put the ancient bus into its grinding first gear, and we launched out of Aberdeen proper, passing White students walking to their white schools. Our bus passed one Catholic elementary school, another county elementary school, and the big Aberdeen High School on Route 40, on the way out of town. I thought we were lucky to be riding, instead of walking in the cold and cutting wind. Watching a small group of White kids fighting the elements to get to school, I would think— boy, this bus is just what we needed, and how fortunate we were to be riding to school every day. I did not understand that, in our case, we were being forcibly bused to maintain segregation, which was fine with the Board of Education and most White people. The bus passed the city limits of Aberdeen, past the brown, barren shoe-peg corn fields along the Pennsylvania Railroad tracks. The trip to school was only about 3 miles and it took only 10 minutes.

The midway point between Aberdeen and Havre de Grace was a Sinclair gas station situated on a small hill at the turn off to our school. Mr. Foots turned onto Oakington Road, and the old bus slowly plodded up a small bridge over the railroad tracks, where you could first gain sight of our nearly new, nearly hidden Havre de Grace Consolidated School. It looked natural in its pastoral setting, framed by maple, aspen, and dogwood trees. It was still looking new, though it was built five years earlier, and then only after many years of battle between the Negro community and the notoriously niggardly, all-White Board of Education. Save for a few old wood framed houses with screened in porches and a couple of newer brick homes, the school stood alone as a monument to one of the most anti-democratic of notions. It was out of sight, out of mind, down a pretty two-lane country road. It was built to keep school children in the county separated by race for the foreseeable future, or for as long as segregation was still possible in the country.

The crescent road, in front of the Consolidated School, was already filling up with yellow school buses. Groups of students disembarked from the buses quickly, to escape the raw weather, and headed straight for their classrooms. Every day I would pass the office where Mr. Roye, the principal, was often seen sitting head down, working at his desk. A little way down the hall of the old school wing, or elementary side of the school, was my favorite place, the athletic trophy case. There were medals, ribbons, and plaques from track and field, cross-country, and the venerated trophies from the Maryland State Basketball Championships for Colored Schools, which were won by Consolidated recently. There were other older trophies won from times before the new school was built. Maybe the best part of going to the Consolidated School was that, even in the first grade, you already had a basketball and track team. The White kids didn't have that.

Now, I was in the 2nd grade, which must have been a relief for my 1st grade teacher, Miss Carrie McWhite. She no longer had to risk the breakage of one of her long, pretty, polished fingernails, helping me to put on my rubber shoes on rainy days. Big sister Pat, no longer had to force me, and my fears, angst, and insecurities, into the classroom. Mrs. Cora Fleming was my 2nd grade teacher and childhood friend of my stepfather, Emerson Griffin. Mrs. Fleming also had previously taught Pat. School was easy for my sister because she was so very smart, popular, and nothing ever seemed to get to her. Pat was tough, fearless and she didn't mind fighting either. But she was a girl, and the world came at me in a different way. I followed Pat's lead on just about everything to do with school, and there was some added protection that came along with being Patricia Ann Ford's little brother. I figured that one day, I would stop being intimidated by the tough Hamilton Court boys. Until then, I always wanted to know where Pat was on the playground at recess, just in case. Recess was when the worst things would happen in elementary school.

This was going to be a school morning like no other so far for me. My teacher, Mrs. Fleming, had selected me and a classmate, Margaret, to be part of the school's official morning program, given over the often shrill and scratchy loudspeakers. Every room had one on both the elementary and high school sides of the building. Our principal, Mr. Leon S. Roye, would be master of ceremonies this early morning, and he always closed with his famous, and much anticipated, remarks about the school day, a particular event or whatever was on his mind that morning. He had been the principal of Havre de Grace Colored School, and now the Havre de Grace Consolidated School since it started in 1930. He was Emerson's, my stepfather's, school principal, as well as the principal for several of the present teachers at the school. Mr. Roye was concerned, colorful, sincere, protective, enigmatic, abrupt, mercurial, and abrasive, sometimes all at once. He appeared to be a very stressed and busy cherub, with his prominent red cheeks and mustachioed smile, running about the school halls as if he had wings. It seemed everybody had a story about Mr. Roye, since he had been the school chief at the Old School, and now Consolidated, for almost two generations.

My favorite Mr. Roye story showed his willingness to do the right thing, even in the face of the utter pettiness, spleen, and paternalism exhibited by the Harford County Board of Education. For many years, the Colored School gave out only general diplomas to its graduates. Mr. Roye, on his own, taught his students algebra when it was not part of the general curriculum for the Colored School. An administrator (a White man, C. Milton Wright) from the Board of Education visited the Old School in the early 1940s one school day to observe. He noticed that Mr. Roye was teaching an unauthorized and illegal subject—algebra. He was ordered to stop teaching it and not to teach it in the future. The Board and the county's White citizens didn't need Negroes who knew algebra; they needed Negroes who knew how to cook and mop. Mr. Roye continued to surreptitiously and illegally teach the dangerous, threatening subject of algebra to his hungry, appreciative students with all its formulae, signs, symbols, powers, roots, and radicals without ill effects on the consumers.

Mrs. Fleming called on me and my classmate, Margaret, to arise and follow her to a small room that housed the school's loudspeaker system. Our six stepping feet echoed out of rhythm down the hall, off the linoleum floors and the institutional green walls of our side of the school. In her soft, reassuring voice, Mrs. Fleming said, "You are going to do just fine. Just remember your lines. Larry, say both parts of it, not just the first part, please. Otherwise, just follow Mr. Roye's instructions." She smiled at us again and knocked on the door of the public address system room. Mr. Roye's voice could be heard behind the door telling us to come in.

"Good morning, Mr. Roye. These are my students who will help you with the program today. I am sure you know them already, Margaret and Larry."

He sat before the lighted console, with the microphone and written notes before him; he looked like the Wizard of Oz, controlling things from behind the curtain. He was distinguished-looking, a very light complected man with wavy, mostly gray, straight hair. His glasses were set on his face in perfect alignment in front of his blue-gray eyes, and he wore a neat, light suit that smelled of fresh tobacco. I thought Mr. Roye was a White man until I was in the second grade, and Pat told me differently. She said, "No, he's a Negro, just like you. He's just real light skin, like Archie Pone, who owned that candy store on Jefferson Street in Albany when we lived down there. Do you remember him?" Yes, I remembered him, and I always thought he was a White man too. I thought that's why he could own a candy store down there.

"Come on in, Mrs. Fleming. How are you young people doing today?" We told him that we were fine, but he could see we were a little nervous in his presence. Our teacher left the room to return to her classroom and left us alone with the Great Oz and his microphone.

Every morning the program was basically the same. A chosen student, on cue from the principal, would say into the microphone, "Please rise for the playing of the National Anthem." Mr. Roye then would start the scratchy, worn vinyl 78 disc, sitting on an old record player connected to the loudspeaker system. He pushed buttons and switches to make various things happen. I was looking on in total fascination at the now steady lights of the console, and the man in charge of them.

He usually stopped the record after the first stanza. But occasionally, the whole school would have to stand through all three stanzas of the Star Spangled Banner, which took more than three minutes. The still-standing students would look at each other, laugh a bit and continue standing. The joke was that Mr. Roye probably got distracted by something or went out to have a smoke, and lost track of time. We stood there until he got back from wherever he was and took the record off.

The National Anthem was followed by the Pledge of Allegiance. I never felt comfortable saying it at the Colored School but didn't fully understand why, until I was in the fourth grade. With our right hand over the heart, we all said it. We said it every day, whether we understood the caustic irony of our being in a school segregated by law, in the "indivisible" Nation we were pledging our allegiance to in 1958.

"I pledge allegiance to the flag of the United States of America, and to the Republic for which it stands, one nation under God, indivisible with liberty and justice for all."

Then the Lord's prayer was said, led by Margaret. "Please bow your heads for the Lord's Prayer." All the school bowed our heads and prayed.

> Our Father, which art in Heaven
> Hallowed be thy Name.
> Thy Kingdom come, Thy will be done,
> On earth, as it is in heaven.
> Give us this day our daily bread,
> And forgive us our trespasses,
> As we forgive those who trespass against us.
> And lead us not into temptation,
> But deliver us from evil.
> For thine is the kingdom, The power,
> And the glory, Forever and ever,
> Amen

Then finally, it was my turn for the thought of the day. I leaned forward near the microphone and spoke, in my still present South Georgia accent and annoying stutter. "Our thought for the day is...do unto others.. Ahh... others...Ahh...Ahhh...as you would have them do... unto you." I stumbled a little but got myself through it with minimal embarrassment.

Mr. Roye took his finger off the microphone button long enough to nod his approval to Margaret and me for the job we had done. We smiled at each other in great relief as he motioned to us, with his finger, to stand quietly by the wall, before he started into his famous self-styled "remarks."

The lunch menu for today reads as follows—

Hot dogs on a bun, French fries, stewed tomatoes, and stuffed green peppers

Jell-O and peaches, for the price of 50 cents for lunch.

And remember, all elementary students will have an afternoon milk break, and the price for a carton of milk is the usual 3 cents.

"And finally," he continued in an ever increasingly playful "Professor Roye" voice. As his eyes twinkled behind his black-framed spectacles, he bent over the microphone to say, "I want to congratulate Mr. Clark and the boys' varsity basketball team, who last week beat a pretty darn good team from Wiley H. Bates High School, over in Annapolis. But you boys, with your captains, Ridgely Stansbury and Early Christy, prevailed to beat a game and talented Bates team 72 to 68. That was a hard-fought game, as well as a well-deserved victory for Mr. Clark and the Havre de Grace Consolidated Eagles. We flew right through Bates, on their home court, and brought home that sweet, sweet bread of victory."

Mr. Roye went on, "Now, this weekend, we face another tough, strong opponent in the team from Harriet Tubman High School, that comes from over in Clarksville. As you know, the whole school is behind you, boys. So this weekend, we expect another great game from the Eagles. And boys, we will win the Maryland State Basketball Tournament championship again. And this time, we will bring home the BACON!!!"

You could hear the cheers, laughter, and hand clapping arising from both sides of the school. The elementary side was laughing, giggling, and clapping, and the high school side was ecstatic and nearly in a frenzy over the words they had heard from the chief, Mr. Leon Stansbury Roye. With that, the remarks were closed, and the official school day began.

1959 boys' basketball team was coached by Mr. William Clark and featured a future NFL and Super Bowl player Earl Christy. From 1959 Havre de Grace Consolidated School Eagle Yearbook.
Photo by: George Griffin
Image: Courtesy of Harford
County Board of Education

MR. LEON S. ROYE
Principal

Mr. Leon S. Roye was principal of the Havre de Grace Colored School
from 1930 to 1952, and of the Havre de Grace Consolidated School
from 1952 to 1965. He was a graduate of Lincoln University, in Oxford,
Pennsylvania, and was a longtime friend and fraternity brother, of the
poet Langston Hughes.
(From the 1959 Havre de Grace Consolidated School, Eagle Yearbook)
Courtesy of Harford County Board of Education

The "Old School" was built in 1930 at 555 Alliance Street, and the original structure was a one room classroom. The Maryland Historical Trust erected the sign to memorialize the importance and significance of the school and its history to the community.

Images: LJF/FORD/GRIFFIN COLLECTION!!!

CHAPTER 2

About C1

With that, the morning program was done, and the official school time had commenced. Margaret and I went back to the classroom with the other students to start our day. Mrs. Fleming, my 2nd grade teacher, was always very nice, friendly, well dressed, and completely prepared to teach her room of 30 or 31 pupils. There were three sections of the 2nd grade, taught by three different teachers, with roughly the same number of students. Our school was only five years old, already overcrowded, and underfunded from the start, just as it had been designed to be by the Harford County Board of Education.

I didn't know it in exactly those terms, but I was aware enough to understand something was not on the square in my environment. Life in school at the Consolidated looked a lot like the "Amos and Andy Show" on television, except every so often, there would be an actual, bona fide White person in the halls or classrooms. The person would usually be a tall man with a pronounced 5 o'clock shadow at 10 in the morning, or a middle-aged, dowdy, bow-legged White lady carrying a lot of papers, trying to smile and not look out of place. They were our overseers, in the parlance of the plantation. The Board of Education sent them to keep an eye on us, as we never saw much observable help from them coming our way. When they were in the school, you had to be on your best behavior.

Mrs. Fleming's classroom was divided into three rows of little aged desks and chairs. The desks forming the rows, like a lot of materials in the school were often second-hand discards from the other county schools. My middle sister, Pamela, would always say the three groups in the classrooms were the smart group, the dumb group, and the smart and dumb group. My goal was to always be in the smart group, but it took a lot of work to stay there. Mrs. Fleming was very helpful and supportive of all her students, whether they were not obviously smart or dressed particularly well. She had her funny side too to go with her classroom seriousness. All of our Consolidated teachers were supportive of us, but a couple had a less kind and tender way of showing it. Still, they all were on your side in education and life.

The tougher side of pedagogical love didn't show up until after the 3rd grade; that's when you got to meet Mrs. Elizabeth Davage. She was legendary, respected, and feared at the school by pretty much everybody. Getting through her class was a test of how elementary school tough you could be, and how you could control your emotions enough to stay out of trouble daily, over an entire school year. You may be lucky and get one of the less scary but equally strict teachers, like Mr. Chauncey Hearst, Mrs. J.P. Turner, Mrs.Christine Tolbert, or, the equally legendary Mr. George Lisby, at some point in your elementary education. They were all old-fashioned believers in the importance of comportment, self-control, personal responsibility, and getting your work in on time.

One day before class, a group of boys asked Mrs. Fleming if we could sing a popular song to her that we had heard on the radio. I was part of a group of five boys who sang so well that our teacher wanted to show us off to the other 2nd grade class. She took us across the hall to sing to the classroom of Mrs. Mabel Hart, who was also a legend, and she was surprised and happy to get a free show before school. We sang a Sam Cooke song, "Wonderful World," the one that goes, "Don't know much about history. Don't know much biology…." We were pretty good and confident as we performed it in front of the class across the hall. The two teachers got a great laugh from us strutting our stuff and singing our little hearts out. Our fellow students got a good laugh, too, to start the school day.

After the performance, a couple of the boys talked about doing the song at the next talent show, which I couldn't imagine doing myself. I told the boys that when my family lived in Georgia, we lived next door to one of Sam Cooke's girlfriends, which was actually true. He was singing gospel with the Soul Stirrers, traveling all over the country singing God's music. The boys didn't believe me, and I didn't blame them.

From Mrs. Fleming, I learned to be a little more social. I still asked the safety patrol on the bus home not to let any girl sit in the seat beside me. But I was getting better about that and being a little less shy. I was also learning to stay interested in things in class, and occasionally I would ask questions when things were not clear. Mrs. Fleming also made me feel that I was almost as smart as my big sister, Pat, and that was fine with me. Mrs. Fleming was a family friend. She grew up with my stepfather, Emerson, and was the big sister of my 6th grade teacher, Mr. George Lisby.

Unlike the 1st grade, in the 2nd grade, I actually had a good friend in my class, and I looked forward to seeing him every day. His name was Dallas and he lived in the Hamilton Court projects, but I was not afraid of him. He would sometimes play like he was going to kidnap me and throw me on Miss Anna Grace's school bus, headed for the much-feared Hamilton Court. He never did it. Dallas was a lot like me; quiet and he was very close to his mom. He moved away after 2nd grade, leaving me friendless on the playground. I never had another close friend in elementary school, but I did finally stop being afraid of the Hamilton Court boys.

I learned to be independent, and to realize that my mother did not come to school with me on any day, from my 1st grade teacher, Miss Carrie McWhite. I felt bad when she broke a pretty fingernail, which forced me to learn to put my shoe coverings on myself. She was a very good teacher to have first in my education. With her, you knew that your best was always expected and there was no excuse for anything less. She ran a coddling free zone. You had to do your work....period.

My 3rd grade teacher was my favorite of all time in elementary school, and not just because Pat always raved about her. Miss Martha McWhite was the serious, and sensitive, younger sister of my tough 1st grade teacher, Miss Carrie McWhite. Miss Martha McWhite made me want to do well, in large part, because I did not want to disappoint her. She had an unshakeable faith in her students' ability to overcome all the obstacles people were going to throw our way, just like she and her sister had done, while living in the apartheid of South Carolina. She was the kindest and most grounded of people, and hardly ever raised her voice in class, regardless of what was going on. I could see in her young face that she had witnessed, and been through, much personally in her life. She knew a lot about people, and even more about making do, and thriving, with what you have. She wanted to inform us early in our lives of what lay ahead of us and how to make our future less painful and more rewarding than her past.

Miss Martha McWhite never talked to us about her growing up in rural South Carolina in the very dangerous and nasty 1940s. This quiet tenacious woman taught me patience, persistence, and to look ahead for better days that were surely on the way for my generation. Whatever was ahead for me could only be a fraction of what she, and her sister, had to overcome, if not conquer, to get to her present place in life. Of course, I didn't see it exactly in those terms back then. But I knew she was there to help and protect us in any way she could, and to make us better students and people. Besides, growing up in a place as proudly Confederate and backward as South Carolina, she probably had to deal with White people that would make Mr. Foots, our foul, ill-tempered White bus driver, look like a regular archangel, in comparison. She survived and came out fine and unbent, as far as I could tell.

I learned my ABCs, penmanship, and writing with one of those big, green, wooden pencils and lined yellow paper that was so raw you could almost see wood chips still present in the minimally processed sheets. We did reading, grammar, numbers, spelling, music, and physical education during our school days. We sometimes talked about the news and current events before class. The topics would be things that happened in Aberdeen, Havre de Grace, or Edgewood that were important in our lives; something funny or offbeat, in a 2nd grade way. Once I gave a report about the fireworks factory blowing up on the hill above the town. Fortunately, no one was killed, but I still thought a building exploding close to my neighborhood was exciting, and a little funny, since nothing noteworthy ever happened in my small, country town.

We would talk about the space race, which was becoming very important in a scary way. The Russians had sent up Sputnik in October, at the beginning of my first grade. Sputnik was the first man-made satellite and was launched from Russia into earth orbit. This worried every adult of all stripes in the country. It was on television, in the newspapers, being talked about at the barbershops, and in the schools. It felt like something tremendously bad might happen at any time to the entire world. But it got everybody talking about science, math, space, and feeling sorry for the little dogs that were sent up later in the capsules, with no possibility of coming back down to earth alive. Meanwhile, at school, we continued to occasionally practice our under the desk, air raid drills to protect us from the nuclear blast and gamma radiation of a Russian hydrogen bomb attack.

I never remembered any teachers addressing why there was a need for the existence of an Havre de Grace Consolidated School, separate from the white school system. Nor was it openly addressed why our school seemed to be a repository for used chairs, desks, and, most of all, the branded, scribbled on, outdated books that we used daily in class. There were occasional pages missing, and a few of the books, and desks, were embellished with a message from its previous users, like "I hate Nigger," or some similar epithet. We had secondhand books to go with our secondhand education, which was, of course, separate and equal in the eyes of White people. The main thing was that we were separate; the rest didn't really seem to matter to them.

You could always tell the old books because the inside cover would show evidence of a pasted label having been removed and another one put in its place. But our books, old or new, had the same label that exclaimed—

PROPERTY of HARFORD COUNTY SCHOOLS.

Handwritten under that was this:

Havre de Grace Consolidated School.....C1

I was in the 4th grade when I asked my teacher, Mrs. Elizabeth Davage, what was meant by "C?" Her answer was short and direct. She told me that "C" is for colored and that 1 meant we were the first Colored School in Harford County. The only other school in the county with a "C" designation was Central Consolidated School, in Bel Air. Its number was "C2," indicating that it was the second Colored School in Harford County. Logically, I concluded that the labels previously ripped out were from a particular white school in the county and had its own coded designation, like W1 or W2, etc. That, along with its better condition, would show the book was definitely from a white school. Not much in

Harford county seemed logical in regards to the education of the races, but maybe that was.

Our teachers at the Consolidated School were remarkable, resilient, and very accomplished in their way. They were people with amazing calm, that should not be confused with a staid satisfaction from their hard won accomplishments. What they had done with their lives was heroic, in the face of a hostile southern world of dangers, threats, limitations of many kinds, obstacles, and struggles, both personal and financial. In a better time, our teachers would have been rewarded for their intelligence, talents, and determination. Some of them would have been professors, businessmen, doctors, lawyers, or the kind of engineers who did not drive trains.

Whatever disappointments our teachers had about their lives and educational struggles, were tempered by their determination to make sure the present generation of Negro students would be confident, prepared, and ready to take advantage of new opportunities coming our way. For certain, one day, even the Harford County Board of Education, and the White people of the county, were going to have to follow the law of the land and the rulings of the Supreme Court, despite their dislikes, anxieties, or the exceptional views they had of themselves, compared to other Americans. But that time had not yet come.

The safety patrol was composed of older high school Student who kept things safe in the halls and on the buses. (From the 1959 Havre de Grace Consolidated School yearbook. Photo by George Griffin) Image: Courtesy of Harford County Board of Education

Mrs. Cora Fleming's 2nd grade class included
Bootsy, Jerry Waters, Doris Durban and Dallas.
Photo by: George Griffin
Image: Courtesy of Harford
County Board of Education.

CHAPTER 3

When I Grow Up

The limitations placed upon the Negro students by the Board of Education, the White citizens of the county, the state, and the nation, made it hard to answer the most elementary of questions posed to students every day, like, "What do you want to be when you grow up?" Ever so often, even at the age of seven, I would run headlong into a limitation that adults knew all too well, though they seldom talked about it directly to their children. They never really told you why you were and what it meant to be colored in the first place. You mostly obtained pieces of knowledge as you needed it, or you bumped into it by accident.

When we moved from Georgia to Aberdeen, Maryland, we lived beside Mr. Herman Hooks and his wife, Miss Leona. They were old fashioned Maryland people who had a very primal take on food. They raised chickens, hunted game in the woods, and fished often. It was not unusual to see the woman pluck a generous bird from her yard, and, in one motion, wring its neck, then fling it flopping back to the ground. Or, Mr. Jimmy, and his brother, may be axing off the head of a larger bird just before it took a final bloody, headless flight of several feet, then landing and tumbling across the barnyard.

One day, Mr. Billy caught a very large terrapin, a snapping turtle. It looked prehistoric, dangerous, and unlike any food I had ever seen. I watched in wonderment on the other side of the cyclone fence as the father and son team wrestled with the armored reptile that was to be their supper. They made a snare out of some cord, then with great difficulty, they used a metal tool to pry open the front of the shell, revealing the blunt head of the struggling turtle. Jimmy placed the loop of cord behind the head and pulled on it powerfully, exposing the vulnerable neck. With the head pulled out of the shell, Jimmy delivered a single fatal blow with his hand ax, going through the soft neck, the hard spine, and onto the ground, severing the head. Just as the decapitated chickens had flown away before their demise, the headless turtle walked about a small patch of ground for a couple of minutes, leaking viscous, red life onto the dirt until it could move no more. And that was going to be supper for the night. These were true old-time Maryland people all the way through.

Often, I would see the bigger Mr. Jimmy, and the older Mr. Herman, come home from working at the Baltimore and Ohio railroad all day. They were clad in greasy overalls, large brown brogan work boots, and helmets. They looked like big and powerful men who appeared to be very important to me. The hardhats on their heads were strapped with goggles with lenses black as pitch. Their faces were black, too, and soiled with railroad soot, but they were smiling, revealing their contrasting white teeth.

One day, I was standing in the backyard at the cyclone fence, in the back of the apple tree with its sweet, yellow-skinned fruit was coveted and guarded by irritable yellow jackets. I was waiting for the men to return from work, so I could tell them something important. We lived less than a quarter mile from the tracks of the Baltimore and Ohio Railroad, and I could hear trains running during the day and wondered where they were headed. At night in bed, I would strain my hearing and listen as the iron behemoths that had slept all day at the end of our street finally started to creek, stretch, and groan their way to mechanical life. I would hear the steel coupler screech and tighten, one by one, down the long line of rail cars. The steel wheels would start to turn slowly on the unyielding rails, adding a pulsing, low metallic murmur to the noise of the night. The unheard power of a distant diesel tugged and jolted the cars until they slunk out of town at the slow pace of a Sunday church cakewalk.

I had decided that I wanted to be a train engineer, just like Casey Jones on TV. It looked like a fun job and not all that hard to do. I mean, how difficult could it be sitting in a high seat, looking out the window as the world passed by, driving a train? When I saw the two men coming from work, I ran over to the fence and said excitedly, "Hello, Mr. Jimmy and Mr. Herman. I got something to tell y'all." I was hoping that they understood what I was trying to say. My South Georgia accent was still thick and made worse by the stutter I possessed, and my two missing front teeth didn't help. I was hard to understand when I started talking about something important, or that really excited me.

"Hey. How are you doin' there little man," said Mr. Herman, flashing a grin and wiping sweat from his brow. "And what is it that you gonna tell us today, Mister Larry? It must be something really important, huh?" The men smiled at each other and then back at me. Mr. Jimmy walked closer to the fence and bent down a bit, and said, "What's shakin' with you today young blood? What you got on your mind?" He was tall, dark-skinned, with a working man's physique and a rich baritone voice, right out of the church choir.

I was very excited, and they could see it too. "I know what I want to be when I grow up now," I proudly proclaimed, in unbridled childhood enthusiasm. "I want to be a train driver and maybe work on the B&O Railroad, just like y'all do." Then I added, "Y'all think I can do that someday?" They were still trying to smile, but it was different. Their lips were kind of happy, but their eyes and voices were not. Mr. Herman stopped pulling at his worn work glove and bent over the fence a little, looking down at my still excited missing tooth grin, and he said this, rather seriously.

"It's good, Mister Larry, you know it's well you like trains and all that. And, you can get.....you know.... work outside jobs like us, but here's the thing...." He crouched a bit lower to my level and said, "Listen young blood, I hate to tell you, but the B&O and Pennsylvania Railroads ain't got no colored train engineers, and neva' had nun neither. There ain't no way they ever gonna let no colored man drive no train full of White people." He was laughing just a little. They looked at each other and then must've remembered what it felt like the first time their ears had received a sinking message like the one they gave me. It was an introduction to how the world worked if you were Negro in America in the 1950s. I had suspected something was up with being Negro, and the two men had confirmed it.

When they looked at the hurt and disappointment in my brown eyes and on my little face, they didn't know if it was their place to be real with me, and prick my dreams of being a train engineer. They didn't know if it was their place to introduce me to the realities, difficulties, and hopelessness that had existed for colored southern children like me forever. There was just no way I was ever going to drive a train in this country without a radical change in sentiments of many regular, everyday White people. They would have to convince themselves that a colored man driving their train was a normal circumstance, which was a very different way of thinking than how they were raised to think. At my age and with my limited understanding of White people, I did get the feeling that it would be a lot to ask of them and even more to expect of them. Sharing in democracy, and the fruits of this country, was not something they were used to doing or required to do.

To be honest, at that time, there would probably be a significant number of Negroes who would also question being in a train driven by one of their own. Most White people seemed comfortable with their lives and not aware that they had a need for spiritual transformation or change on their part. The idea of seeing a black face sitting high in a train cab, driving all that steel and power was something no one, White or Negro, was familiar with in 1958.

Mr. Jimmy and Mr. Herman told me they were sure I would find something else to be or do. Or, I could be a porter or clerk if working on the tracks was undesirable. That's about all you could do if you were a Negro and worked for the railroads at that time. "You can think about doin' something else. You got time," they said. And with that, the two hungry working men went off to supper in Miss Leona 's house. They left me alone, under the apple tree, with my thoughts, hopes, anxieties, and the irritated yellow jackets.

If I had not known it before in such a direct way, I would know it now and into eternity. Being colored, Negro, or Black was always inconvenient, sometimes confusing, and often dangerous. It wasn't about to change anytime soon. I thought there must be a list somewhere of things colored men and colored women can and cannot do, depending on where they lived, and how White people there may be feeling that day.

It seemed that in Maryland, you could be the smartest little colored boy in your neighborhood, town, or county and still end up working on a garbage truck or in jail. Dreaming big would likely end in disappointment, and obstacles would surely be coming your way, from various directions and sources, to help ensure your failure. At the age of six, you cannot know the nature of the fight that you're already in, but you know you are in a fight, in an unknown round. That was all that I could take. I turned from the fence to walk back to the house for supper, head down and dragging a little.

I was not very hungry, but I had to sit at the table with the family and eat after Grace was said. My Mom and step-grandma, Mary Griffin, who Pat and I always addressed as Miss Griffin, made dinner that night, as usual. I ate my chicken, hominy grits, and white bread, in spite of a lack of appetite, and my total disdain for hominy grits. After dinner, Miss Griffin would retire to her television room, with Pat and me following. She would turn on her large wood cabinet Zenith TV, which started with a single white dot in the middle of the screen, and it took forever to warm up.

She loved watching the 15-minute national news shows, and then "Amos and Andy." It was a comedy show about colored people, acting humorously colored, from the perspective of the White people of the time. Miss Griffin laughed heartily at the antics on the show, in which usually everyone was Negro; the cab drivers, the families, the businessman, the doctors, and the lawyers were all colored. In the end, it did show the challenges and futility of being urban and Negro, in their Sisyphean effort just to get through the day without being rolled over by it. They lived apart from the complacent, unaware majority culture of the country.

The "Amos and Andy" show was moderately entertaining, but I felt a lot of confusion about the situations the "King Fish" found himself in and the methods he used to extricate himself. I never saw a Negro train engineer on the show, even with all those other Negro professionals around. Maybe there just weren't any colored engineers since there were no colored railroads. That could be the problem.

I had gotten small whiffs of the reality of what being colored meant, in measured shocks and traumas, since I was little. I will always remember the White city bus driver in Albany. It was about 1954. Mom had taken Pat and me downtown to shop. On the way back home, something happened that became my first unforgettable, haunting memory of being a Negro.

We gathered our packages and prepared to exit the bus from the back door at the next stop. The bus came to a rest at the curb, and the back door opened. Mom was holding me, with Pat trailing, as we stepped into the door well. Mom and I cleared the door, but the driver closed it quickly and immediately after Mom's second foot touched the ground. The closed bus door trapped my screaming sister between the blunt edges. She was frantic, and Mom was yelling at the driver to release the door to free her. The driver quickly realized his mistake and released the back door.

Mom grabbed Pat from the door well while still holding me in one arm. The driver stepped out of the bus and came over to check on Pat and to talk to Mom. I was standing on the ground by the bus at the curb, watching what had happened to my sister. As Mom was giving the driver a piece of her mind on what he had done, I found myself upset in a way I had never been before. I truly believed that had I been older and bigger, I would have taken a swing at the big White man, who was in a hurry that day and dealt with the consequences later. I hated him at that moment, and I knew he was a White person. I was getting an elementary understanding of what that actually meant and what to expect from them sometimes. Pat recovered from this incident. I never did.

HARFORD COUNTY PUBLIC SCHOOLS

PROGRESS REPORT

GRADES TWO THROUGH SIX

NAME _Larry Ford_

SCHOOL _Havre de Grace Consolidated_

GRADE _3_ YEAR _1959-60_

TEACHER _Mrs. B. White_

PERIODS FOR REPORTS

Reports are sent out early in November, February, April, and at the close of school in June.

P R O G R E S S   R E P O R T
G R A D E S   T W O   T H R O U G H   S I X

SUBJECTS	NOV	FEB	APR	JUN
Reading				
Spelling	B	B	B	B
Handwriting	A	A	B	B
Language	A	A	A	A
Arithmetic	B	B	B	B
Social Studies	B	A	B	B
Science	B	A	B	B
Music	B	A	B	B
Art	B	A	A	A
Physical Education	B	B	B	B
	A	A	B	A

Explanation of Marking System

A - Excellent
B - Good   D - Poor
C - Fair   E - Failing

GRADE LEVEL AT WHICH PUPIL IS WORKING

SUBJECTS	NOV	FEB	APR	JUN
READING	Grade 3 Book - 3	Grade 3 Book - 3	Grade 3 Book - 3	Grade 3 Book 3
ARITHMETIC	Grade 3	Grade 3	Grade 3	Grade 3

Ms. McWhite's unshakable faith in her students made them want to do well for her. In Ms. McWhite's comments she noted problems with my writing composition.

LJF/FORD/GRIFFIN COLLECTION!!!

CHAPTER 4

I've Got Mine

I've got mine, and you've got yours to get. And to get it, you have to come through me."

That's what Mrs. Elizabeth Davage used to tell every one of her 4th-grade classes, year in and year out. It was her well known motto and creed. She was not a warm, nurturing type of teacher, not in the least. She was fabled, around the school, for her near dictatorial classroom management, red hair, freckles, and frequent bad attitude days. It was a rite of passage, at the Consolidated, to survive four quarters in her room and come out mostly intact. I got a perfect attendance award that year, for my feat of endurance in 4th grade masochism. She was like castor oil was said to be, an unpleasant temporary experience, but good for you in the long run.

There were two other 4th grade classrooms, but I knew I was going to be in her class. Pat was her student two years before me. My sister thought she was a demanding, tough, very good teacher. Pat told me, "You just have to get used to the way she is, stay on top of things, and out of her way. That's all." She also told me I would enjoy reading the stories about the "Tar Baby" and "Bartholomew and His 500 Hats" in Mrs. Davage's class.

The school looked a little different that year because we had a family of Filipino-American students enrolled at the Havre de Grace Consolidated School. Their father was in the Army and stationed at the Aberdeen

Proving Ground. Even though the students were not regular "colored" Americans, they were not White either. They were dark-skinned Asian-Americans, but by the standards of the day, they were "colored" enough, for the purpose of segregated education in Harford County, Maryland, in 1960. They fit into their forced school environment very well. The girl in the family was in my class and she had a couple of brothers, with nice wavy, black hair, that all the school girls liked. The older brother was in a school talent show once, singing the bass part of the popular song "Blue Moon." The girls screamed loudly for him at the show as he bellowed the protracted coda in the lowest register he could find — "Bluu-uue Moo-oo-oon!"

From time to time, the county had to face the problem caused by the proximate Army bases and its students, Black and not White, in need of education. They lived in an integrated community on a base surrounded by a sea of entrenched, historical segregation. Some of the fathers of the students were officers who did not get into the Army to send their kids to an inferior, underfunded, crowded school with no trigonometry course, academic diplomas, only one foreign language course, and little up to date learning materials. It must have been difficult and disappointing, for an educated, well-traveled, modern, non-White serviceman to be forced to put his children into a segregated school just because he was transferred to Aberdeen Proving Ground or the Edgewood Chemical Center. Some of the Army families fought the school board on a yearly basis over the segregation of their children. They were the Board's constant problem and made it increasingly difficult for them to defend and extend segregation for as long as they wanted.

But most of the students in the school were the same ones from the year before, and the year before that. There was a student from the Consolidated School who was able to transfer out to the white school the previous year. He managed to get over every obstacle the Board and Aberdeen High School, threw at him and his family. There were several Negro families around the county whose children, to my amazement, had never experienced or been forced to go to segregated schools. Perhaps, the county had a secret list of acceptable traits that would make some of us tolerable in small numbers. Admitting a few colored students would probably give the Board a fig leaf to hide behind, and make some of the Board members feel better next Sunday morning, at 11 AM.

All the Negro families had a right to petition for transfer if they did not mind putting themselves, and their families, through every indignity the Board could think of, including IQ tests and psychological evaluations. The Brown Supreme Court ruling did not call for such evaluations, but Harford County customized the ruling, in many ways, to placate their White citizens, and ease their fears of the change that was coming too fast and too soon. Mom did not want us to transfer to a white school in that climate. It was clear to my mother that the whites, in general, did not want us in what they considered their schools. Why would she put her child into a governmentally sanctioned, guaranteed hostile environment?

But my teacher, Mrs. Davage, was a problem for me. She was a problem for just about every student in the class at one point or another during the school year. I never heard anyone admit to liking her, except for Pat. She liked Pat too, of course. It was hard to see the benefit of sitting in her class and being told how lacking we were in our academics and brain power, and that was partly responsible for us being in the Colored School, to begin with. She didn't say it too often. When she did say it, it stung and bothered me a lot. I wasn't sure whose side she was on sometimes. We had enough baggage to tote around, and we didn't need any more negativity from her.

I don't think she was ever very happy in school, except when Mr. Roye was doing his traditional monthly money stroll around, to personally hand out the salary checks to each teacher. Mrs. Davage would smile then, for as long as Mr. Roye was in the room. Her modus operandi in class was discipline, intimidation, and then more intimidation. If all else failed, collective punishment for the class was her tried and true go-to move. She would tell us, "the just must suffer with the unjust," right before she handed out the latest class penalty, for a transgression by an unknown perpetrator. She made it sound like a Biblical prophecy, something beyond her control, preordained and strictly called for in her personal canon of behavior. I disliked her superior tone, but it wasn't like I could do anything to change her. She must have been put in my school life for a reason. I just didn't know what it was at that time.

One day in class, she was being particularly abrasive during an arithmetic lesson. She badgered one of the Aberdeen boys without mercy because he just wasn't getting the math concept. She was haranguing on him to excess, turning the lesson into a cudgel, with which she continued laying into my defenseless classmate. Gregory lived in the same neighborhood that I used to live in Aberdeen. He was a very nice and kind of quiet person; not the kind of schoolboy tough I always feared. It was like the teacher was taking her frustrations out on him, as she did with the class on occasion. It bothered me to see Gregory so upset. But it bothered me more to see my teacher making the situation worse, for no good reason that I could see.

At the next class break, I walked over to Greg's desk, where he was still sitting and recovering from the arithmetic lesson. I bent my head a bit toward him and softly told him if he wanted, we could get together instead of going to the playground for recess. He nodded when I told him I might be able to help with the classwork. It wasn't like I was all that great in arithmetic at that time, but I thought I recognized the mistakes Greg was making because I had made some of them too.

At recess, I gave him a couple of tips and tricks to understand the lesson better. It was a good talk, and he caught on quickly, as how to approach the problem and solve it. Both of us felt better; Gregory, for the obvious reasons of getting the lesson down, and Mrs. Davage off his back. And I, because I had a difficult time sitting by and watching senseless wrong at work. If you think about it, you can usually come up with something you can do to help your circumstance, even a little bit. I did what I could to help Greg, and he appreciated it for a very long time.

The major daily concern I had in school in 4th grade was trying not to cross Mrs. Davage for any reason, at any time. But it was difficult to keep my noisy mind from wandering off on its own in class. I'd occasionally find myself looking out the window of the classroom as random fugitive droplets of thoughts condensed and flowed in my head; are the Colts going to beat the Packers?; what is my first car going to be?; do White people and Negroes pray to the same God?; when will the bituminous coal mines in Pennsylvania run out?; is Heaven segregated too? There was lots of other interesting thought debris flowing placidly through the runs, creeks, and branches in my head. Most times, I enjoyed the cerebral free ride, but not in school, especially in Mrs. Davage's class.

The most enlightening happenings during the school year involved my right arm and getting help with my annoying asthma and tenacious allergies. Dr. George Stansbury was the town's only Negro doctor. He graduated from the Havre de Grace Colored School in 1939, with its limited math courses and no science labs. He then went to Morgan State College, before going to medical school at Howard University. He graduated at the top of his class from Morgan State, with a degree in chemistry, without ever having a chemistry class in high school, due to the limits of segregation in Harford County.

We were all very proud of Dr. Stansbury, and he served the Black community for over 4 decades and struggled to protect us from the worst excesses of segregated medicine in our community, at that time. Also, he saved my little sister's life, by coming to see her at home every day with an oxygen tent, when Pam was very sick. The hospital was also segregated and services for Negroes were limited. So, you took your chances going there. Little Pam showed her thanks to Dr. Stansbury by being deathly afraid of an office appointment, merely hearing his name, or seeing his car around town for many years.

After he had done as much as he could for me and my allergies, Dr. Stansbury sent me to Dr. Theodore Kaiser, a pediatrician in Havre de Grace, for further treatment of my allergic condition with desensitization therapy. Dr. Kaiser was the first White person I ever knew on my own. I was also playing Little League baseball with White boys from the town for the first time. I'd spend all day navigating the sometimes choppy waters of 4th grade life at a colored school with Mrs. Davage, and then have several evenings a week of baseball practice, trying to figure out my new White teammates.

I liked Dr. Kaiser very much and so did my mother. I had never been one on one in a room with a White man before. He wasn't like others I had been around, had seen on television, or in the movies, except for Gregory Peck. Dr. Kaiser had a kind of towering, chivalrous presence, that cut through skin color and superficial characteristics, to define what a good man should be. Certainly, he was not like any of the white men I still remembered encountering in Georgia. He was naturally patient and always concerned about how I was doing, and what was happening in school. I went to his office on Union Avenue for several years. Dr. Kaiser was always the same at every visit. He was never in a hurry, always organized and adorned with a faint trail of sweet pipe tobacco.

He gave me five shots in alternate arms, twice a month for a couple of years, trying to desensitize me to living in Maryland. I seemed to be allergic to everything in the air, especially in the spring and fall. He would always save one of the spent syringes to enjoy without the needle. I told Mom that Dr. Kaiser seemed very different to me. He wasn't mean, loud, bossy, uninterested, or short - tempered with anyone. He seemed to enjoy every second of what he was doing in the office in his slow, measured, lowkey manner. I thought that he was very cool.

The thing I noticed most was that he didn't seem to mind touching me like some white people did when they were giving you change at the store or passing you in a small aisle. And he smiled at me like he was enjoying my presence. Mom said that part of the reason Dr. Kaiser appeared so different to me was because he was a Jewish man and not just another regular White man. His beliefs about some important things were different. Otherwise, she said he was basically a very good person, which was rare and wondrous on its own. I told Mom, okay, but I really didn't know what being Jewish meant. I was glad Dr. Kaiser was Jewish, and I wished more people were like him, too, regardless of their religion or race. I knew that was asking a lot, and it wasn't going to happen.

Whenever the good doctor gave the burning series of five subcutaneous shots in my right arm, I couldn't pitch a baseball for days, which was not good for my team, the hapless Indians. I was the only Negro on my team. Several of the other teams had friends of mine from the Consolidated School. Some of the White coaches would get us confused and call any of us Tasby; after Willie Tasby, the only Negro player on the Baltimore Orioles at the time. Our coach was a kindly, heavy-smoking, middle-aged man, Mr. Fredricks. He was glad when I could pitch, and he was always encouraging me to do the best I could. He was very patient with all the athletes on his team.

My teammates were fine, but our team was bad, lacking in skills and overall athletic ability compared to the other teams in the league. The boys were just normal kids who could not run, throw, catch, or hit very well. The one exceptional thing I picked up on was they sounded differently from people I was around regularly. They had White Marylander accents, nasal and a bit harsh, chocked full of mangled vowels, and swallowed consonants. I had never heard accents like theirs up close before, not in the church, the barbershop, or my school. None of the boys seemed to be mental giants or walking around with any unexpected exceptional qualities or powers, as they were rumored to have. We all got along on the field and in the dugout.

One day before a game, I was both surprised and a little confused by seeing what our water source would be. There was a solitary water bucket and a single ladle tucked in the corner, near the entrance to the dugout. I was looking around for cups, but none were to be found. That's when I realized the communal intent of the water bucket and ladle. I was thirsty, but not that thirsty. I grew up in a family that did not eat, or drink, after one another, except in extreme circumstances. So this was unexpected, unwanted, and comically ironic to me.

I had to think hard about it, in between my suppressed chuckles, because it did not make any sense. My White teammates were willing to drink water from a bucket after me but, supposedly, unwilling to sit by me in school. And I was willing to sit by them in school but was definitely unwilling to drink water after them or anyone else. I did not get the impression that most of my 4th and 5th grade baseball teammates would actually have a problem sitting by me in their schools. It was likely that many of them didn't even know where the Consolidated School building was or why it was there in the first place. The White boys were just flowing comfortably in their safe bubble, not looking for any insoluble social riddles to consider today. They had no reason to know a lot about my particular existence, championed by their school Board and their beloved superintendent, Dr. Charles Willis.

We only won 2 games all season and lost a total of 12. My teammates were much better at losing than I was. As the team's main pitcher, I racked up most of the losses and all of the wins. When the arm discomfort from Dr. Kaiser's shots wore off, I could pitch again, usually to get another loss. It was a relief when the season was over. I never played Little League baseball again, but I was glad to have met and played with the Indians that one time. I learned something important about myself; I really hate losing.

Dr. Theodore Kaiser eventually went back to The Johns Hopkins Hospital to train as a child psychiatrist after practicing pediatrics in Havre de Grace for many years. His patients and their families were very sorry to see him go because he had helped so many people in the town. His staff was wonderful, especially his nurse Gay, who made me feel special every time I was there. Also, it was important for his Negro patients, that his waiting room was integrated, which was not true for all medical offices in the town in the 1950s and the early 60s. But at Dr. Kaiser's office, you could sit anywhere there was a seat, no matter who you were. You could talk to anybody in the waiting room if they wanted to talk to you, even if they were White.

Dr. Kaiser must have been perfect for his new, special discipline of child psychiatry. It was difficult losing my doctor, who kept me breathing. I was lucky to have known such a grand person in a confusing period of my life. It was good to know there were a few people in the country who seemed to get it naturally and didn't mind acting like it.

It felt extraordinary to be out of Mrs. Davage's class, and it was soothing knowing I would never be terrorized by her again for the sake of education or anything else. I still bore some psychic contusions from the yearlong encounter. But I learned something that was important: how to survive a prolonged difficult situation that was not in my control and to still come out on the positive side. It would not be the last time I would need to call on that knowledge.

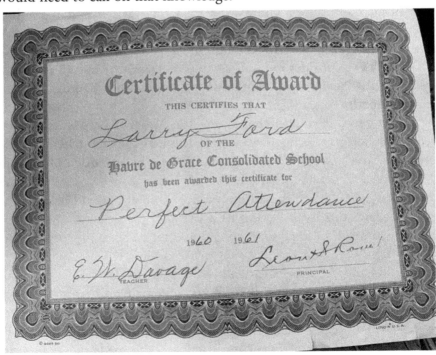

Getting this award in Mrs. Davage's class was a
major feat of comportment.

LJF/FORD/GRIFFIN COLLECTION!!!

CHAPTER 5

Thinking about Lumumba

The best thing about being in the 5th grade was that I was no longer in the 4th grade. This meant, I had survived Mrs. Davage, and her Sego-powered, redheaded, freckled reign of terror, and I had a perfect attendance award for the year to prove it. I did learn that fear can be a powerful and useful motivator in small doses. I certainly didn't want to fuel my entire school career on fear. Anyway, it was summertime in 1961. John Fitzgerald Kennedy was President and Roger Maris was chasing Babe Ruth's home run record all July and August. He finally caught and surpassed "The Sultan of Swat" in September with his 61st home run of the season. The Russians had built a wall, topped it with razor wire, and divided the city of Berlin, Germany. It threatened the post-World War II peace and stability of Europe and the rest of the world. Harper Lee won the Pulitzer Prize for "To Kill a Mockingbird."

What got my attention the most during the summer was watching Adolph Eichmann, in a glass box, on trial for his life in Israel. There was some of it on the television, or I read about it in the newspapers or Mr. Lisby's Time Magazine. I did not know much of the dense, complicated history that involved him in the killings of a multitude of Jewish people in the war. Eichmann appeared to be a passive, troubled, fearful, middle-aged German man, in black-rimmed glasses, wearing a headset tuned in to his fate. He knew he was in very serious trouble for what he had done in World War II. The Jewish people wanted him badly, and they searched for the murderous demon all over the world until he was found in Argentina. They snatched him from South America and spirited him away to Israel for trial. I was very glad they got him.

The other event that I had been watching, and had been trying to understand for a couple of years, was the overdue disintegration of the European nations' stranglehold on practically the entire continent of Africa. How did a small country, like Belgium, come to claim the physical ownership of the Congo on the African continent, its treasure, and control of its people? I was struck by the black and white photograph on the Baltimore Sun's front page. It showed an inconsolable African woman sitting in front of her house, knees akimbo and arms flailing, upon learning the news of the assassination of her husband, the Prime Minister of Congo, Patrice Lumumba. The murder was done by the Belgians, with the apparent knowledge and acquiescence of Dwight Eisenhower, the Dulles brothers, and the United States government.

The same could be said of the English in South Africa and the French in North Africa. Before WWII, the Germans, and their Italian allies, had claims of ownership of a large area of the southwestern coast and the Horn of Africa. In the 4th grade, it appeared to me that wherever in the world, White people met people who were not White, even in their own country, the assumption was that the White people were always in charge, just like in America. For centuries, almost everyone had been going along with this dogma until now. Now America, and a lot of the world, was trying to put some limits on the historical majesty of whiteness that had controlled much of world history for the last 1000 years. I was rooting for anybody with dark skin living in their own country and fighting an invading plunderer from Europe.

On some warm summer nights, you could hear a few of the older Consolidated School girls walking down Erie Street from the highway. They would be singing and harmonizing in time to the Shirelles' song, "Will You Love Me Tomorrow?" Or, they would doo-wop to this is "Dedicated to the One I Love." They sounded good, and they knew it as they strutted down Erie Street headed for their night out. But mostly, I enjoyed listening to music on the radio and talking on the steps with my sibs and Peety, our next door neighbor. We would drink soda, munch on chips and candy, and swat bugs away constantly. Then, we would be amazed at the squadron of acrobatic bats diving into the gray moving feast of gnats and mosquitoes flying around the street lamp in front of the house. My little sisters, Pamela and Pelbea, would run about chasing each other and catching a few mystical, magical lightning bugs, until it was time to go inside for the evening.

I was still in the Havre de Grace Consolidated School, C1, with no imminent prospects of going anywhere else, not if the Board of Education had their way and Dr. Charles Willis remained in charge. The conditions caused by the American caste system of segregation were personal, demoralizing, degrading, and petty most of the time. The Brown decision of the Supreme Court was now seven years old, fraying and getting stale. Negroes didn't realize, but were not surprised by, what the "all deliberate speed," prescribed by the courts, actually meant. It had nothing to do with speed in the mathematical sense, as most normal people understood it. The leisurely pace of integration was well tolerated, if not encouraged, by the federal court rulings. The defendants gladly used the time given by the courts to devise new methods of subterfuge and delay of total school integration.

The body politic of southern White people never seemed in a hurry to address the concerns of Negroes, that was their nature and their privilege. Some of them congratulated us on being indestructible people, considering the cruelty, abuse, rape, torture, and Christianity we had survived at their guiltless, holy hands. Then they said, okay, here's some more abuse, and kept doing what they always had done to us. Deep inside, some of them admired and, grudgingly, respected us for being able to survive the very worst of their lot, for almost four hundred years. But most of all, they physically feared us one on one, and man-to-man. Some of them knew they had a 400-year comeuppance that was way overdue. Whites, historically, seemed more comfortable confronting Negroes with guns, in fixed legal proceedings, mob settings, police actions, or extra judicial lynchings. The more of them present, the braver and more dangerous they became. That's how it appeared to me, from the colored school.

Mrs. Jan Pierce (J.P.) Turner, my 5th grade teacher, was another institution at the Consolidated School. She went to college in Virginia, at the Hampton Institute. The venerable school was founded by Booker T. Washington, in 1874. She was old-fashioned and strict in school, but she liked to laugh and sing gospel too. She got a big kick out of some of the misspeaking that I would occasionally display in class when my brain backfired. She once taught us about the different modes of thinking: abstract and concrete. The following day she asked the class, "Who remembers the two kinds of thinking that we talked about yesterday?" My hand shot up immediately, accompanied by, "I know, I know!!" The smiling Mrs. Turner called on me and my excitement. "The answer is abstract and cement!!" Her eyes nearly teared up with surprise and laughter at my answer. She used that story for years, telling it to her other classes. But, it was an unappreciated window into my brain's congenital problem.

I loved her voice and her unusual accent. She could have been dropped into one of those 1930s black and white movies, with Myrna Loy, and William Powell, and the little terrier dog upstaging everyone. No one would know she was Negro, as long as they kept their eyes closed. She did not have the soft, country southern inflections of speech like many of the people at the school. Her elocution was clearly delivered with the flawless diction of Ella Fitzgerald, the jazz singer, and with the passion of a Baptist preacher. She sounded more sophisticated New York City to me than anything else. She, too, was a past teacher of my sister, Pat.

I would occasionally see Mrs. Turner across the street from our house at the beauty shop. She would park her large, four-door Dodge sedan with white wall tires, get out and wave to me before going into the shop, to get her hair done. She would comment on Mom's roses in the front yard, still blooming in late September. She said, "Your Mom's roses must think they are still down south in Georgia." She was a well-traveled and very classy person. As a teacher, she did not have to count on instilling fear to do her job. But she was fearsome in her own direct, resolute manner. She didn't mind letting you know when there was a problem. She had no hesitation in bursting into the boy's bathroom with a clutch of rolled up "My Weekly Readers" as a weapon. The commotion in the bathroom was quickly quelled by Mrs. Turner and her "puppy trainer."

By the time of 5th grade, in the Consolidated, most students had been homeroom classmates with most everyone else at least once. We had been together so long it felt like we were all distant relatives, with at least one major thing in common, segregation. There was not much infusion of new blood in the school except for the rare new student from the Aberdeen Proving Ground. I was seated in a group of reliable, serious pupils. Bertha Bond was very smart and confident in herself, as was Charles Warfield. They both seemed to get it and retain lessons better than I did. Bertha read very well and was unstressed reading aloud in class. In fact, she was the best reader in the whole class and one of the best students. I would hate being called on to read and expose my biggest academic deficit. I knew I had a significant problem with reading, but I didn't know what it was caused by or how bad I sounded to the rest of the room. It was embarrassing at times.

It took forever for me to read stories or assignments, then I still may not understand them until I read them again and again. In 4th grade, the work was generally slower and easier, and there were fewer completely new concepts to wrestle with. Sometimes, I would have to look at words hard before they made sense. It didn't happen often, but there were times a page in my book was a picture of incoherent, nonsensical symbols for a while. There was always a threat the spell would come just from me thinking and worrying about it too much. That was the worst part of 5th grade. I never talked to Mrs. Turner about my problem, but she knew something was discordant when it came to my reading and comprehension.

I did fine with the work in Mrs. Turner's class, but it wasn't the Pat Ford sharpness she had seen with my sister. She never said that, and she didn't have to; I already knew it, and it was simply a fact. After the Maryland statewide test of 5th grade, given in the spring of the year, Mrs. Turner did have something to say to me. One day she kept me behind when the rest of the class went to recess. Her voice was soft, which did belie the gravity of the words she wanted to deliver. Mrs. Turner was serious was serious in a way I had never seen before, and she got right to it.

"Larry....You did not do as well as I had hoped you would do on the recent Maryland state achievement tests," she said in a concerned voice. I agreed with her but didn't tell her about my problems with reading, brain clarity, or taking a long test for two days. My brain hurt, and my concentration vanished by the afternoon. I just wanted to finish and get outside. I kept having to read the same sentences over and over again. It was quite frustrating.

She continued, "Not all students can learn and compete at a very high level. But those who can...must, for all of us to advance. Do you understand?" To which, I said, "Yes, ma'am." It gave me a lot to think about for a very long time. It was likely not the first time Mrs. Turner gave that speech, but she obviously didn't give it to everybody. I had to get my problem under control very soon, and not just for me. One day I would be out of the Colored School, and I needed to be ready to compete with White kids, regardless of their advantages over me or their personal feelings about me. That's what Mrs. Turner was saying. Neither one of us knew when I would get to compete with White students. It was my job to get to the point that I was ready for integration and whatever surprises and opportunities it brought.

Fortunately for me, Mom had bought us a new set of World Book Encyclopedias, and she sat them beside the television in the living room. It was an alternative to Rocky and Bullwinkle and an adjunct to the news I watched nightly on the television. Very good move Mother dear, or Mudea, as we used to call her. It made a very big difference in my growing brain problem.

The Consolidated Schools had sports teams in only cross country, track, and basketball. We never had a football or baseball team. The colored and white schools were not allowed to play each other in basketball, for reasons known best to the Board of Education but fairly easy to guess. But competing in track and field did have their blessing since there was no physical contact between the students. In the spring, track was on everybody's mind on both sides of our school. Even the elementary and high school girls ran track. Other than the Maryland state track and field championships, the big track event was the annual bus trip to the Pennsylvania Relay Carnival in Philadelphia, the Penn Relays. The trip was only about 70 miles away from Havre de Grace, but it was across the Mason-Dixon Line, which was always nice to traverse. You were allowed, by law, to contend with less everyday Jim Crow racism for a little while and be treated, more or less, like a person.

The Relays were the oldest and biggest deal in the world of USA track. There were many running and jumping events for high schoolers and then college athletes later in the day. All the Consolidated folks were sitting in the same section of the ancient, medieval-looking Franklin Field stadium and having a very good time with each other. Mr. William Clark, our coach, gym teacher, and model of Black manhood, was there with Mr. Lisby, and a few other teachers. It was like an outdoor family party, with a track meet in the background.

There were marvelous athletes from everywhere; high schoolers from all over the country, really fast White church boys from Abilene Christian, Texas Christian, and Southern Methodist. There were Black colleges from the south and fantastic field event contestants from everywhere. There was a beautifully sculpted Black man from Villanova named Billy Joe. He threw a 16-pound shot put over 60 feet, and he looked like John Henry, the mythical Black steel drivin' man of American folklore, come to life on Franklin Field.

I saw Brian Sternberg, the world record holder in the pole vault from the University of Washington. He was reaching unbelievable heights of over 16 feet using a new fiberglass pole. From across the stadium, I could see the pole bend like a fresh green twig under his weight. He was spring loaded, just before his powered pole slung him cleanly over the bar. He rode gravity back to the earth from the dizzying height with a controlled fall into the padding. I was impressed by his strength, daring, and the science in that fiberglass pole.

The final event of the day was the college mile relay. I didn't know much about the teams who were running, but it didn't matter. The four laps of the track, by teams of four men, risking three high-speed exchanges of the baton, made the three minute long race a changing, frenetic play on spikes. After the second exchange at 880 yards, the crowd was loving the battle, as the teams were very competitive coming down the backstretch.

I could not contain my enthusiasm as the final baton pass was done. I was yelling and screaming to the point that Mr. Clark, our gym teacher, turned around, flashed me his manly smile, and nodded approvingly at my fanatic state. The final race was finished, to the delight of the fans, and the athletes celebrated on the field one last time. The Relays were over just as the sun was fading, and the first hint of chill was noticed in the late afternoon April air. It was time to go home.

We boarded the bus home as satisfied fans and very hungry people. After loading and counting heads, the bus turned south out of Philly toward Maryland. A couple of the teachers, and an older student, were going around the bus asking people how many hamburgers, fries, and drinks they wanted. They were organizing and getting ready to cross the frontier, the Mason-Dixon Line, into Delaware. It wasn't the true Mason-Dixon line. It was an arc of 12 miles, drawn on a map with the center at the courthouse in New Castle. It was fixed by an agreement between Pennsylvania and Delaware in the 1700s. It eventually met up with the real Mason-Dixon Line to the south to complete the border between the North and the South. Regardless of the imaginary geometric entity you crossed, the result was the same; it was always hard for a Black traveler to get fed once he crossed the arc or the line, and that was not imaginary.

This was a yearly trip to the Penn Relays, and many people were accustomed to, if not comfortable with, what it took to get something to eat traveling back home. The line to the other side was only about 30 minutes away from Philadelphia. We crossed the southern frontier at the odiferous, flaring refineries of Marcus Hook, Pennsylvania, on into the industrial town of Claymont, Delaware, just on the southern side of the border. We found a small family dining establishment just off the highway. Our bus turned into the restaurant's dark, small parking lot, and our driver brought the bus to a stop and parked. The several cars in the parking lot indicated they were fairly busy but not packed, which was good for us. They might need our money more than they thought they disliked our skin color.

A teacher and a student got off the bus and walked a short distance to the restaurant's back door. They knocked and waited for the door to open. A White man in an apron came to the door and talked briefly with the teacher. It was not so much an order our teacher was giving to the White man as it was a request for consideration to be allowed to do business with him and his restaurant. He didn't have to serve us if he didn't want to, in or out of his building. It came down to whether they wanted our money or not. The White man said yes, and the period of breath holding for the interested, hungry spectators on the bus ended with the knowledge we were going to get something to eat now.

We ate the food and talked with each other about the happenings of the day at the track meet as the bus rolled home. A couple of comments were made about the indignity of having to go to the back door, but not many. All the adults and most of the students, understood that this was just one of the several indignities you may face on a typical Negro/Black/ colored day. Our teachers were always there helping us to find our way through the haze and maze of segregation and, when possible, to protect us from the worst of it. We did not have the luxury of ruminating on any one of the slights for too long. You just had to register it and get ready for the next one, which was probably already on its way. We were glad to get home, well fed and still standing tall, despite Jim Crow.

NOVEMBER

TEACHER'S COMMENTS:

Larry is a conscientious student. He has good reference books which he uses to bring in extra assignments to share with the other children. His work is well prepared and he shows a deep interest in all of his work.

We are trying to help him to read more smoothly orally.

Times Tardy	- Year to Date	
Days Absent	- Year to Date	0
Days Present	- Year to Date	38

PARENT'S COMMENTS:

In the future I will see to Larry reading orally. I am very impressed with his performance.

Parent's Signature

In the 5th Grade, Mrs. Turner was concerned with my difficulties in reading aloud, which was quite embarrassing to me.

LJF/FORD/GRIFFIN COLLECTION!!!

PROGRESS REPORT
GRADES TWO THROUGH SIX

SUBJECTS	NOV	FEB	APR	JUN
Reading	C	C+	B	B
Spelling	B	B+	A	A
Handwriting	C	B	A	A
Language	B	A	A	A
Arithmetic	B	B+	B+	B+
Social Studies	A	A	A	A
Science	B	B	B	B
Music	B	B	B	B
Art	C	B	B	B
Physical Education	B	B	B	B

Explanation of Marking System

A - Excellent
B - Good
C - Average
D - Poor
E - Failing

GRADE LEVEL AT WHICH PUPIL IS WORKING

SUBJECTS	NOV	FEB	APR	JUN
READING	5¹	5¹	5²	5²
ARITHMETIC	5	5	5	5

Mrs. J. P. Turner noted the reading problem in this
5th grade reported card. (Photo by L. J. Ford)

LJF/FORD/GRIFFIN COLLECTION!!!

Dr. Larry James Ford

My class picture from 6th Grade

LJF/FORD/GRIFFIN COLLECTION!!!

CHAPTER 6

Mr. Lisby: 6th Grade

The start of the 6th grade began with the usual school hopefulness, happiness, angst, and fall fashion show. I was getting used to being in Mr. Lisby's class and the new expectations it brought into my life. All those school concerns were quickly swept away and replaced with thoughts about imminent, instant death and annihilation, not just of me but for all of nature and mankind.

In late October, President Kennedy announced the finding of offensive nuclear missiles in Cuba, 90 miles from Miami and about 1000 miles from me. I could read maps and also knew there was a difference between a plain nuclear bomb and a hydrogen bomb. I knew enough to understand that being in the middle of the east coast, 70 miles from Washington, 70 miles from Philadelphia, and 130 miles from New York City, if the shooting started, it was going to be a very short and sharp transition from my daily assumptions and visual earthscapes to something hellish and apocalyptic, if I survived.

The President gave his speech on Saturday, the 22nd, and anxiety and bad thoughts pervaded the nation, but the crisis had been playing out slowly for a week already. I was watching the TV news and reading the newspapers over the weekend, but what happened on the bus going to school Monday morning, made everything vivid, and the true stakes were brought into focus.

When our school bus stopped at the end of Revolution Street, at the light on Route 40, a solid phalanx of drab green Army vehicles of various sizes and deadliness cut a path from horizon to horizon, from the direction of the river bridge to Aberdeen. There were Jeeps with a couple of men in them and larger filled personnel carriers, as well as heavy military equipment on flatbed trucks. They were all headed south toward Florida because it was very close to Cuba, and there was a military quarantine to enforce.

It was probably the only time in my life I was sorry for knowing a lot of news. The adults were going to play it down, but we were in the deep. It interrupted school and all of life that week. Mr. Lisby was completely on top of it, of course, and he mentioned it in class. He was very worried. Otherwise, we just stocked up on food and prayed a lot. I mean, it could actually be the end of the world. It was hard to sleep at night, worrying if you were going to wake up again or do anything ever again.

Through political gamesmanship, common sense, luck, and not wanting the responsibility of killing the entire world and destroying all of civilization, mankind barely squeaked out of a very bad one. It emphasized to me that I am very small, insignificant, and not in control of much of anything of consequence, as well as the grandeur, wonder, and lightness of our fleeting, gossamer existence. Then school life resumed, but none of us was the same, having peeked into the abyss, and survived.

It was preordained from my very first day at C1 that Mr. George Daniel Lisby would be my teacher when I got to the 6th grade. Pat had him too. She did complain once, or twice, to Mom about having to see him all day in school, then to see him again when she got home, sitting at the kitchen table. She was just yapping. She liked Uncle George as a teacher, and she just had to accept that everybody loved Mom's cooking, even her teacher. Mr. Lisby was one of my stepfather's best friends, when they grew up across the Baltimore and Ohio railroad tracks from each other in Aberdeen. They played ball together, went hunting with their .22s, snow sledding, and whatever else they could think of that didn't cost much money.

Uncle George was a single man, and we saw him often. You always knew what you were going to get from him for Christmas or your birthday — books, and then more books! They were mostly about United States history, sports, the Supreme Court, and who was on it. He told me that being a Justice on the Court was one of the top jobs in America because of their power and influence. We talked a lot about politics after he told me what it was— "horseplay." I didn't understand all of the content sometimes, but that wasn't the point. Mr. Lisby wanted me exposed to the concepts, so I could figure them out for myself later.

On the first day of school, he let me, and the entire class, know that I couldn't expect any slack from him just because he came over to my house sometimes. I always thought he said it for the benefit of my classmates because I never expected anything to be easy about being in Mr. Lisby's class. I knew him much too well for that. Mr. Lisby was very smart, and, if given the opportunity, he could have been, and done, anything he wanted. When he was growing up, his options were few, just like mine, but even worse. He graduated from the Havre de Grace Colored School in 1948, at the age of 14. Everyone knew he was an exceptionally intelligent young man, and the whole community appreciated him. Whether in school, church, or on the athletic fields, he was a special presence, excelling at everything.

Mr. Lisby went to teacher's college at Bowie and came back to teach in Harford County at his old school. His principal, Mr. Leon Roye, was also there when he was in high school. We heard a lot about the legendary Mr. Roye, and everybody had a personal or family story about the "Professor." He had gone to college at Lincoln University in Oxford, Pennsylvania. One of his close friends and fraternity brothers in college was the poet Langston Hughes. Mr. Hughes visited the Old School a time or two, gave lectures, and left some of his autographed books in the library.

It was hard for me to digest how many decades Mr. Roye had been at the Colored School. He was a great storyteller, in addition to his other talents. He told us once, in an assembly, about the Civil War battle of Gettysburg, and the surviving men seeing the creek run red with blood in the morning, after the previous day of killing. It was not that long ago, not quite 100 years, and less than 100 miles from here. Mr. Roye had a way of connecting the students to history and how it still affected our lives daily.

The teachers were not free to talk directly about race, integration, or White people too often, for fear of their jobs. The important, infrequent, indirect messages delivered to us at school were unintentional, or unexplained. There were the occasional sightings of a few white faces in the hall with Mr. Roye in our school several times a year. I came to call it "Overseer's Day," and it made it feel like we hadn't advanced all that much since the battle of Gettysburg.

Not every Black kid had around him a serious, learned man who seemed to be able to analyze anything, like Uncle George Lisby. I was lucky, and I knew it. There was no using poor English or not being up on current events or sports around him. You might get unexpected information coming your way or questions about anything; like "what do you think about that," or given these circumstances, "how would you handle that?" You needed to stay on your toes around Mr. Lisby and think quickly on your feet. He never tried to embarrass you, but his expectations were very high.

It may have been a good thing that my worst year in school would happen in Mr. Lisby's class at the Consolidated School. That year, I was lost some days in class for various periods of time, and it was getting worse. The work was difficult in some cases, but manageable with extra time and effort, except for "the new" math. I just had not figured it out yet. As things got tense in school, there was more unhelpful chaos interrupting my attempted brain functions. I thought if I was at the white school now, they'd probably find a way to put me in special ed or something. I had a lot of straightening out to do, and not a lot of time to do it.

In the 6th grade, the school day usually got off on a good prehistoric note because of our class pet. Somehow, my class science teacher had come into possession of a small alligator who the class had named Alfred. At first, he was about a foot long and spent most of his time in a glass tank at the front desk. Alfred was now about two and a half feet, from his prehistoric snout to his scaly tail. As Alfred got bigger, Jerry Waters, who always seemed to be devoid of fear and impervious to pain, would fashion a neck leash for the reptile and walk it down the hall on the elementary side of the school for exercise. The girls took a while to get used to the sight of his daily primordial ramble.

A good day in school might be when the class got to see a real movie, with good animation and sound, instead of the old, soporific film strips, accompanied by a phonograph record for sounds and beeps, to indicate when to advance the film strip. The first time I saw "Hemo,

The Magnificent," I was amazed to see how blood and hemoglobin worked through the animated action of the film. I wondered if it would be possible for me to get a job working in a lab, doing science as a career. The days of inspiration at the Consolidated School were few. Even with the encouragement of the teachers, I could not see very far into the future and where I fit in it.

Once at Smitty's Barber Shop in downtown Havre de Grace, I was waiting to get a haircut. A collection of older town men was holding the floor and talking about all manner of subjects, including the Baltimore Colts, the Orioles, and the coming presidential election. When the men finished discussing Lenny Moore, Brooks Robinson and venting their collective displeasure with Barry Goldwater — the unlikeable, John Birch Society-loving, out-and-out racist—Republican nominee for President, they turned their attention to the "young bloods" sitting in the shop. One of the men started talking to me directly. I was surprised by being suddenly questioned, but it was the barbershop way, and it was my turn. He asked right off, "Well, young man. Have you decided what you want to be when you grow up?" He had a kind face and a deep churchy baritone in his voice. He was interested in what I had to say. It was always intimidating when you were young, to speak up center stage in a barber shop. It was a place where a young man was seen and not heard until he was invited to speak.

I gathered myself and gave him the best answer I could, given my present state of confusion on the matter. "I want to graduate from high school and then probably get a job at the Aberdeen Proving Ground." I was happy that I was able to get a crisp sentence out without slipping. But on the other side of my success was silence and a quizzical expression on the man's face. When he saw I was finished, he gave a jocular smile and loosed his serious baritone softly on me. "Son, somebody has given you some bad information. Your objective should not be graduating and quickly getting a job and then working forever. Do not be afraid of staying in school for as long as it takes. Work will always be waiting for you. Don't be in a big hurry to start working." Don't be afraid to stay in school as long as needed and that was the message received from him.

Everything came to a head late one night at Mom's kitchen table when I was struggling to finish my homework. Pat had helped me earlier, but she was asleep now. I had a screaming, endless cacophony and discordance of unrelated words, numbers, and events swirling in a toxic, indecipherable stew in my brain. The harder I tried, the less sense it made, and the harder it got to do anything. Mom watched and tried to support me as best she could. She felt sorry for her son in a battle with himself. I cried, spilling briny tears on my homework paper, running the ink on the page. Mom asked if I wanted a little something to eat to distract me some. I knew I had to clear my mind and get this done. It was 12AM and Mom was tired.

I cleared and reset my mind enough to get Mom and me through the night. I knew this could not keep happening. It was starting to affect the frequency of the asthma and itching rashes the allergies would bring. I got through the night and did my homework okay. I dragged through the next school day and thought a lot about the night before. I had to be more organized and get to the point that reading was not such a fear filled, time consuming chore. The math was something I was going to have to break down and teach myself. I needed some shortcuts in the math work that I could understand and give some general direction to my untrained, unruly digital thoughts. Mom and I never had another bad night of homework travails and confusion after that.

Since I had a reading problem, I started to read all the time. Many days I would take a book, usually an encyclopedia or a Time Magazine, to the dinner table. At some point, I decided to read the entire World Book Encyclopedia as treatment for whatever it was that I had. I seemed to be able to help with the problem of reading and poor comprehension with periods of forced attention and trying to slowly increase my speed, without getting lost. My comprehension improved moderately by Christmas, and I was feeling better about myself and school. I still knew I was disappointing Mr. Lisby. He once told me, as he got in his car leaving our house, "I wish you would get heavy for me. Do you know what I mean?"

I told him, "Yes, Sir." I understood that he knew intellectually I could do the work. But I had to decide it was important enough to want to do well for me, and then figure out how to do it. He may have had misgivings about how hard he could push me without making things worse..... and risking his frequent sumptuous home-cooked meals.

Perhaps doing it for someone other than myself was a key to my motivation, inspiration, and direction for a while anyway. It took a couple of years, but I eventually read the whole World Book Encyclopedia, not that I understood all of it. I had all kinds of new, disconnected notions to play with in my head and use in school or just to entertain myself with novel, unusual, radical thoughts. With my improving brain function, I started to think I may be a scientist someday, and I may be able to do it, even if I never got out of the Havre de Grace Consolidated School, C1. I was starting to feel better, and math was starting to make sense.

All fall and winter, my class was raising money to take the Pennsylvania Railroad Tour to New York City. Although Maryland was comfortably Confederate in many ways, it was still only about 130 miles away from the sophistication and liberalism of New York City. Everybody was looking forward to the trip, and we had raised money by selling Christmas cards earlier in the year. But the big push came two months before our trip. We spent a whole weekend delivering the meals some of our parents had made for us to sell. What we were selling, and smelling, were chitlin' dinners, with their subtle barnyard essence right there on your plate. We never ate the "wrinkle steak" at home and I was glad for it. The chitlin's were a hit and we sold enough for the whole class to go on our trip. It was fun delivering the porcine delicacy to the waiting customers, and some of them dove right in, fingers first.

I was not sure I was going to make the trip to New York City because of a bad ankle sprain. My middle sister, Pamela Elizabeth, had wanted to go on the trip, but she was told there was no room for her. She decided if my ankle was bad enough, I wouldn't be able to go, leaving room for her. She put her plan into effect by grabbing a broomstick and whacking me on the injured ankle a couple of times while I was sitting with my leg elevated. She had a clean shot and she, took it. One wack landed squarely on the joint and hurt, but the look of determination on Pam's little face made me laugh as she delivered her coup d' grace. She was very serious about what she was doing and she was not in a talking mood. Mom grabbed her and the broomstick, allowing me to avoid strike three. We all laughed it off except for 6-year old Pamela. She wanted to go to New York and she may have missed her last chance. I kept my eyes on her, just in case she had any other enterprising thoughts before the trip.

When we boarded the train at Aberdeen on a Saturday morning, everybody was enthused and prepared to get going. The parents and grandparents were as happy to go as their kids. I loved getting out of the

South, even for a short stretch, to experience life without the pressure of Jim Crow and his enforcers in blue, breathing down your neck. They tried to control everything, including your thoughts about yourself. The train was filled with groups from several other local schools also taking the Pennsy Railroad tour. When fully loaded, the train engine tugged all the individual car linkages tight, and we smoothly, quietly eased out of the small railroad station down the tracks headed for Wilmington and Philly before our final destination, New York City.

On the trip, we were scheduled to go to a restaurant, like you see on television, and sit down and eat— in the restaurant. That was going to be a new experience for me and many other of my fellow travelers, since I had never eaten in a restaurant. Previously, I was shocked when I saw Emerson go into a Woolworth store last year, in Philadelphia. He ordered a BLT, sat down, and ate it....on the seat....at the counter. Nobody tried to stop him. You couldn't do that in the South, on the other side of the line, or the arc, dividing how far White people could go in exercising their conscious, domineering racial desires when protected by law and tradition.

Our tour bus had took us around Manhattan to the famous tourist sites; Fifth Avenue, with all its impressive shops, the United Nations, and the Empire State Building. We also passed through the heart of Harlem and by the Apollo Theater on 125th Street. We went into the United Nations building for a tour, and it looked just like it did on television. We passed the residence of Althea Gibson, the famous Negro professional tennis player. It was in a very nice area where individual homes had fancy doors leading directly to the street.

I especially liked seeing the rather worn appearing Hotel Theresa in Harlem. Fidel Castro stayed there during his visit to New York to address the United Nations. He gave the address a year after taking over his country and a year before he embarrassed the United States at the Bay of Pigs in the first year of the presidency of John Kennedy. He didn't want to stay in any Yankee, capitalist pig hotel on Park Avenue. So, he went uptown, to be with the people of West 125th Street, in Harlem.

We passed the enormous, one-block square city library, whose entrance was guarded by two massive carved stone lions. And there were people everywhere; in the doors, the stores, walking fast on the sidewalks and swimming like tadpoles, through the crowded intersections of the streets. It looked a lot like it did on television or in the movies, and unlike anything you would ever see in Havre de Grace unless it was the Fourth of July. In Harlem and Spanish Harlem, the people on the street were a multitude of Negroes and brown Hispanic people. Land-wise, the two areas were very large by Baltimore standards. There were no marble stoops in front of block-long row houses. There were no row houses at all in Manhattan. People lived in large tenement buildings of many stories like I had never seen before. People were hanging out the windows, trying to catch a breeze, along with their laundry, trying to dry. Lots of unfamiliar Spanish music was heard in several of the blocks that we passed on the bus, and it added a different kind of score to go along with the unusual sights of the day.

My ankle hurt, and everybody was tired, hungry, and looking forward to our real sit-down meal at Lindy's Restaurant. It was a relief walking through the door and seeing White people not looking shocked, disgusted, confused, or otherwise piqued by our presence. No, they were more than happy to seat us, take our money, and treat us like normal people. Well, the food was another issue. Whereas selling "wrinkle steaks" helped pay for the trip, Salisbury steak was on the menu that day. One of the younger kids looked at what was on her plate and proclaimed, "This don't look like no steak to me. It looks like just plain old hamburger."

Our waiters were nice and they didn't appear afraid of us in any way. They seemed to enjoy our country kid enthusiasm about being in the Big City. The waiters were mostly tan to brown in complexion, and many spoke in distinct, pleasing accents, not heard in Havre de Grace. They encouraged us to have some of their "famous" Lindy's cheesecake, and some did. I had never heard of cheesecake before that day. The thought of the two foods, cheese and cake, eaten together didn't sound very appetizing.

We finished our food and headed back for the train to go home. It was an outstanding trip for all, and I was sorry my little sister missed it. But, Pam did not forgive Mom or me for making her miss going to New York City for the first time. It was amazing, as well as disturbing, to see how different things were not that far from Havre de Grace. There was a good explanation for it, plain old American racism, that was as real as the change you felt crossing the Mason-Dixon Line. Crossing it southerly was like falling off a political cliff, back into racial quicksand. That seemed to be okay with most White people, at least they didn't talk about it as a problem that concerned them. It was difficult to know if they didn't get it, and thought things were fine for everybody. Or, if they didn't care about understanding our situation, as long as we didn't disturb them. It was hard to know when whites really didn't get it, or if they were just shining you on because they didn't have a good answer at the moment. It was very hard to know.

Mr. George Lisby eventually became the president of the Harford County Board of Education in 1991. This school was named in honor of him, my 6th grade teacher and family friend

LJF/FORD/GRIFFIN COLLECTION!!!

CHAPTER 7

In the Streets of Annapolis

The end of the 6th grade was marked by a Harford County elementary school rite of passage, a week at Fresh Air Camp. It was something everyone had been looking forward to since early elementary school when we saw our big brothers and sisters return home dirty and smelly after a week away in the woods. The camp was a forested retreat, with barracks space enough to accommodate all the 6th grade students from both the Havre de Grace Consolidated and Central Consolidated Schools, C1 and C2, at the same time. One week a year, the camp was reserved for us, the Colored Schools. It was the first time many of us had social contact with our Colored School cousins from the middle of the county, who were going through many of the same educational and social challenges.

Still to me going to Fresh Air Camp was a lot like going to "Colored Day" on the Buddy Dean show, a popular daily teen, dance television show from Baltimore. Once a year, we would rush home from school to watch some of the older Consolidated High School students dance, eat Gino's hamburgers, fries, and drink sodas on "Colored Day," which was the only day Negroes were allowed on the dance show. It was special seeing people that we knew from school actually on the television screen, in our living room. All the other days, the show featured White high school kids from Patterson Park, Highlandtown, Dundalk, Essex, and the other white working class areas of Baltimore. Some of the regulars on the show were well known locally, and minor TV stars around town, in their own right. Colored Day on the Buddy Dean show and Colored Week at Fresh Air Camp were accepted and welcomed little, limited crumbs of grace rarely cast our way. The show did not want White and colored kids dancing on the same day or with each other. Fresh Air Camp and Buddy Dean must have had the same booking agents.

The Central Consolidated kids were a lot like us. The girls were nice, at least to the boys, and the boys were always competitive with each other at everything. They had gone to the same basketball games between the two Consolidated Schools in the county and witnessed the fierce battles over the years, just like me. During the week, we had classes on nature and took hikes in the woods. There was a lot of flirting going on between the schools. It was refreshing for everybody to meet new people who you hadn't seen every single school day for the last six years. I even got into the flirting game a little myself, and it was noticed by Mr. Lisby, who teased me about it without mercy the whole time.

We also went fishing, saw a rifle shooting demonstration, and the boys peed out the campfire on the first night after the girls were dismissed. That was not something I could have come up with on my own. The tall White man in the straw hat, who was head of the camp, assured us it was a camp tradition, and every school did it. So, we did it, but I was hoping we didn't have to repeat it since it was only the first night.

One night later in the week, the tall, boss White man was upset with us over some breakage of protocol, tradition, or something. As he talked down to us in the cafeteria about his distress, I was uncomfortable with the tone and aggressiveness of his words. He finished his rant by taking a paper straw that he held in his right hand and forcing it through the raw Irish potato held in his left hand. It was a not-so-subtle implied threat as to what would happen to us if we got out of line again. Our teachers were present but had nothing to say to the boss man in response to his threatening message.

After that demonstration, I was ready to go home. It was hard to imagine the boss man would give a similar threat to White students under any circumstances. I hoped that I was wrong but was fairly certain I wasn't.

We finished the week, packed up, and were bused back to the Consolidated School. We unloaded our bags and went back home to our families after the rites in the woods. We all needed to take a long bath and shampoo to get rid of the embedded dirt, crust, grime, and insects from the camp. Being gone for a week was a new experience, but I was happy to be back home, not breathing dust, finally eating Mom's food again, and watching my siblings do whatever they had planned for the day.

The school year ended shortly after camp concluded. I had made a lot of progress in reading, comprehension, and even math during the year. I was surprised at how much of the World Book Encyclopedia I had read and remembered. But I was still a work in progress, with quite a ways to go.

That summer, America was still a place trying to descend into self-immolation rather than evolve into a more democratic entity. Ten years after the Brown Supreme Court ruling, school segregation still had a firm hold on the South and Boston, too, which I always found curious. Maryland was just south enough to be part of the historical problem. The only hope we had was to get enough power at the ballot box and find enough reasonable White people to join us to effect some degree of change. Then we needed to get White people, in general, to do things and act in ways they had been disinclined to do for several hundreds of years; to share democracy equitably, as their Constitution promised.

We were marching to increase voter enrollment and against the continued segregation of schools in many parts of Maryland, the "Free State." Many southern White people never liked the idea of large numbers of Negroes voting and had tried many creative or violent ways to limit it. It was a natural part of the voting process for them, the Constitution notwithstanding.

Pat and I had been to meetings about elections and voting before. I had gone door to door in Havre de Grace handing out flyers in support of fluoridation of the water supply last year. Some people thought it was a communist-inspired plot to do something, or another, to the unsuspecting, carious American people. But I didn't know that at the time. I got the door slammed in my face more than once by people unhappy to see me. Doing something to decrease cavities and dental disease sounded like something everyone could be for. I was just learning there is nothing, regardless of how pure, reasoned, thoughtful, or rational, that everyone wants.

My sister and I had never gone on a march in the streets before. There was a large demonstration planned for Annapolis, the capital city of Maryland, in mid-summer. Of course, Pat was ready to go and do her part in the struggle and have a good time doing it. I was less enthusiastic, but I was always a good follower when it came to my sister. Mom packed us lunch and then drove us to meet up with the group heading to the demonstration from Harford County.

We were with Mrs. Janet (Morehead) Grant and her husband, Mr. Woodrow Grant. The then Miss Janet Morehead was a graduate of, and now a teacher at, the Havre de Grace Consolidated School. They were both committed to the fight for integration, voting rights, and social justice in our backward county and state. She had been educated at the Maryland State Teachers College and the University of California -Los Angeles, UCLA. She chose to return to Maryland and help us with all she had learned. And we were her little foot soldiers, trying to help make things better for everyone, especially for ourselves and our futures.

Fresh in my mind was what had happened in Birmingham, Alabama, earlier in April. Many White people in the country got to see, for the first time, what Black people already knew; that the viciousness and racial animus of those empowered to enforce Jim Crow laws, and cater to the leftover desires of the Confederacy, was limitless. Violence was the main feature of their beliefs and a useful tool to keep control of matters extrajudicially if needed. They would attack defenseless, peacefully demonstrating children with German shepherd police dogs. Torrents from water cannons would crush the children against brick buildings or wash them down the street with irresistible high-pressure blasts. The enforcers of Jim Crow did this without compunction or hesitation. To them, the kids were just little colored piccaninnies anyway, and there were plenty more replacements around.

The same people would have lynched the children's fathers, grandfathers, brothers, or uncles with the same human detachment if given a chance in the dark. It was something the country needed to see and not be allowed to pretend like it was a rare occurrence, delusion, aberration, or another one of those "colored people's lies." I didn't think anything bad was going to happen to us in Annapolis, but you could not assume that would be the case dealing with White southerners.

Thankfully, Annapolis was not Birmingham, and Bull Conner, the police chief of that city was 900 miles away in Alabama.

The day was hot, but not too oppressive, as midsummers go in Maryland. There was a light breeze coming from the Bay, just enough to keep you mostly dry while standing still in the shade. Our Harford County group met the other marchers in a Negro neighborhood close to downtown Annapolis. The adults planned our route through the bricked ways of the central city, and the narrower streets of the neighborhoods. There were many people my age and a few younger. They were organized and serious about the mission, especially the girls. We got our stick signs and the handout materials ready to go. We marched, a couple of hundred strong, down streets with fancy names like Duke of Gloucester and other streets with more forgettable tags. There were people lined up and looking at us as we marched and chanted:

Oh, oh freedom,
Oh, oh freedom,
Oh, oh freedom over me,
And before I'll be a slave,
I'll be buried in my grave,
And go home to my Lord,
And be free!

There was hand clapping and cheering from the mostly Black people who lined the route. The few White people we saw mostly looked on with mild curiosity, but some approved and nodded so. There were a few cops around, but they seemed interested primarily in traffic control and not bothering us at the time. I was holding up my fairly large sign to encourage people to register and vote in the next election. The sign was big enough to hide my face from the onlookers or provide shade from the sun. At different points during the march in the streets, I used it for either. I was not used to being the center of attention of strangers. It was unnerving and unnatural, being in the streets, but there was no other choice, and nowhere else to go, to get something done about our futures.

After the marching, we reassembled in the parking lot, and the older guys started planning their next step. The leaders were in their 20s and 30s and seemed to know the layout of the streets of Annapolis well. I was close enough to hear much of the conversation before they broke the huddle to tell the rest of us their decision. The main man told the group, numbering about 25, to listen up. The plan was to have us march down to a local restaurant, known not to give service to Negroes. A couple of the older heads would go into the restaurant and try to get served. They told the "young bloods" in the group to stay back because you never know how White people are going to choose to be, on any given day.

And march we did, a couple of blocks down the street to a little standalone eatery, on a quiet neighborhood way. It was an Italian restaurant, with an inconspicuous front and an old screen door at the entrance. The group stopped the march, and the two big guys walked across the street approaching the door, while the rest of us stayed on the other side. There was no sign on the building that said whites only, no coloreds, or no Negroes, like you would see around sometimes. It was obvious that many local marchers knew the reputation of the establishment, and they wanted the owners to know how the community felt about them.

The big guys opened the flimsy screen door and went inside. There was quiet and uncertainty for about a minute. Then the yelling of one irate person could be heard in a tenor, above the rustle of the street noise. The one-man tirade continued a few seconds more, and the screen door opened again, with the back of one of the big guys pressing against it. In short order, both of the young Black men had retreated from the store and found themselves facing off with a very upset, middle-aged, balding, roundish White man. He had a long butcher knife in his right hand pointed at them. The standoff went on for a minute that felt like an eon. Being close to potential violence was unfamiliar and frightening to me. Trying to get food at a restaurant could cost you your life. Yes, it could, and it had before.

The sound of approaching police sirens didn't alter the tension of the scene. I was hoping that when the police got here the chance of someone getting hurt would decrease. I was standing across the street fixed in a safe spot when the screaming cars arrived. The round White man lowered his knife, as he prosecuted his way of seeing things to the multiple policemen now on the scene. The two young Negro men remained calm and did not seem particularly surprised by what was happening. It was disappointing, but not unexpected, when after a couple of minutes the police handcuffed the two men, put them in the back of a patrol car and took them off to jail; their crime was trying to get something to eat while being a Negro in Annapolis, Maryland, in 1963.

A smaller subgroup of the original marchers walked down to the city jail to see the men. We waved and chanted our support to a couple of unidentified men waving back from a second floor window. I hung around for a couple of minutes more and then headed back to the demonstration pick-up spot. I found Pat, with her friends, ready to board the bus back home. We were both tired but satisfied we did as well as we could on this day.

When we got back home, we told Mom what happened marching in the streets of Annapolis. She was glad we had a good time and were safe. Then in true Mom style, she let me have it after Pat told her I was hiding behind the big sign I carried. Mom was laughing, smiling, and having a good old time giving her son the business about trying to hide in the middle of the street.

The March on Washington, with Dr. Martin Luther King, was a month after the Annapolis march. I couldn't see myself in a crowd of a million people, and I didn't want to tag along with Pat, who would not miss a gathering like that for anything. I would only slow her down from having a good experience and enjoying herself with her friends. On the morning of the big march, I saw Pat off and then walked down Erie Street to the Route 40 highway. I watched for several minutes and waved to the many buses filled with smiling, determined, well-dressed, hopeful Negro men and women heading south to D.C. to see Dr. King.

All the street marches, and other demonstrations in the country, were negatively affecting the mood of the dark underbelly of White American society, especially below the Mason-Dixon Line. There was an element in the South possessed of racist craziness, hate, vicious sadism, and cruelty, along with a very short memory and the ability to believe, or to pretend to believe, in just about anything. It was always a part of what made the South so volatile and dangerous. It was hard to imagine that many everyday kind of middle of the road non-southern White people ever had a naked, direct conversation with the very worst of their race. In reality, going to an Elks, Oddfellows, or Rotary meeting might net the same goals in the end for White people, with a softer tone.

But Negroes had to interact with the unreasonable, purportedly Christian, White people all the time, every day, all over the country.

Bad interactions were neither rare nor imagined. They were quite real and frequent, judging from the number of similar encounters of myriad Black people for hundreds of years. Sometimes you know exactly who they are, or at least you suspect them. Other times, you don't know and just have to guess, or risk being surprised. My working assumption was that 25% of the country was irredeemable when it came to matters of race; that assumption was probably a bit optimistic.

In the second week after the start of the school year, four White men, members of the KKK, put nineteen sticks of dynamite in the basement of the 16th Street Baptist Church on a Sunday morning in Birmingham, Alabama. Before the blast, a man called during the church service to tell the congregation they had 3 minutes to get out of the church building. But the bomb went off within 30 seconds of the call. Four little Black girls, in their Sunday best and carrying their pocketbooks, had attended Sunday school. They were killed by the blasphemous, impious explosion set off that morning by criminals and murderers, purporting to be men of faith and followers of Jesus Christ.

As illogical as it seemed to me, a person had to be a White Christian, non-Catholic, to join the Ku Klux Klan. The men in the Klan brought death, desecration, and an unmistakable non-Christian message to the Negro community at large; if we will kill your children while they are praying in church, what do you think we wouldn't do to the rest of you? The church bombing was an exclamation point on a mean, remarkable, unforgettable summer in the streets of America. It was also a stark reminder that the country I lived in had no limit as to the violence it would allow, accept, or acquiesce to on Negroes. In some of their eyes, it was a defensive move for the Klan to protect their country, heritage, and way of life from the existential threat presented by people unlike themselves.

It seemed we, Black people, were not actual people to some of them, and killing one of us was like taking down any other type of wild game in the woods or getting rid of loathsome vermin in an alley. The clamor, commotion, and violence with them seemed to have been going on my whole life because it had. It was a continuation of how things had always been, and I was feeling tired of it consuming my time, energy, and 12 year old spirit, as it had done to many before me. I was stuck in their shell game, with nowhere else to go.

CHAPTER 8

Leaving C1

Shortly after the March on Washington, with Dr. Martin Luther King delivering his historic "I Have A Dream" speech, I started what would be my final year at C-1, the Havre de Grace Consolidated School. We did not learn about the partial collapse of school segregation in Harford County, which would free most of us until very late in the school year. Until then, the students toiled on, and the teachers kept fighting the Board, trying to free us all.

Thanks to Uncle George Lisby, I had a ringside seat for much of the show. He was exasperated by the official positions, double-dealing, and antics of the Board officials, pretending to care about what was best for Negro students and teachers. He would come over to the house and bring his soap box with him. Mom was usually his main audience, as he would systematically check off all the lies and double talk that the Board was cooking up. With an eloquent, ecclesiastical, avenger voice, and like a preacher in a righteous pulpit, he sought to intellectually and verbally sleigh the local fossilized White devils of pedagogy.

I enjoyed the show and learned a lot about the machinery of racism and segregation in schools and how the system worked. There were people behind this making it happen, and Mr. Lisby knew all of them. It was an ongoing act, unlikely to end soon.

Miss Jane Gates was my 7th grade teacher. She was from Cumberland, Maryland, and had graduated from the revered Howard University, in

Washington, D.C. She was different from my other teachers, with the possible exception of my 4th grade teacher, Mrs. Davage. They were both kind of prickly, authoritative folks. But there seemed to be a class difference with Miss Gates. She seemed a cut above the rest of us in some ways. I'm sure being able to go to a school like Howard could mold you and your expectations in life in a different way than going to a state school like Bowie or Morgan. The teachers, and the people you interact with, would be very different, I suspected. She carried herself strongly and proudly. She was very smart, with an easy command of English, without a trace of a recognizable regional accent. I just didn't like the way she projected herself sometimes. But I learned important aspects of English and writing skills in her class that were making me a better communicator.

The beginning of the school year was normally hopeless. There was talk about which students were trying to transfer out of Consolidated to the white school. People had talked to my mother about the possibility of Pat and me going to the new John Carroll Catholic School that was going to open in Bel Air. Students were trying to get out of Consolidated, a school with no future, which was a rightful fate for a nondemocratic institution, in a supposed democracy. Mr. Lisby's soap box tirades in the living room gave me an insight as to what was happening to us, why, and who was doing it. Uncle George called them out by name; Charles Willis, Charles Reed, Virginia Pate, Clark Jones, Ernest Vogel…And he threw in Federal Judge Roszel Thomsen too. So, I had a very good idea who they were, what their part in it was, and, generally, what was going on.

We had been doing the usual daily colored school grind for a few months when it was suddenly interrupted by events in America. I didn't go to school that day. I was watching my baby sister and trying not to give her my cold. The television was on Mom's favorite soap opera, "As the World Turns," when Walter Cronkite changed everything. It was just after 1:30 EST, the afternoon of November 22nd, 1963, when Cronkite reported to the country that President John Kennedy had been shot in Dallas, Texas. The President of the United States was pronounced dead at 2 o'clock EST. Within 90 minutes, the Dallas, Texas, police had arrested Lee Harvey Oswald for the murder. Lyndon Johnson was sworn in as the 37th President of the United States at 2:38 CST. Lee Harvey Oswald was killed the next day while in custody in the basement of police headquarters, by Jack Ruby, a Dallas nightclub owner. The shooting was beamed on live, grainy, black and white television into our homes. The time was 11:21 CST.

Almost everybody was shocked and saddened by the death of Kennedy, who took the hopes of many Negro Americans with him when he was felled. The country came to nearly a full stop overnight, with a deep pall cast in all directions of the compass. He had been a refreshing ray of hope that meaningful change was possible, even in a country like this, stuck thickly in denial of its own racial history and buoyed by self-proclaimed ignorance of the existence of a significant race problem presently. We had hoped to see John Kennedy lead White people kicking and screaming into something that looked more like a democratic society, but it was not to be. It would be for others to take up the historically difficult task of getting White people to believe in democracy for themselves and everybody else.

The music of the funeral procession was a solemn dirge fitting for the steel gray autumn day. The passing caisson was drawn by a team of white horses, towing the flag-draped casket of the fallen President. They were followed by a riderless horse with boots turned backward in the stirrups. The horse seemed agitated, like he was looking for his missing rider. After the interment at Arlington National Cemetery, a great sadness engulfed the land for many months. We did not know if we could trust President Lyndon Johnson, a Texan and southerner to carry on and do the things needed to be done for advancement to happen in the country for Negroes.

I was doing okay in school, but I knew I needed to do better. Many people were expecting me to do better. I just didn't have a goal driving me forward. I didn't have something to fight against other than the fight I was born into, which sometimes was not enough. The everyday background racism was there permanently. You couldn't spend too much time thinking about it, and you couldn't escape it either. I was academically floating but generally in a positive direction.

The math was becoming easier with Mr. Griffin. The distributive property was finally making sense, and I even knew what a google was, a 10 followed by 100 zeros. Mr. Griffin was very stern, but I liked him anyway because he was completely fair. If you knew the answer, you knew the answer, and you got the credit for it. If you didn't know it, Mr. Griffin was there to help you in his no-nonsense way. I always laughed when he would go into a full-on tizzy, after catching someone playing "X's and O's", or tic-tac-toe to everybody else. He was genuinely offended and spitting mad that anyone would do such a thing in his math class.

I was getting to the point where I could translate the math lessons into a brain package I could understand, even if I couldn't explain it to anybody else. Mr. Griffin had a large black and white slide rule hanging on the blackboard. I was mystified by all the numbers, the movement of the slide and cursor, and how the rule was used to do calculations. He didn't teach us to use it. But I figured, if I could operate one of those one day, I would have to really know some math.

My favorite new teacher that year was Mr. Rudolph Norton, from North Carolina Central College. He was young, a bit brash, and very certain about his abilities in math, science, and most other things. And boy, could he handle a slide rule. I would hang out in his room before the bell, picking up pointers about the slide rule, equations, molecules, and anything else in science that he was offering. He challenged me in ways I had never been, like designing a way for him to grade papers faster. It was simple for my brain to do, applying a little easily mined imagination, and common sense, and getting through the ambient head noise.

Mr. Norton and Mr. Lisby were good friends. They would carry me to all the science fairs they could find, as well as basketball games and track meets. They wanted me to know what the good students were up to in science and math in the white schools. I was extremely ready to get out of the Consolidated School, with our inferior facilities and accepted limitations. I was stunned by the quality of the science projects produced by the students of the white schools, even if they did have help from their accomplished parents. The level of scientific thought was beyond what I believed was possible in a high school. When I thought about my little Gilbert chemistry set at home, the lab equipment, reagents, and knowledge available to the White students, who did those experiments, were impressive. Our tax money was definitely helping to give them every chance to get ahead, while we were making do with one Bunsen burner for the entire science class.

The other reason I wanted to get out of Consolidated was I never fit in, anyway; and I didn't want to. Maryland boys were louder and less respectful than I was used to seeing or being around. The boys in my neighborhood were always into fighting each other and throwing rocks, their favorite pastime. They were surely like that before I moved to Aberdeen. There were woods across the way from our house on Dorsey Street. The trees were thick enough to obscure the activities inside, which the children loved. But you could still hear when a couple of the neighborhood tough kids were fighting each other and hurling rocks. I had little contact with those boys, which was safer for me, and fine with my mother.

Pat had a lot of friends in the neighborhood, and she even spent a little time at their homes. She got along well and didn't have any conflicts with her girlfriends that she couldn't handle. But Pat could fight. Her opponents were usually one of the boys in school who got fresh with her, or who was at the bus stop annoying her. She never beat up a boy who didn't deserve it. Fighting physically was the last choice. As a boy, fighting usually got you more people to fight and a negative reputation to go along with it. As we passed through the 4th grade, the differences between me and my Consolidated boy classmates were widening. I seemed to have less in common with most of them every year.

There was only one threatening situation, last year in 6th grade when some of the big downtown boys surrounded me in the bathroom. They pushed me around a little before one of them told me what the deal was. The boy, who stood a head taller than me, let me know that they didn't appreciate my sitting beside Barbara on the bus home. And if I did it again, something might......

That's when one of the teachers, Mr. Brashears, came into the bathroom and broke it up. I was confused, and I thought Barbara would be too since we were like neighborhood cousins. She was a very nice person, liked by everybody. But the boys in the bathroom were not playing around, in their quest to send me a message. I was shaken by the encounter, but I still realized the silly ridiculousness of what had just happened. Getting beat up in the bathroom, for sitting by a girl classmate on a school bus home—Come on. I wondered what made them decide to confront me in such a gangster manner in school. Why did they think it was a good thing to do? I knew that this probably did not enter into their calculations. I did not understand them and never had. I had known for a while that one day, I was going to come face to face in school with somebody I would probably have to fight. Some people thought I could be picked on. I couldn't figure out why a person would want to spend their time picking on someone unless they had a problem with themselves, or were jealous for some reason. There was an unofficial pecking order of badness among the boys in school. Your place in the order would depend on several things; your size, your friends, if you had a big brother, where you lived, and the name of your family.

I only had to throw one punch in school, and I didn't have a choice. A boy, not too high in the pecking order, decided one day to try to bully me, in the hall between classes. It was hard to believe that the particular boy did it because he was not a tough kid at all. You could easily imagine that the boy would be a target for bullying himself. That day, he was acting a little loud and slightly bad in the hall. He walked in my path, as I was going to class, mouthed something, and pushed me on my shoulder. I replied with a meaningful straight right to his chest, and to his great surprise. He was looking for someone to bother, to make himself feel better, and, perhaps, to move up in the schoolboy pecking order. If so, he was not looking for me.

That incident was merely annoying. The most serious unwanted interactions between boys usually occurred in the gym class, the bathroom, on the bus, or the playground. There seemed to be a desire, or need, in some of the 8th grade boys to bother the younger, smaller students and not the known class toughs. There was one boy who, for some reason, developed a dislike for me and decided to do something about it one day. We were playing softball on the playground against the 8th grade boys, who were mostly from Aberdeen. I was playing catcher and was situated much too close to a group of boys who had decided to have some fun at my expense. The group of 4 guys was being instigated by one with an especially hazing, taunting manner. It was mostly sophomoric trash talk and a few ad hominem insults, with some family stuff thrown in, rising steadily in aggressive playground silliness.

I was bent at the knees behind the plate, waiting for the pitch to be thrown and trying to ignore the boys. The batter swung at the next pitch and hit a soft pop-up a couple of steps to the left of home plate, in foul territory…... My ball! .….I moved under the ball to catch it for the out. That is when both of my legs gave weigh from a sudden, sweeping force delivered from the side and behind. I fell on my back to the ground and heard the laughter of the playground mob. I looked through the sun's glare to see the face of the main instigator, pleased with what he had done, and looking like a laughing, inappropriate chipmunk through my squint.

I supposed that my other more Maryland classmates understood these boys better than I did. All I wanted was to stay away from them and be careful the next couple of days in school. I had never cared for their lack of manners, and I could only imagine more friction like this if I continued in this school. The lunch bell rang, the ball game was over, and I was back in the relative safety of my classroom. I couldn't wait to leave this school, in large part because a few of the boys here, and my relationships with them, that were only going to get worse. I'd take my chances with the White boys in the white school, with more educational opportunities along with it. As far as the laughing 8th grade boy went, like Mom said, "Son, every dog has his day. You just have to wait until yours comes around." And, one day it did.

During the latter part of the school year, there always seemed to be a bit of commotion, and some contention, between the teachers and Mr. Roye. It was obvious our teachers were very restricted in talking about school integration, the Board of Education, or the subject of race in class. But that didn't stop important things from happening and the news from getting out. Of course, I knew more of what was going on because of Mr. Lisby's impassioned rants in Mom's living room.

One afternoon in the spring, my 7th grade teacher, Miss Jane Gates, was late coming back from lunch, to start our English class. She walked in about 10 minutes after the bell, to find a restive, talkative classroom full of her students. She was not pleased with our behavior, especially since the teachers were having a meeting about some important school matters, and our immediate future. She was serious with us, but not angry like she could get sometimes. We settled down into the lesson without any explanation for her tardiness. She looked like she had something heavy on her mind but couldn't speak of it to us. Shortly after that, the county school board announced the provisional demise of the segregation of public schools in Harford County, Maryland.

There was no ceremony, grand proclamation, or mea culpa; it was just suddenly, curiously over. Like Mr. Lisby told me, money was the key to just about everything in life, including sports, love, politics, and racism too. The Board had run out of money and declared the game over. It was, of course, more complicated than just that, and other factors were involved. But they didn't develop a sudden Christian calling to educate young Black kids or eschew whatever they had heard around their family dinner tables, in their churches, at the frat houses, or at the Rotary Club meetings all these years. But in the end, they simply ran out of funds to continue the separate and unequal school systems that some had coveted as if it was a precious stone. They wanted it preserved or kept around in Harford County at least until 1970, regardless of what the Supreme Court had to say on the matter. And you couldn't do that without some money to keep a contrived, dysfunctional system running; racist desires aren't dollars.

As we were getting the news of our apparent liberation from the talons of segregation, the Civil Rights Act of 1964 was winding its way through the byzantine, arcane rules of the United States Senate. It was a major advancement for Negroes in protecting our constitutional right to vote, thereby protecting us from the worst natural inclinations of some White people. If there was anything that White southerners were afraid of, it was massive numbers of Negroes voting in any election. Since most Negroes in America lived in the South, they were willing to do anything to keep their sacred vote away from Blacks, and murder was always an option. It was their custom, self-given right and some of them enjoyed it.

The bill had been originally proposed by President John Kennedy, and it was going nowhere at the time of his assassination. Congress was then jawboned, cajoled, and browbeaten by President Lyndon Johnson until the bill passed. The slice of democracy it finally ceded to Black Americans was first filibustered for nearly sixty days by members of the President's own majority party, a rare occurrence in American history.

As expected, the Democratic Southerners used all available methods in their quest to hold back time just a little longer. The South had never proclaimed its love for the concept of democracy, the quaint notion of one man-one vote, or ever showed any desire to extend the rights that they seemed to enjoy very much to others. The decision in Plessy vs. Ferguson was an inside joke. White people didn't actually believe things were going to be separate and equal, not the non-delusional ones anyway. They had no intention of providing the considerable amount of money it would take to attempt to make accommodations equal. But they could pretend like they believed it and be amazed or offended when Negroes couldn't see things exactly as they did, and that the Plessy decision was actually good for everybody.

It took another southerner who spoke their language and, for much of his life, had some of the same thoughts on certain social issues. President Johnson knew how to beat them at their own cynical game. The Democrats had less and less appetite for the support of Jim Crow (the policies and laws that essentially criminalized the state of being Negro in America), the KKK, or the continuation of letting things play out as God's will, just like they had in the good old days. Johnson knew he was going to lose the South to the Republicans for a generation, or more, with the passage of this democratizing law. The Democratic Dixiecrats were in the wrong party, and they knew it. It was only a matter of time before the civil rights movement drove them into the big, accepting arms of the GOP, the Grand Old Party. The Republicans were growing increasingly receptive to thinly disguised, somewhat deniable racism in their party, and the acceptance, into their fold, of the believers in the political, historical, and cultural supremacy of White Americans over everybody else — as long as they didn't say it too loudly.

With the help of twenty-seven Republicans counteracting the drag of the Southern Democrats, the Civil Rights Bill was passed and signed into law on July 2, 1964, and it was a very big deal. It sought to make America closer to a true democracy for the first time in its history. It put into the legal code that discrimination on the basis of race, sex, religion, color, or national origin was illegal. I took that to be an admission that all those anti-democratic processes had been allowed to exist, flourish, and were in play all this time, just as we suspected, in spite of what they told us about being too sensitive to things.

We had been lied to, hoodwinked, and shined on about democracy since enslavement, the Civil War, Reconstruction, and Plessy vs Ferguson. The fix was always in for whites when it came to matters of race in America, they just pretended like everything was equal, and Negroes were the disobliging, delusional, dissembling entity at play in politics. The bill outlawed racial segregation in America's schools, which I thought had been done already by the United States Supreme Court in 1954. But parts of America needed to hear it again.

My personal segregation ended suddenly in a whimper. One day in the spring of 7th grade, it was immediately finished, without warning, fanfare, or celebrations. It had seemed that most of the students in the Deep South were going to integrate before us, in Harford County, which was barely in the South. I was tired of being in the Consolidated, and I was willing to deal with whatever nonsense, arbitrary treatment, new teachers, and unfamiliar obstacles that lay ahead, to escape the obnoxious capriciousness of institutional segregation.

It was only a partial victory. None of the Black teachers would be allowed to transfer with us. The Board, especially Dr. Charles Willis, showed how small, petty, venal, unchristian, and mean they still were, by going after Mrs. Janet Grant, in large part for her activities in the civil rights movement. Mrs. Grant, a graduate of Morgan State and UCLA, had applied for a transfer to teach at a white school each of the last six years. That was a personal affront to a man like Willis, who was not about to forget it and would try anything to block her.

Dr. Willis, and the Board, seemed to think the exercising of constitutional rights by a Black teacher, involved in the civil rights movement was tantamount to sedition or breakage of some law or another. Dr. Willis wanted to make sure that Mrs. Grant was not included in the first group of Negro teachers to be transferred when segregation finally ended. Dr. Willis' gracelessness was thoroughly and effortlessly on display at all times because that is who he was, which was easy to see if you happened to be a Negro.

In a remarkable show of spiritual strength and grace in the face of evil, Mrs. Grant stated she would continue to do what was necessary for Negro advancement. If the Board was miffed by Mrs. Grant's participation in the civil rights march in Annapolis last summer, I was happy to say that I was there too, in the streets, engaging in what they called "sedition," right along with Mrs. Grant.

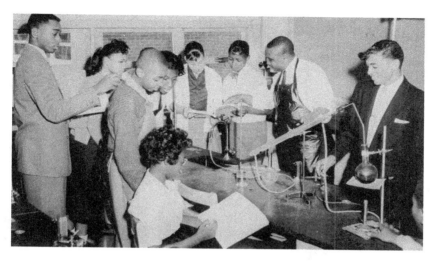

Mr. William Taylor is holding chemistry lab for his class with a single
Bunsen burner.
From the 1959 Havre de Grace Consolidated School Eagle Yearbook.
Photo by: George Griffin
Image: Courtesy of Harford County Board of Education

Mr. George Griffin teaching math class. He was the main reason we
were not behind in math when integration came.
From the 1959 Havre de Grace Consolidated School Eagle Yearbook.
Photo by: Bobby Parker
Image: Courtesy of Harford
County Board of Education.

Russell Stansbury
Maryland State College, B. S.
New York University, M. A.
Industrial Arts

Mrs. Florence S. Stansbury
Maryland State Teachers
College, B. S.
Core, Math, and Science

William L. Taylor
West Virginia State College, B. S.
West Virginia University, M. A.
Science

Mrs. Bernice H. Turner
North Carolina College
at Durham, B. S. C.
English and Business Education

Mrs. Gertrude A. Washington
Morgan State College, B. S.
English and Librarian

Rose D. Weems
Morgan State College, B. S.
Physical Education (Girls)

Mrs. Bernice J. Williams
Morgan State College, A. B.
New York University, M. A.
Social Studies

Some of our beloved, accomplished teachers of the Havre de Grace
Consolidated School.
(From the 1959 Havre de Grace Consolidated School,
Eagle Yearbook.)

BOOK II

CHAPTER 9

Trying to Understand White People

"It may be possible that the continued segregation of school children may continue here if the citizens of both races desire it."

Bel Air Aegis, 1956…..From a newspaper article, 2 years after the Supreme Court struck down school segregation.

In the spring of 1964, state-sanctioned school segregation was finally finished for me and my family. The school year usually started after Labor Day. But that year, the holiday came late in the first week of September, and the county public schools opened earlier than usual. Patricia and I started classes at the Havre de Grace High School for the very first time in the last week of August. It was the second time we had been to the school. The first time was when Mom took Pat and me down to the old red brick building on Congress Avenue. It was a small renegade act to walk through the doors and up the stairs to the second-floor administration office. We did what was objectionable and unthinkable to many; register for classes at Havre de Grace High School, the white school. There were probably prayers from all over pastoral Harford County, from Level to Jarrettsville and Abingdon. Many White people, and some Negro people, prayed that the day of integration would never come. But all the time, they feared it was an inevitable, irresistible, unwanted political and moral force on the way. If they could just convince Negroes segregation was best for them, too, then everything would be fine again, which seemed to me an irrational thought for any sane person to have, but they did.

This was 1964 America, just below the Mason-Dixon line. It was full to the brim with scared rural, God-fearing White folks, for whom change was not a friend but an existential threat. On a base level, they felt that they had the right to segregate in any social context by custom, if not by law, as they had always been free to do. On a political level, the whites in power used fear, denial, and distortions of reality and common sense to disguise and deodorize the foul potion they had peddled for so long. It made it easier for their undiscerning, less educated followers to get behind them in unquestioning lockstep. The local newspaper editorials and articles were slanted heavily toward continuing school segregation (as if it was their choice), mirroring the common beliefs of White county residents, and, probably, a few Negro readers.

The Bel Air Aegis Newspaper of June 1956 summed up the wishes, prayers, hopes, and delusions of some White people for Negroes to be reasonable, see their side of it and appreciate the things that had recently been given to them; their new consolidated schools. The article was referring to the Brown Supreme Court ruling outlawing segregation in education. It mentioned the two new schools and further said:

"The decision of the US Supreme Court banning segregation of races in public schools, is apparently being calmly received by school and county officials here. Harford is very fortunate in…. that it has two new consolidated schools for Negro children, which are as good and in some cases better than those for the white children… It is probable that many Negro leaders will regret the change, if segregation is stopped in Harford … the school leaders are very enthusiastic over their new consolidated schools and would probably be disappointed if the control of the schools were divided, if used by children of both races. However….. there are no racial problems here."

The article displayed the full-on mendacious paternalism, delusional clairvoyance, and the total White cluelessness of the time; they had convinced themselves they knew more about Black people than Black people knew about themselves. Some of them had convinced themselves they lived in a county with no race problem, and they conveniently saw no connection to race on the issue of the schools in the county being segregated by race. In addition, they thought it reasonable to expect Negroes would find it in our best interest to agree to voluntarily and happily continue second-class citizenship, personal degradation, violence, and death at their hands while erasing any guilt on the part of the perpetually innocent, self-deluding White people. It seemed like little Harford County was carving out a racial fiefdom for itself within the United States. They just had to get the courts to let them do it...... After all, the Supreme Court's Dred Scott decision originally said they could feel any way they wanted about Negroes, and act on it sometimes, without much consequence. And they liked that feeling and power, and then it was taken away. The Court took that right away from White people, but not the urge and itch to do whatever they wanted to Negroes. — Anyway, they said we had our brand-new schools, and that ought to be enough for now.

Another article in the Bel Air Aegis from September 13, 1956, stated this:

> "It has been generally recognized that practically all of the Negro school patrons of the county have been delighted with their new schools..., and it is probable that for many years to come there will be very few classes of mixed races in the county. The situation is most pleasant as compared to the troubles and confusion which have occurred in the other states and in several counties in Maryland."

To be fair, the high school had several Negro students already enrolled. There were a few former students from the Consolidated School who had transferred and another group of students mostly from New York, who had never attended segregated schools. Ten years after the Supreme Court's Brown ruling, you would have hoped that Harford County schools would have already enrolled a few Negro students into the white schools. And they did, a very few. Some of the families jumped through the onerous transfer process for "colored students." This process included IQ tests and a committee evaluation for fitness for transfer by an all-White panel. The committee was not envisioned by the Brown Supreme Court ruling, but the Board of Education gave it a desired customized rural Harford County touch.

And then, there were the New York Negro kids. The school board seemed to produce an acceptable exception to allow them admission into their sanctum. Perhaps the Board felt that exposing these New York "colored students" to segregation so late in life would be unacceptably harmful to them, as students and people... Maybe... Even Mr. Lisby didn't know the answer to why the Board did that with the New Yorkers. It annoyed me that the New York boy, who lived behind Erie Street in my neighborhood, could move here and enroll in the white school, no questions asked. The rest of us who had been fighting for that right were continually told no. I got the feeling that the New York boy took that as a sign that he was better than the Colored School kids too, just like most White people thought.

Lastly, there was an even smaller group of Negro students in elementary schools who had never attended the Consolidated Schools from the start of their education. The Board must have kept the workings of that process of admission a closely guarded secret. And, I imagined the Board had a list of certain Black families they didn't want to mess with and didn't want to fight.

When we went to register in the summer, I couldn't tell if the office staff at the high school was happy to see me and my family, or if they were irritated by our presence in their school, and were just acquiescing. My parents had paid taxes for the functioning of all the county schools, even this one. The Harford County Board of Education had unconstitutionally kept me fettered in inferior, racially segregated schools for seven years after the Supreme Court told them to stop. Only a fool would voluntarily pay for the facilities to benefit others, while those facilities were off-limits to themselves. That is exactly what Dr. Willis, the Board, and many White citizens expected us to do, and to be. We simply came to collect what we had already paid for.

Mom, and many other Black adults, felt that their children had a right to go to a school that had trigonometry, foreign language courses, real science labs, academic diplomas, and even glass backboards in a full-size gym. Still, the look on the face of the middle-aged White lady registering us was not all that welcoming. It was neutral at best.

We signed the papers for our classes, said thank you to the office staff, and left the school. Mom made sure we were put in the correct academic courses, and not accidentally put into general classes, industrial arts, or special education. To Mom, there was no reason to believe that the county Board of Education, or this school, suddenly had sincere concerns about the best educational interest of Negro children, in addition to their happiness and well-being. No. We could have been going to the white school a long time before this if the good Christian folks of the county had read their Good Book, practiced what was inside it, and accepted that Jesus was unlike them; He loved all of humanity without exception, tended to the poor and the sick, and He was not a bigot. That's what Mom would think.

We could not be sure what to expect from the teachers and the administrators of the school. It should have been apparent to everyone the Harford County school system had been erected in a way to benefit White children preferentially and eternally. They built inferior facilities for Negroes, and then fought like the dogs of hell to keep us from escaping the educational graveyards and spiritual catacombs they had so carefully dug for us. The county could concentrate our numbers, paying as little as possible to keep us contained. They provided as little education as they could get away with, at the least cost, and educated us to fit their needs. What was in their schools that was so important and valuable that we had to be kept apart? Was it the education or something else they were afraid of Negro students being too close to? Something that some of them seemed willing to fight to my death to preserve.

When I started at the white school, it had been ten years since the Supreme Court ruled that segregation in public education in the United States of America was illegal and the educational system based on it should cease. Furthermore, school integration should proceed with "all deliberate speed" to make it happen. In the case of Harford County, "all deliberate speed" turned out to be a leisurely 3,772 days from the court's landmark ruling. It took that amount of time for the county to accommodate equal education to the original 2000 students in Colored Schools and the subsequent students put into those schools after the 1954 Supreme Court ruling. It took 10 years to absorb the 2000-plus Negro students into a student body of 16,000 whites, with all deliberate and conscious lack of speed.

A citizens consultation committee, composed of 36 county citizens, including 5 Black members, was convened in 1956 by the Board of Education. It provided cover and notoriety for some people. A sub-committee on the social aspects of desegregation was chaired by Mrs. Jason Pate, a resident of Havre de Grace. Mrs. Pate and the committee concluded that the ideal ratio of "white to colored" students in the county schools should be 10 to 1, mirroring the demographics of the County. Nothing in the Supreme Court Brown decision allowed for the use of this ratio, and there was no explanation of what would be done with the remaining Negro students, who did not numerically fit into her formula. Dr. Willis, the Board, and their lawyers continued to use logic not expressed by the Brown case. They performed customization of the case to fit the sensibilities and comfort of their rural, fearful, godly White constituents, which was the basis of their sandbagging, time-wasting, ostensible "Step Wise Plan." This plan called for the county to integrate certain grades one year at a time, with completion around 1970, or so. They did not try to explain why the Deep South had already initiated court ordered integration, sometimes under threats of force, yet little litigious Harford County stood as an island of unbent resistance to Brown, and school desegregation, to an effective degree in federal court.

The County had been involved in a string of five lawsuits brought by Negro students seeking transfer to white schools. The cases were Moore (I and II), Slade, Pettit, and Christmas. Dr. Willis had a difficult time ever seeing students and teachers in integrated classrooms across the county, as long as he was in charge. Willis was a man blissfully stuck deeply in the past, and he wanted the Board, the schools, and Harford County to stay there with him.

Both the state of Maryland and the counties knew what was coming but were stalling for as much time as possible. The federal court seemed to be dancing along with them most of the time and cutting near maximal slack to the county often. Finally, Federal Judge Roszel Thomsen had enough of the county lawyer's specious arguments, involving how much the desires and anxieties of the White county residents should play in the proceedings. This was not a valid point of argument in the case, so the lawyers were "estopped" from bringing it up again, but it was all they had. The legal tricks and sleights of hand had served them well in the courts all these years, but they were of little use once the Board finally ran out of money to fund two parallel, unequal school systems. This part of the game was over, with more games to come, but it was the undeniable historical lay of the land as I started the once-white school.

My mother, Mercides Robinson Griffin, was taken in
Albany, Georgia, in 1952.

LJF/FORD/GRIFFIN COLLECTION!!!

Mom and my little sisters, Pelbea and Pamela,
was taken in our home in 1986.

LJF/FORD/GRIFFIN COLLECTION!!!

CHAPTER 10

Enter To Learn

The first morning of school seemed amazingly normal, considering the magnitude of what was getting ready to happen. Pat was preening in the bathroom, while Wayne and the girls were eating some breakfast with Mom in the kitchen. I was ready and was getting my pencils and tablets in order and trying not to forget anything. The radio was on WANN and playing the summer's Motown anthem of protest, "Dancing in the Streets." It sounded as good as when I first heard it back in the spring. I told Mom goodbye and she wished me good luck as I left the house for school, just like it was a normal day. She didn't give me any final words of wisdom. This day had been a long time coming, and Mom knew I understood what was at stake and what I needed to do about it.

I passed the corner of Erie and Juniata Streets, the former bus stop for the colored students, going to the colored school. No one was there. All of us were walking to school today for the first time. There were still yellow school buses coming down the hill, still filled with White students who were now my schoolmates. That gave me a lot of new things to think about on my little walk to school. Most of what I knew about White people was from the news and Mr. Lisby. Mom hardly ever talked about them, in general. What I knew, saw, and read about them was checkered, and that was being kind. There were magnificent and awe-inspiring achievements in science and the arts from the same group of people responsible for slavery, blowing up churches, killing children, lynchings, and mutilations; not to mention two world wars, the Spanish Inquisition, eugenics, The Trail of Tears, European Colonization, the Catholic Church, Pat Boone, and barbecue sauce made from mayonnaise. I remained astounded by their ability to believe patently untrue things, apparent to any person able to sense the world. Small wonder they could concoct the doctrine of separate but equal and pretend Negroes were being unreasonable when we didn't want to play along in their insulting, rigged 3D shell game of non-reality, all taking place in their Potemkin village of racial harmony.

I passed the stop light at Otsego Street and headed for the halfway point of my short walk. The old Pennsylvania Railroad bridge was supported by large brawny, aged stones, moist and partially colored green from lichenification due to the constant dripping of water, or something, from the tracks. The dank, musty odor was familiar to me from the many times I had walked this way. The last thought I entertained before my final destination was something I had recently heard on the radio. It was late at night this summer in the kitchen. I was tuned to a nighttime AM talk show, and given the accents of the callers, they were from the South. The topic was the recently passed Civil Rights Bill, the demonstrations for voting rights, and all the commotion the Negroes were causing in the country that was upsetting so many White people. The young man, probably an older teenager, had called in to tell the moderator about something he didn't understand, and it was bothering him:

> "Why are all these colored people marching and protesting and making noise in the streets? I don't get it. They are really ungrateful.
>
> I mean, we gave them their freedom already. Right? What else do they want from us?" —-

It was frightening to hear that from a young person. But he went on:

> "And, I really don't think those colored people can give believable opinions on a lot of social things, because the stuff they are talking about is happening to them at the time. Their opinions are not reliable like other people's who would be looking at a situation from the outside and not being personally involved.

You know what I mean? Right? Right?"

He was followed by an older man who wanted more information from the moderator about Negroes who had owned White slaves in the South before the Civil War. There did exist a large subset of people, especially in the South, who you could get, willingly and with bliss, to believe most anything negative about Negroes, and who knows what other matters.

That was my last disturbing thought before turning on Congress Avenue, walking by the industrial arts building and the old clapperless victory bell on its red brick base, to the doors of the school, into my new world. Over the door was the inscription, "Enter to Learn, Leave to Serve." I was thinking — that's nice. We'll see what that actually means.

Mrs. Dinger was my homeroom teacher, and her room was on the second floor near the office, where we registered for school in the summer. It was easy to find. She was a fresh-faced young woman, eager and ready to get the school year going. She had gone to a teacher's college in Pennsylvania, and she had the kind of non-southern accent that you heard in people from that area; a little flat, moderately nasal, but twangless. The main thing was that she likely didn't carry the below the Mason-Dixon Line baggage that some of the long-time teachers at this school might have.

After spending seven years at C1, the Colored School, it was strange to sit in the homeroom listening to a voice on the public address system that was not Mr. Leon S. Roye, the longtime principal of the Consolidated School. Instead, it was Mrs. Gorsuch, who I had seen at registration in the summer. I didn't think I could expect her to be as inspiring and entertaining as Mr. Roye. That wasn't the only difference I'd see on the first day.

But after all the buildup, nothing particularly memorable occurred on day one at the former white school. Mrs. Dinger, my homeroom teacher, also taught math. My homeroom was designated 8-2, as in section number 2 of the eighth grade. There were five Negro students in 8-2, and about 20 other ex-Consolidated students in the other sections of the grade, except for section 8-1. There were no Negroes in 8-1, the top academic section. Karen Lilly, Doris Durbin, and the Christy cousins, Jeffery and Elroy, were in 8-2 along with me. Out of a class of 30, I only knew one White student, Jimmy McFadden, who played on my Pop Warner football team. I had just recently met him. He was very nice and a good teammate too. But he was the only non-Consolidated student I knew. There were a couple of other students known to me by face, as I had seen them around town or in the stores shopping. I had also seen the names of many of the older Whites students on the pages of the local newspaper, The Havre de Grace Record, for various reasons.

It was a very official kind of day, with papers being signed, stapled, folded, and handed in, repeatedly. Roles were taken, books passed out, and people watched each other quietly. Consciously or unconsciously, we all watched each other that day, looking for a difference, a sameness, a brilliance, or a flaw in our new schoolmates.

Meeting the new teachers was a major part of the first day, of course. I did not know it at the time, but I would never again have a classroom Negro teacher, for any subject, in the school system of Harford County. The new instructors would have to be sized up, one by one, to see if there was anything that needed my immediate awareness. It was not possible to put all these historically conflicting forces and people together after years of contentious interactions, from the dime store to the courtroom, and count on nothing to happen. When things did happen, not all of them were going to be worth fighting about. If I were going to have a problem with someone, it would probably be from one of the teachers who had been at the school the longest, with the most to defend or lose. But I was trying to be aware of potential friction from all areas of school life until I got a better feeling for my new environment.

I didn't have to wait long in the school year to find out what foul attitudes were lying shallowly beneath the veneer of school normalcy. They were not buried deeply, were not dead, and could erupt with minimal or no, provocation. Music would have been low on the list of classes that I thought could be my first problem in the school. It was the last period of the day, which meant I was taking every moment to do some homework to get ahead. Some of the girls in the class, and Mrs. Hutchison, the teacher, had started some small talk and a bit of school gossip, waiting for the final bell. That's when I got my math out, trying to do a couple of problems in class and get ahead of my busy evening.

My math book was opened on my desk with a few papers on top of it. Then unseen, and from behind me, came the long arms of Long Leg Lee, who quickly snatched my book and papers. With a couple of quick steps of his long legs, he was in the front of the room, near the distracted teacher and the trash can. He quietly dropped my classwork in the trash and innocently walked back to his desk laughing, very pleased with himself. He was just having some 6th period fun at my expense. He probably figured I deserved it for being so irritatingly studious. I thought it was a little funny too. It was just Lee being his old jokester self; if he didn't like you, he wouldn't bother you. Everybody knew that about Lee.

Mrs. Hutchison was still engaged with the girls, talking about some rich girl in the school being a "Golden Child," which brought laughter, and agreement from some of the girls. I got out of my seat, went to the trash can, and retrieved my work, as Lee kept enjoying himself. I went back to my seat thinking it was over and I could finish the math. When Lee initiated his second sortie, I was surprised again and was getting a little annoyed, because I wanted to get a couple of math problems done. It was the same play on a different down. He filched my book and papers, took two steps, and deposited them in the trash can again, then chuckled to himself on the way back to his seat.

Fun is fun, but I was running out of patience. It looked like not bothering me was not on Lee's mind at the time. I got up again and walked to the trash can to retrieve my goods, and I could have gone back to my desk, closed my math book, indicated to Lee that he had won, and I'd do my math when I got home after football practice. I didn't do that. I did what I would have done at the Consolidated School since those teachers had a special problem with students interfering in the learning of others, even if it was a joke. Mrs. Hutchison didn't feel that way, especially with people like me and my kind, and she had no problem saying it out loud to the whole class.

It was probably a mistake to try to get an audience with Mrs. Hutchison right at that time, but what she did was a good thing for me to see so early in the school year. She let me get seven words out of my mouth, including her name, before she went off.

Mrs. Hutchison, could you please tell Lee…..

And that was it. She had enough of my kind and was up to her limit of tolerance. She let me, and the class, know exactly how she felt about certain things, and certain people being in the school this year. Her eyes were alight in an angry glow. There wasn't one wrinkle of kindness or understanding, on her small angry white face. She hit on me like she'd been carrying a burdensome thing for a while and had been looking forward to unloading it on some susceptible person. She looked upon me as if I was some detestable, sub-human refuse, standing objectionably in her line of sight and unwelcome in her classroom, school, or life. It seemed I had taken something from her, to which she dearly claimed unquestioned ownership in perpetuity. She had the appearance of an enraged gargoyle that you might see spouting water from the corner of an ornate building, looking squat, bug-eyed, menacingly medieval, and potentially savage. She seemed possessed of something close to hate, and she was ready to blow. I would not have been surprised to see her head spin around at that point. She said:

> You see, this is what I mean. You colored kids have no business in our school messing things up and causing problems like you do. You should have stayed at your own schools and left us alone in ours. You should not be here……

She went on for a bit more before the bell saved us. She showed how she felt, and that should have been abundantly clear to all within earshot, and with a basic working knowledge of English. I wondered how the scene in class was received by my new classmates, if received at all. I was glad to leave school that day and was even happier that I was going to see Mr. Lisby at football practice to get a little needed reality and grounding. Having music only once a week was a blessing.

But, Mrs. Hutchinson was not finished venting on her colored students yet. Toward the end of the grading period, she let the class, and especially the colored kids, know of a decision she had made, affecting only us, the Negro students. She delivered what she had to say with all the compassion and concern of a plantation overseer, in an antebellum field of cotton. She told us:

> I have thought about how I was going to grade the colored kids this first quarter.

> Since I don't know you all, or your abilities well enough, I have decided to give all the colored students a grade of "C" for the grading period.

It was definitely a colored "C," and, perhaps, I was lucky to get that. It was my first colored "C" at the white school. She intimated that she didn't know us well enough to give us any other grade. And she did. She gave me a "C" as a grade on the first quarter report card. Her excuse for doing it struck me as a ridiculous and lazy way for a teacher to think, and then it was outrageous and insulting to announce it to the class.

She did it because she could, with no cost to her, and likely it decreased her stress and anger caused by the Negro students for a little while. Being that close to a white person having difficulties controlling their racism and then blaming it on me, was dripping with serious pathology. There was enough black humor there to activate the more inappropriate regions of my brain and force me to beat back the funny stuff trying to make its way to my mouth. There was no penalty Mrs. Hutchison would incur for her classroom rant, and there was no one to complain to about things like this unless you wanted to start World War III in the school today. I wondered what would have happened if Mrs. Hutchison had said something equally degrading to one of the white kids. But there was nothing she could say to white kids that would equally attack them for the color of their skin.

The music teacher, like a lot of other white people, liked to use that word.... colored. They used it as a shield and a weapon at the same time. It certainly differentiated us from them and everybody else. What words did they use when we were out of range? It wasn't too hard to guess. Like Mom said, we would have been at this school years ago if they had wanted us here. They didn't want us then, and there were many people who didn't want us now.

That was a very bad interaction with a teacher, and it was easily the worst memory of the first year at the white school. Mrs. Hutchison was angry, aggressive, aggrieved, and dismissive of the Negro students in general. She was very direct in letting me know what was wrong with me being in her classroom or her school. It was a sure bet that she was not alone in her way of thinking. She didn't want to hear that we, the Negroes of the county, had paid for the functioning of her school, without having any access to it for decades.

It was a good thing it was just music class and not something more academically important. We were easy targets in the school, and there wasn't much to do about it. We couldn't hide who we were all day. Transferring Negro students without transferring our Negro teachers exposed us to the whims and attitudes of the White teachers and staff, without any adult backup of our own. We were in hostile territory for a year by ourselves. The white school just wanted us to trust them to do what was right for us, like on the old plantation, in the good old days. It didn't look like they were planning on doing anything to earn our trust, but they wanted us to act as if they had. And we could show a little gratitude and understanding of their difficult position and some appreciation towards them for a change.

CHAPTER 11

The Perfect Hit

The first semester at the former white school was going as expected. I appreciated all the wisdom, spoken or implied, imparted to me by the wise and tested teachers at the Consolidated School. They taught me the meaning and importance, of self-esteem, comportment, and dignity, to get through hard times. (Pat told me just don't ever let them see you sweat, that's all.) I tried to limit my encounters with just about everybody in school until I had a better grasp of people and the way things were in my new environment. I felt like I was being watched or being disproportionately noticed and observed, like a lab rat, because I was. Some people were just looking on to see what was going to happen in the new social gumbo at school. However, some were more active in the game negatively but not transparently. No doubt about it, dealing with White people was a game of the head soul and not for the fearful or faint of heart.

It would be hard to miss me or any of the other few Negro students in the halls, shops, and classrooms. The majority of the Consolidated School students had gone to Aberdeen High, which was a larger school. I didn't know if the size of the school was a factor in how my friends there were getting along. Of course, they had all White teachers too. When more of their adults were around, in general, more things happened to you; some good, some bad, some obvious, some subtle, and many occurrences questionable. What did the teachers see when they looked at us? Most of the teachers appeared fine on the surface, but most were not all. At least my music teacher revealed herself to me early on, and I had no interest in trying to change her mind not in a music class in junior high school. Fortunately, the original colored "C" that Mrs. Hutchison had bestowed on my record would not count in my high school grade point average, GPA.

It was a blessing to have football as a release valve to the aggravation of school and the dealings with some of the new people. I had a lot more control of things playing on the field than sitting in the classroom. And after dealing with the condescension of Mrs. Hutchinson during the week, I got to beat up on a few slow, unsuspecting white boys every Saturday at the football game. It was therapy. Mr. Lisby was still teaching at the now cadaverous Consolidated School. No Negro teachers were allowed to transfer to any of the white county schools as part of the Board of Education's tepid surrender plan to the forces of integration and reality. The mass of Negro students from the Consolidated Schools invading their consecrated spaces was galling enough. Dealing with those long suspected, very educated, potentially seditious Negro teachers in their schools, teaching their own children, was not something the Board of Education, and many White citizens, were ready to accept.

Mr. Lisby, Uncle George, was the coach of the new Pop Warner football team in Havre de Grace. Our team was integrated, and there was no confusion on anyone's part as to who was in charge. Most of the teams in our league were all-White, including the coaches. We practiced twice a week and had games on Saturdays at the town's old race track, where the immortal Citation ran in the 40s. I looked forward to practicing to get physical, let off some steam, and see Uncle George.

In spite of the disorienting changes, I felt calmer and better about life, knowing he was still around and close by. He kept an eye on me to make sure I hadn't seen anything I couldn't handle at school, like nasty curveballs, spitballs, brushbacks, or beanball pitches from any direction. I told Uncle George that I had taken their first pitch and saw what they were bringing. It was a chin high, hard one, a purposeful message pitch to move me off the plate. That was in the parlance of baseball, which George Lisby dearly loved, and it was an apt metaphor for my situation in school.

I was a reluctant football player at first. One of our better players got hurt early in the season, and he stopped playing. That forced me to come out of hiding at the end of the bench. We had a good team, so hiding was easy. My ex-Consolidated friends, Bobby Harris and Robert Ware, were on the team, and both were excellent athletes. Bobby was fast, and so was Danny, our quarterback. Robert was country strong and showed it at every game and practice. Our team was composed of town boys from the lower grades of the high school, except for Danny Bungori, who went to the Catholic School in Bel Air. He was the fastest running White boy I had ever seen on an athletic field, and he could motor. It was always a jolt to the other team to realize Danny was the fastest player on the field. And he was completely unflappable like he was used to being in control of things. Nothing ever seemed to bother him. All the boys on the team knew Danny and his dad, who was a Sergeant in the Havre de Grace town police department. Sergeant Bungori had a very good reputation in the community, and he was a vocal, encouraging presence at our games.

I eventually enjoyed playing very physically on Saturdays, especially after realizing my body wasn't made of fine crystal, and a little pain and discomfort were survivable. It was a balm to me for being at the High School all week and dealing with everything new and different there. But watching Uncle George in charge on the sidelines, his poker face studying the field, looking for the next best move, was a big part of my Saturday joy. He was a master tactician on the field – just as he was a master teacher in the classroom – who liked to throw in some ambitious trick plays occasionally as an exclamation point.

The White coaches, on the other sideline, had no clue as to what type of Black man their adversary was. They had no idea of the kinds of endured experiences that had brought Mr. Lisby to this moment, now intersecting with their lives. There was no doubt in Mr. Lisby's mind of his abilities to outthink, or outwork, whoever was on the other side. And even as the Harford County Board of Education cast doubts about the qualifications and intelligence of Negro teachers and students, on Saturdays, Mr. Lisby didn't have to fight a system; just another man on the other sideline. It was the most democratic activity in his week, and in mine too.

This was Saturday, and school was out. The schooling that was going to take place would be on the field when stoic Coach Lisby was going to enjoy beating the stuffings out of the other team with his marvelous mind. If he got a chance to use our special play, the "dip-si-doo," late in the game, he would do that too. It was a final stylish stiletto in the opposition's heart, with a twist, to let them know they just got beat and who just beat them. But through the entire game, Coach Lisby never changed the dour look on his poker face. He was all business on Saturdays and all the other days of the week too.

By midseason, we were undefeated and having more fun than I could have ever imagined. After a while, being one of the smaller players on the field didn't matter as much. I had the tackling technique down and had learned to use my speed and agility to make stops with surprising physicality. By the third game, I had learned the key to survival on defense was to accelerate into the tackle. Because—Force = Mass x Acceleration; Newton's second law of motion, which I had seen in the encyclopedia, and it seemed to apply to football.....I was dangerous and safer with that appreciation of elementary applied football physics. I could not change my mass, but I had control over my acceleration. Once or twice in a game, everything would line up just right, and I would get to make a very satisfying tackle on one of the opposing players that would get their attention. Or, if I had good speed and it was a straight shot, I'd aim for just above the boy's waist and try to accelerate right through him.

That is exactly what happened in the last Bel Air game– a dream shot straight at the punt returner. He was looking away from me, trying to find a path out. He pulled the ball down, turned, and ran directly, squarely into me as I accelerated with the last push of my right leg and boom! The impact was loud, and it immediately stopped the boy's forward motion. I felt the hit a little but kept moving forward after the contact, still churning my legs. It was perfect - like hitting a baseball on the sweet spot of a hickory bat. There wasn't much vibration, all crack and pop. The impact drove my bigger opponent back about 3 yards, where we landed on the dirt. I rolled over on my back, thinking, "Wow! That was a really good one. The form was just about perfect."

At first, I was not aware of the stir in the crowd the noisy hit had caused. People were clapping and cheering like they had seen something special. When I went off to the sideline, Mr. Lisby came over to me to see if I was okay, which was a surprise. That is when I knew the hit must have looked even better than it felt, and I was sorry I was never going to get to see it. Even my teammates were a bit amazed and excited by it. Mom enjoyed coming to the games, too, once she realized she was watching a different version of her son. She was surprised and pleased with some of the things I could do. But mostly, she was happy to see I could protect myself and have a good time at it. Even the referees enjoyed our games, and that was a very high compliment to our style of play and to our coaching.

We had only one difficult game the whole season, with the team from the Patterson Park area of Baltimore. They came to Havre de Grace to play us when they, too, were undefeated. They were gritty, urban, White boys who were so tough that their uniforms did not match. They looked like a mixed group of hyperactive harlequin and calico cats in their motley incongruous jerseys, pants, and helmets. Nobody laughed or even mentioned it after the initial shock of seeing them. Those boys came to play, and that is what they did. We found out right away why they had not lost a game in the league; teams were afraid of them.

At halftime, we found ourselves in the unusual position of being behind by a touchdown. I had made a very big mistake early in the game, missing my pass coverage assignment and then having to watch my undefended man streaking alone down the sideline. He extended his arms to catch the fairly soft, arching pass coming his way. Danny was playing defensive back, and I was the safety, the last line of defense. We watched in real - time, slow motion as the ball reached the Baltimore player's fingers. He turned his head to run an instant too soon as the ball glanced off his digits, falling harmlessly to the ground. Audible groans and gasps from the big crowd filled the air of the field at the old town race track.

Danny looked at me with an unruffled little smile. We both agreed that I had nearly really messed up, and we shared a private deep breath about it, standing in the middle of the field. We knew what to do; switch positions, which we did without asking Mr. Lisby. I was more aggressive than Danny, and I wanted to be closer to the line so I could hit somebody on every play. Danny was better at waiting for the play to develop and reacting with his incredible speed. My aggression had almost cost us a touchdown.

We learned our lesson in the first half. We were a little tight, and nervous before the large crowd that had come to see our big little game.

I don't think Baltimore had faced a team before in the league that was not afraid of the city boys or had a coach as smart as Mr. Lisby. We ground them down in the second half with our speed. Bobby and Robert each scored rushing touchdowns in the half. Baltimore got tired later in the game and couldn't keep up with us. We beat them; not bad, but bad enough.

There was one more game after that, which we won, finishing the year undefeated. We had our team party at Danny's house and got our championship trophies there. Mr. Lisby had not expected our team to be as competitive and physical as we turned out to be in our very first year. But neither did his players. Well, maybe Danny did. About a week after I had put my cleats away for the last time, Mr. Lisby contacted all our team players to give us the news; the Baltimore coach had invited our team to a championship game on their home field in 2 weeks. They were having a hard time believing they got beat by some country boys from little old Havre de Grace. I had mixed feelings about playing them again. If they beat us, they would be champs, and that didn't feel completely fair because we had already beaten them. But it would be another chance to beat up on some pretty good city boys and watch Coach George, in control of the troops and the game, one more time.

It was a spectacularly sunny, early November Saturday in Herring Run Park in Baltimore. A large group of parents, family members, and fans showed up from both sides. The adults were just as excited as the players, maybe a little more. Danny's dad, Sergeant Bungori, was there with his family, as were some of my neighbors and many other people from the town. This was a very big game, and both sides were loud, a little aggressive, and expecting a good contest. Even the referees were excited because they knew there were some very good athletes in the game they were calling.

We took the kickoff after winning the coin toss and started on our 20-yard line. The first play from scrimmage was a simple 6-yard square out pass to me, directly in front of the loud Baltimore bench, backed up by their rabid fans. Their best player was covering me, but he was not a factor in my dropping a perfectly thrown ball from Danny against the sideline.....Okay... First play of the game; a little nerves; early yet; so what; wake up...I told myself.

I winced at my gaffe and turned to rejoin my team when I felt a firm tug and spin of my shoulder pads. The touch was not friendly, but authoritative, and rather disrespectful. My helmet turned and revealed part of a wrinkled white face, with poor dentition, and a mouth full of white trash talk. He held on to my shoulder pads and shook me a little, as he gave me a very personal message. "Hey boy! That's the old butter fingers, boy!" which was followed by a hardy, raspy Lucky Strike laugh. "Keep it up, boy! Good job." I pushed his hands off of me and went back to the huddle.

The whole incident took no more than 6 seconds. I couldn't believe that he had touched me and seemed to think it was a natural right of his. He was the second aggressive adult White person who felt comfortable getting in my face and spewing their take on the world, since the start of school. But I had a lot of control this time around. Mr. Lisby once told me that the difference between me and my brother, Wayne, was this; "If Wayne got mad at you, he'd just take a couple of swings, and then it's over. But you, Larry, wouldn't do that. You'd go back to your room and think about it a while, and then come out with the perfect plan to really get the person back, twice as bad," which was absolutely true. That's probably what Mr. Lisby would have done too. I was just coming out of a brief visit to that special headspace of mine, in time for the next play. I wasn't mad at what happened, only because I couldn't afford to be.

This was all cold-blooded business now, and I knew the work I had to do. I was glad we had more than three and a half quarters left to play in the game, so I could get even and maybe a little more. I was in a good position to influence the outcome of the game and deliver a message to the White man, with the bad teeth, who actually touched me.

I got my chance on defense the second time Baltimore had the ball. Their main player was a boy named Frank, #11, who ran with crazy leg and arm movements like he had chorea. He would try to juke and jive his way clear because he couldn't do it with flat-out speed. He had scored a touchdown on us in the first game, and he was dangerous enough. But he was the only one we had to watch out for. If he was on our team, he would be the fourth fastest, after me. I had been in on a tackle of him with another player earlier, but the chance to really hit him had not presented itself yet. If we stopped Frank, we would win, and the Baltimore team, and their fans, knew it too. He was good, but he couldn't beat all of us.

Baltimore threw a little flare pass out to Crazy Legs in the flat. He caught the ball, turned, and danced a step before I launched off my right leg, and cold-stoned him, right in his bread basket, with more force than #11 expected. At the time of the hit, my right cleat caught and came off my foot. I was grabbing so hard with the toe of the shoe, in an effort to generate as much force as possible, that it went flying backward, like an arching rooster tail. I ran out of my shoe, doing my best to run right through Frank and meet up with myself on his other side. It was a very good purposeful hit, loud, clean, ringing, and I thought it probably hurt. I wanted the fans on the Baltimore sideline to think about how it must have felt to their boy, and what the rest of his day was going to bring after a hit like that.

I put my shoe back on and hoped they ran the play again. I got to re-shoe myself two more times before halftime after more solid collisions with #11. He was slowing down and looking like he was in a very tough brawl. It was likely he had never been hit that hard before, and there was more to come. At the end of the half, the teams were tied, and Bobby had scored a touchdown. It was the excellent game everyone had expected.

The second half of the game was downright contentious. We got a quick score the first time we had the ball, and another one on a defensive mistake by Baltimore that gave me the easiest touchdown I had scored all season. The Baltimore boy fumbled the ball in the end zone on a kickoff. The ball was just laying on the ground, and I just fell on it for the touchdown. I left the scoring of that game up to Danny and Bobby because my only desire was to stop Frank. Our score was followed by a couple of questionable calls by the refs, and our parents being a bit rowdy and vocal, which included Danny's dad, Sergeant Bungori, and probably my Mom.

One of the referees called a 15-yard penalty on our fans and parents. It got a little tense on the field after that when some of the Baltimore boys were overly happy about the penalty call and were clapping, but not Frank. The boy that I had been unsparingly pounding all afternoon told his team, "Come, on guys! We don't want to win like this." I was impressed by his words and desire to win correctly and not steal it or have it given to them. But I was still going to hit him hard again the next chance I got.

At that point, we were ahead by two touchdowns, and we were beating them soundly. Being intimidated in a football game with country boys, was probably a novel, uncomfortable feeling for the street tough city boys. The penalty did help them to score on us late, but it wasn't easy for them. Nothing was easy for them that day. Our defensive end, Joe Scherer, was getting in some cringe-inducing hits on anybody on the other side of the ball lining up against him. I was very happy that I was on Joe's team. He was the only player in the league I was a little afraid of because Joe was tough and a little crazy at game time. He liked hitting people in a way you can't teach.

The last time I tackled Crazy Legs, I knew he was hurt, but he was still coming on every play. He was a load all game long. In the last play of the game, Joe laid another big hit on Frank on the other side of the field, which made me cringe again. Wow! Joe drove him to the ground hard in a final pancake tackle, in an exclamatory coda for the day. Joe sprang up from the dirt with a trophy. A fluttering, black number one was held high and proudly in his right hand. It was from the jersey of Frank, previously #11. Joe ran off the field with his war booty, laughing heartily with his old man's raspy voice. I was glad Joe never hit me.

Game over, undefeated, and still champions of our league. Uncle George was pleased and satisfied. We were happy we would not have to play Baltimore, or their fans, ever again. But we would if we had to, and we'd beat them again. They knew it. Toward the end of the game, the Baltimore side of the field had been very quiet as the clock ticked down. I didn't bother trying to find the touchy Baltimore man with the bad teeth, who had grabbed me on the first play. However, I did want to find #11, Frank, and shake his hand. I found him walking toward the parking lot by himself, going in the same direction as me. We noticed each other at the same time, with simultaneous, respectful side glances. Then we made full eye contact, and I headed toward him. He raised his head as I approached and extended his hand to meet mine. I shook his hand firmly and told him he was a very tough and worthy opponent and who played an excellent game. He shook my hand and returned the compliments on my gameplay. We smiled, nodded, parted, and continued our separate walks off the field.

On the way back to the bus, Mom was laughing because my shoe kept coming off during the game. She said, "Every time I looked up, your shoe was flying up in the air, Boy. So, I was saying, why don't you just tie your shoe right the first time, so it would stay on and stop flying off." I did explain the shoe problem to her later, as well as some of what was happening during the game. Over the season, Mom thoroughly enjoyed the games, and she showed her very competitive side that I had seldom seen. She was glad to know I could be that rough when called for and take care of myself. That game was one of the best things that had ever happened to me, and I felt a new confidence and control in a way I never had before. I was going to need it.

CHAPTER 12

Slave Day

The High School, unlike the Consolidated, didn't present me with ongoing forebodings of possible imminent physical harm from unexpected or expected sources. There always seemed to be a presumed pecking order among the boys, roughly based on your size and reputation at Consolidated and whether you had a tough big brother or not. But here, you still had to be aware of your company and where you were on the school grounds to remain safe and free of conflict, regardless. At Consolidated, if two people weren't getting along, something might occur in the bathroom, on the bus to school, in gym class, or in the hall, but not in the classroom.

That place was the sacred temple of seriousness and learning. Even the tough students, and the hard heads at C1, knew certain boundaries existed, and there was a price to be exacted for certain transgressions. The idea of starting something in the classrooms of Misters Lisby, Griffin, Taylor, Brashears, or Clark could only end poorly for the instigator, and that was before his parents or grandparents got a hold of him at home. I found out that things were a bit different at the Havre de Grace High School.

I had taken my seat in Mrs. Dinger's math class after what I thought had been an uneventful gym class session. That's when a boy from the previous gym class came walking very purposefully into the classroom like he was pushing through a pair of imaginary swinging hinged doors, at a Wild West saloon. He headed straight for me and started to raise his voice above his usual dull monotone, and glared at me through his rectangular eyeglasses. Evidently, something that I had done to him in gym class had left him feeling...slighted? Angry?

Violated? Disobeyed?.....Belittled?....Or, God forbid, was he made to feel inferior by the new kid from the colored school? Did he feel that I had disparaged, or even discriminated against him, in some hurtful way that called for atonement, or apology, for some sin committed by me? He never said what I did, but he acted as if he had been born on the right side of everything. I didn't know what his problem was, but I was thinking it probably dealt with something before and beyond gym class with me. And, more importantly, the problem was his, not mine, as long as he didn't touch me.

He was standing over me as I was still seated at the desk. I arose to face him, just in case he wanted to step across the line. I gave him the South Georgia death stare to let him know what no fear looked like in a Black face that was very close to his White one. If he felt so strongly about things and if he wanted to go, then we could go. I had spent a good part of last fall crashing into the bodies of white boys on the football field. I already knew that particular feeling on several levels, and I was not impressed by his puffery or concerned about what he thought he had seen in gym class. I doubted that he knew that physical feeling at all and that he didn't want to find out about it right now.

He wanted me to start the fight, so he could sidle off to the office to claim....what?...victimhood?.... harassment?....assault? It was surprising that this very average unassuming boy would feel that he could take me without some help from a couple of his friends. I supposed he wasn't paying attention in gym class. He probably didn't see me showing off when I won the trampoline basketball dunking contest over everybody in gym class, including him. I thought I could fly, and I wanted everybody to see me.

We stared off at each other a few seconds more, then he said, "Come on, Ford. I can afford it.... Can you?" He was pretty confident that the fix was in on his side, and he would come out of whatever happened between us just fine. After all, he could "afford it." Why?

I was thinking — Mark, you punk. You are the one who is upset with me, and you want me to start a fight about something that offended your frail, tender sensibilities in gym class. I don't even know what irked you to this state of near agitated delusion. But, if you touch me, I am going to give you all you want, and more, for a very brief time. — At that point, I lost all interest in him and sat back down in my seat. If he wanted a piece of me, he knew where to find me. And if he was that aggrieved, then hit me instead of trying to con me into hitting you first, to give yourself a get out of jail free card with the principal, Mr. Banick. It didn't make any sense. He could have been trying to impress a girl, which is always a possibility with a boy in the 8th grade. Still, it was a punk move. Maybe I would have been more accommodating of him if I had known what I had supposedly done. It was over, and I wouldn't have to bother looking over my shoulder to watch out for him. Because I could afford to, with a boy like Mark.

I got along with my new classmates fine, and I was friendly with several of the boys. There were a couple of girls I would occasionally share a chat with. I was the same way at the Consolidated; friendly enough, but I wasn't trying to see how many people I could get to know during the day. It was a very pleasant surprise one day to hear my new classmate, Sharon, mention to another student that her Mom had worked a long time for my old pediatrician Dr. Kaiser, when he practiced in Havre de Grace. Then I realized that this was Sharon who Dr. Kaiser's nurse would call on the phone practically every time I was in the office. Gay, the nurse, would check in on her daughter at home, Sharon. I said to her, "Oh, you are that Sharon." We laughed about the coincidence and connection, and I told her to tell her Mom I said hello. She was a very nice lady and ran the medical office like a clock.

Every once in a while, I would show a bit of what I knew in class, or display a little "colored" academic leg, if I felt moved or mischievous. Our science teacher was Mr. Grove, a kind, rather odd looking man who happened to be a very good scientist. He told us in 1964, that in our lifetime we would have computers in our homes, which was an amazing statement. He wasn't talking about the big IBM machines, but smaller ones that were yet to be made. Everyone was aware of large, mainframe computers seen in ads, or stories about IBM on the television. Those machines could take up an entire room. Someone, in the future, was going to figure out how to shrink down a mainframe to fit on your desk, or in your hands, according to Mr. Grove, in 1964. I hoped that he was right.

It was the one class in the first year at the High School, that I had with some of the smart 8-1 section kids. There were three of them in my science class with Mr. Grove. His tests were fair and reasonable in his expectations of what we should know, and he was not trying to trick anyone. I could see that there was a difference in the 8-1 students; they kept up with the lessons, were more articulate, and well-spoken in class. I am sure they did well on the tests too. I wondered if they noticed there was a step down in being in class with the 8-2 section students, which was probably true. I wanted them to know that 8-2 was okay, if not dazzling, and that we had brains, too, including the new Negro students.

The science classroom looked like a lab, with a large black top desk in front. There were raised seats in the back of the room, so students could see the teacher. I sat in the lower section, below a smart section 8-1 students. Mr. Grove had just handed back the test he had graded the previous night. I did very well on it and thought it would be interesting to see what would happen if the smart girl behind me saw the grade on my paper. I didn't care if she knew I was doing it on purpose. After all, this whole thing was one big game, and since it was the only one in town, I wanted to bring my monkey wrench and play too.

I took my paper with the "A" on it and moved my body to the side a bit to provide an unobstructed view to anyone directly behind and above me. I wiggled the paper bait a little to attract the prey. Hit!!..... After a few seconds, I heard an unsettled "Well, hmmm," from the mark behind me. I don't think she cared if I heard her. The shock probably made it impossible to suppress her utterance. I put my test paper back in the pocket of my notebook and felt pretty good about myself for the rest of the class. I just wanted to give the girl some different and new possibilities to think about and perhaps, to discuss at her home dinner table. Score one for 8-2, and C1.

The first field trip I took with my 8th grade section was back to Annapolis. The social studies teacher, Mr. James Davis, took us to see the state legislature of Maryland, the General Assembly, in action. He sounded like he was from the Eastern Shore with his accent that was decidedly southern for Maryland. He seemed to know all the characters in state politics very well. The politics in the state were the rough, corrupt, cartoonish, base type, employing the dirty "horseplay" that my 6th grade teacher, Mr. Lisby, spoke of when I asked him what was politics? There were always grafts, grifts, and payoffs in Maryland that were frequent, and no one was surprised when the pols got caught. Mr. Davis never talked directly about the dirt in state politics, but he implied strongly about the historical corruption and hinted at some of the ongoing funny business of more recent times.

I was not keen on returning to Annapolis so soon, still remembering the disturbing demonstration Pat and I had gone to the previous summer. When we boarded the bus, I saw that my Erie Street neighbor, Mr. Franklin, was driving. I said hello to him and took my seat toward the back, near Jeff Christy. The bus filled up with my classmates, the doors closed, and we eased out of the parking lot of the school to start our vacation day. The whole class seemed happy and ready for a school day without being there.

I hadn't been going to school with the white kids very long, but sometimes the things that they assumed they could do, and often did, were things we would not assume were ever in bounds at the Consolidated School. They were routinely used to doing things that would be considered near capital offenses at C1, the Colored School. By the time the bus had turned the corner onto Revolution Street heading for the highway, a quarter of the occupants of the bus had already pulled out their butts and lit them up. I was stupefied but realized I was also fairly sheltered and, according to my big sister, completely lame. Last year, a boy at the Consolidated got sent to face Mr. Roye for just smelling like smoke, after a visit to the bathroom.

White kids seemed used to their freedom and apparent coddling, as an expected natural given rite in their young, innocent lives. Their view of acceptable and permissible behavior was quite different from mine sometimes. But it was sanctioned, since Mr. Davis, the teacher, was smoking too. This would have been a major scandal at Consolidated, eclipsing any other news of the week, and would have been the center of attention and conversation for some time. I was dumbfounded and amused by the differences between the two schools and the expectations of the people in them. Pat was right. I am lame without being bothered by it. I eventually recovered from my jolt of reality.

We rolled into Annapolis onto the very familiar tree-lined, cobblestone streets to the beautiful brick-domed Georgian capital building in the center of town. We exited the bus and filed into the lobby of the Assembly building, and climbed the stairs to the seating area to watch laws and sausage being made. The students sat in the gallery watching the speaker of the Assembly, and future convicted criminal governor of the state of Maryland, Marvin Mandel, with his pipe in mouth, and gavel in hand. The floor seats were filled with fifty or so elected delegates. Mandel was the main man in control, and he seemed very comfortable in his role on the floor. The happenings on the dais were fast paced and sprinkled with important sounding words that made it hard to follow in spots. They were debating, concurring, disagreeing, and voting on the motions or a bill after the discussions were done.

As we were sitting in the dark gallery, I noticed a small, undistinguished looking man wearing glasses, seated alone several seats away, appearing to be very interested in the day's proceedings. Though it was dark, I knew who he was after a second glance. It was J. Millard Tawes, the Governor of Maryland, sitting a few feet from me. He was on the news quite often, so he was instantly familiar. I grabbed a piece of paper and scooted over quietly toward him to get his autograph before anybody else noticed who he was.

I said hello to the Governor and asked for his signature. He signed my little piece of paper and smiled at me, as a small line of other students started to form behind me. I surprised myself by having the courage to be the first one to go up to him, such an important man, which was not something I was comfortable doing. I was taught not to bother people, and it was a trait that was difficult to break. But I was beginning to think some of it needed to be chipped away. Still, I was proud that I was the first person in the gallery to recognize such a well-known man and get his autograph.

I tucked away the prized signature, of barely legible scrawl, into a notebook for safekeeping. On the way back home on the bus, I showed Mr. Davis the Governor's autograph, and he was pleased that I knew who he was sitting in the dark. My classmates on the bus were very happy too, after our day immersed in state politics, instead of being in real school. It was interesting seeing and meeting people that I saw on the news all the time. They were famous, or infamous, enough in the state of Maryland.

If I had to pick the single most un-Consolidated School kind of day in the first school year at the once-white school, it would have to be Slave Day, which happened once a year. They also had a Sadie Hawkins Day, which we did not have at the Consolidated either. On that day, a girl would rent the services of a boy by tagging him to carry her books and be obedient for a day. The school used the "special days" to raise money for the student council activities. Making a game of chattel slavery is a subject that would have never come up at the Consolidated School in any form, especially as an entertaining, money making project.

I was surprised when I came to school one morning in the spring, and lots of people were excited. They were going down to the bookstore, paying their buck, and getting a tag that would allow them to claim and own a person for the school day, thereby, enslaving a fellow schoolmate. The oppressed student would carry books, get lunch for the owner, and deal with light high school abuse and humiliation for the day as if he, or she, was a slave. The boys would have their chance, and then the girls had theirs the following day. The enslavement could be by agreement, or it could be under more hostile or comical circumstances, as slavery goes.

On the girl's slave day at lunchtime, I was the only unenslaved boy left in my class. A couple of my Consolidated classmates had enslaved each other and were having a good time laughing about it. Karen was ordering Jeff Christy around, who was indignant at being shackled by a paper tag. I was happy not to be a slave, even a play one. However, being the only boy in the class not tagged was only a limited honor. I felt a bit odd being untagged, or untag-able, in a negative way.

After lunch, my dilemma was resolved. Sandy, with the big blue eyes, came over to me in the hall before class. She was very shy and tentative, but she held a paper tag in her hand. She told me that she had bought it in the morning and still had it. She wanted to know if I wouldn't mind being tagged. For an enslaver, she was very sweet and accommodating. Well, I did mind it, but I'd make an exception in this one case. I didn't feel all that odd, and I enjoyed carrying her books and getting to talk to her a bit. She was a very nice person and fairly courageous in her own way for enslaving me, with some in the school watching.

Fortunately for all of us, that was the last call for the celebration of Slave Day at the High School. The next year we did not have it, and nobody seemed to notice. I would have hoped that the inappropriateness of the day finally fell on the adults of the school. The other way to look at it was that the administration didn't need, or have, an epiphany since they always knew Slave Day's inclusion in the school year calendar was insensitive, questionable, and indefensible. But they did it anyway, for one more year.

I had survived my first year at the erstwhile white school, and it was illuminating, to a painful degree sometimes. But still, I was more comfortable here than at Consolidated in a couple of important ways. I felt less stress here from the students, which was not the same as thinking that everybody liked me. It was a larger building with more space and less crowding; there was less chance for a negative interaction in school during the day. Mainly, though, the books, materials, courses, labs, and equipment were just better here. On the last day of school, our class had a fun end of the year election for class titles, like the funniest, best dresser, or most likely to do something. My 8th grade classmates at the White school selected Karen and me, the two new students from the Colored School, as most likely to succeed. I was surprised and deeply appreciative that they noticed and were fine with what we had done in school that year.

As Mr. Lisby said, "Things were always separate and unequal at Consolidated, exactly like it was planned." If the board wasn't spending its money on the Colored Schools, it must have been spending it somewhere else, like here, on their kids.

I did miss the experienced, stern, solid, no-nonsense attitudes, and gentle guiding hands of the teachers from the Havre de Grace Consolidated School, C1. When you went to school, you knew you would be taken care of and protected by our teachers until you got home, to the best of their abilities. You would never have to fight to keep the grade you earned in any of their classes. Negro teachers didn't come to school every day to be obstacles or a force of drag on the learning of their students. They were in it with us all the way and supported us until we could fly on our own. That was not true for all the teachers and staff in the High School. I was not sure their plan was ever to be all in with us on much of anything. But I was trying to keep an open mind about the matters, which is the minimum my Mom expected of her children.

CHAPTER 13

Parallax View

The summer of 1965 was the summer of "My Girl," the signature song by the Temptations. The tune was everywhere, and its three minutes of pentatonic perfection and hopefulness stopped people in their tracks, caught up in a much-needed musical breeze out of Motown, and sweeping over the airwaves of a steamy nation. It was hard to find a person who did not like "My Girl" or a 1965 Mustang back then. It was a very good thing that the tune, and the car, were around to deflect from the ongoing, unfinished, bottomless nastiness in the country.

It was now 100 years from the end of the Civil War, and we were still fighting it, as far as I could tell. It was an unfinished engagement, with the victor still in doubt. Also, there was the looming Vietnam problem, a key tile in the domino theory of Southeast Asia that must not fall, according to some. Troops from this country were half a world away and were being increased to 125,000. We were being "Maxwell Taylored and Norman Mailered" with no end in sight.

It was easy that summer to think about my recent school experiences and my knowledge of history and come to this conclusion; you get to have an opinion about it when a boot is on your neck. I was having more opinions and was getting to the point where I would have to ask myself occasionally, what is wrong with White people in this country anyway? Do they really believe the craven nonsense they peddle as the Gospel truth coming from their putative Christian mouths? It seemed some of them always needed to have someone to look down on or something to be afraid of, depending on the situation and their fluid needs at the time. They wanted to believe that all of the worst they had heard about Negroes was categorically true and even more dreadful than they had first thought.

My increasing pubescent cynicism and disappointment were tempered a bit when stories came from the Deep South about people being there when they didn't have to be. The southern white people truly hated those turncoat northern, latter-day carpetbaggers, sticking their noses where they don't belong and dealing with things beyond their Yankee comprehension.

The year started with the introduction of the transformational Great Society social program of President Lyndon Johnson and was quickly followed by the assassination of Black Muslim Malcolm X, in New York City, on February 21st. Three weeks later, there was the Bloody Sunday beating of marchers by police in Selma, Alabama. John Lewis, and many other activists, were mercilessly assaulted by mounted police wielding batons and, presumably, enjoying themselves at work on a Sunday.

The crowd, mostly of Black people, was trying to cross the Edmund Pettis Bridge, marching to the state capital, Montgomery, 60 miles away, in support of increasing voter registration. But the White people were having none of it. — No democracy for you! — The Negroes were routed back into Selma and to their church to regroup. They would be back for two more attempted marches and more confrontations with the police. As soon as a Negro child is born, he is a suspect. He or she attracts suspicion from those in charge for looking different and for, assumedly, being descended from a lesser stock than the normal, morally superior beings who enslaved his or her ancestors. Any protest by or claiming of rights for Negroes was automatically of questionable legality and enforceability in the South, the Constitution notwithstanding. The police were historically free to be as vicious, inhumane, sadistic, and violent as they pleased since they were protecting all of Southern history, culture, White womanhood, and privileges for themselves against the ungrateful descendants of chattel.

Shortly after the Selma police riot came the beating death of a White Unitarian minister from Boston. He had come South to support the marchers and the ongoing voting rights campaign. To a certain White native of the South, there was no lower form of life on earth than a man like this, who would turn against his white color in favor of "those people." Minister Jim Reeb was killed at night on a street in Selma. He was a fearless man of God who didn't accept how the God of the South supposedly worked.

The sad, heroic story that got to me most was that of Viola Liuzzo, the White mother from Detroit who decided she had to drive her car down South and get involved. She had never forgotten what it was like growing up White and poor in the South and still being aware of the different ways Negroes were treated, even if they were in a similar financial way as White people. Even as Mrs. Liuzzo advanced and bettered herself throughout her life, she always remembered how things worked in the South, and how sometimes who you were and what you looked like was what mattered the most. She could not stay uninvolved.

Mrs. Liuzzo was murdered after the third Selma March. She was shot to death by a man in a car containing four members of the Ku Klux Klan, as well as an FBI informant. The FBI engaged in a smear campaign against Mrs.Liuzzo to cover the agency's involvement in the murder, calling Mrs. Liuzzo, among other things, a heroin addict and casting aspersions and innuendo upon her assumed sexual relationships with Black men. This was during the time the FBI was wiretapping Dr. Martin Luther King and threatening him with salacious material they had gathered over the years. The FBI suggested, in a note to Dr. King, that he should kill himself as a solution to his mounting personal problems.

The country was nearly inured to the reports of mistreatment and deaths of Black people in the South that appeared on the television, or in the newspapers, with increasing regularity. Some White people even thought it was comical to watch little "colored kids" being washed down the street by powerful fire hoses or to imagine how satisfying it would be watching the hated and feared Malcolm X being assassinated in a hail of bullets, in the Audubon Ballroom, in Harlem. It took the death of one of their own, from time to time, to remind the country that the everyday, common, gratuitous cruelty exacted on Black people was historic, unending, and morally indefensible. Some of the same physical abuse or murder would be meted out to members of their race if they got in the way of things as they were. The killing of another Negro would scarcely make a dent in the day of most of America. But the senseless killing of an innocent, good, young White person would give some of the country pause for a little while.

The best thing that happened in the summer was the passage of the 1965 Civil Rights Act, which prohibited discrimination in voting, public accommodations, and education. Suppressing the Negro vote was a cherished Southern tradition, like lynchings; they both had the same goal in mind. And, as with many things with Whites southerners, voter suppression turned into a blood sport and merely another fixed game. Literacy tests (including detailed questions about United States history, civics, and clauses in the Constitution), poll taxes, guessing the number of jelly beans in a jar, and other clearly anti-democratic practices were common and well tolerated in the South.

It was all cloaked in a thin, palatable, non-racial veneer, and it was as old as Reconstruction. Sometimes, Congress had to at least pretend to address this recurrent political canker. It had to be codified and reiterated for all to know that this country, in fact, is not and has never been an actual functioning democracy for Black Americans. That should have mattered to all Americans who professed to believe in liberty and democracy, but on certain matters, like race, it did not. They just didn't like being reminded of it or hearing foreigners point out the rank hypocrisy of America promoting democracy abroad while tolerating untended, anti-democratic decay at home.

It was summertime, and I had taken off my Timex watch and stowed it in the desk drawer until September. It was my big sister's party season too. The only parties I ever went to were the ones in my house. I hardly ever went to anybody's house anyway, except for Jeff Christy. He lived two blocks away up Erie St., just past the candy stores owned by two old Italian brothers who truly hated each other. But when Pat gave a party, it was a rare chance for me to see people outside of the school setting. Also, it was a chance for me to make a little money.

We bought our house new in 1959, and it had a full basement, which was the party room. Pat was cool, fly, with it, and she loved to dance; the Boogaloo, the Stroll, the Twist, the Frug, and the Mashed Potato were her favorites, with a few James Brown "Night Train" steps thrown in. On the party nights, I was very proud of being the little brother of a very smart and popular girl.

It was odd, and a bit unnerving, to see a lot of people in my house, especially since I never went to theirs. There were students from the neighborhood and also downtown who came to the party. Pat seemed to know everybody, so there were also people who had gone to the rival Central Consolidated School in my house! I recognized a couple of guys who were on the Central basketball team, and they seemed pleasant and mannerly enough. For the few who needed it, Mr. Lisby, Uncle George, was there to keep everybody in line, like no smoking in the basement or foul language. That's when I had a thought. I didn't like dancing or hanging around with a lot of older students. So, I went upstairs to help Mom and Miss Margaret in the kitchen with the party food. Miss Margaret was Mom's best friend and our official other Mom.

She lived next door with her son, Alan, who was my little sister's age, and our official other brother. We called him Rock because that's what he wanted. Once, Miss Margaret took me to a White church in Aberdeen to see Dr. Benjamin Mays, who was the first very important Black man I ever saw in person. I knew he was special since he was speaking in a White church on a Sunday. He was the president of Morehouse College, and he was the intellectual architect of the modern civil rights movement. All the college educated adults knew who he was. Miss Margaret thought I should know him too. She was from West Virginia, where she went to West Virginia State College and majored in mathematics. She worked on the Aberdeen Proving Ground, calculating the trajectory of military projectiles. She was very smart, and we loved being around her.

A lot of the boys, and some girls, would come up from the basement and go outside to smoke a cigarette in the front yard or the driveway. That's when I saw my chance to make some money. I got my freshly filled bubblegum machine bank out of my room, and I took up a spot near the front door. As the smokers came from the outside to return to the party, I was ready for them. "You guys want to buy some gum from my bank (that doesn't give change)."

They, especially the boys, wanted to have good breath when they resumed rapping to the girls, sitting expectantly along the wall downstairs. I sold a lot of penny gumballs that night and extracted many silver coins, mostly dimes and quarters, from the fuming partygoers. There was a little fun grumbling from the victims, but they knew Pat's little brother had them this time, and they paid up. It was a nice haul of about 6 dollars and change. Everybody got something out of the deal, especially me.

It was entertaining and instructive to watch Pat and her friends interact and party. There was the occasional drama that came with popularity, but Pat never sweated much about that or anything else. Still, it looked like it took a lot of work to be popular, and I could not see the benefit in it for me, and besides, I couldn't dance. Pat, and her crowd, enjoyed socializing regularly. She even had her Prom breakfast in Mom's kitchen. She knew the benefits of having fun that I never picked up. Or, as Pat once put it, "The problem with you, Larry, is that you are just lame, unlike your brother, Wayne....who is cool." Which was all true and still okay with me.

There was one other important thing I learned a lot from that summer; I was not very good at making new friends or hanging out. One torrid dog day in August, I struck up a conversation with Anthony, the Italian boy from across the street. He was my age, but I had never talked much to him. Jeff Christy was his friend, and they seemed to enjoy each other's company. We had started talking a little when he was sitting in his front yard, and I was on my house steps. Then I went across the street to continue talking to him. Anthony was with a friend, a small boy from the neighborhood, Mike. We kept talking about unimportant, inconsequential things, trying to stumble upon some subject of common interest. It was difficult, and Mike was just listening.

We started walking down the street, half a block to the corner of Erie and Juniata, by the Villa Roma restaurant. Our halting conversation kept limping along about school, the best submarine sandwich in the neighborhood, and cars. The two boys took seats on the concrete curb on the street corner and looked comfortable there. I had never sat on any street corner before and was not looking to do it then. There were a few cars on the street passing by the corner headed for downtown. I finally did take a seat by the boys on the hard curb as the awkward chat went on, and more cars passed by.

After a couple of minutes, we noticed a familiar figure riding an old Schwinn bike, with an attached metal wire basket, passing in front of Tilley's candy store. It was Sammy from the Alley, riding slowly in our direction on the other side of the street. Everybody knew Sammy, who was a White boy around my age, a bit slow, harmless, and he rode his

Schwinn all over Havre de Grace practically every day, waving and saying hello to everyone. Just past the store, Sammy stopped the bike and stood astride it on the sidewalk. He reached into the metal basket to retrieve something. The three of us watched as he picked it up in his hand, cocked his arm, and side-flung it toward us. It bounced in the street and took a couple of irregular hops, finally coming to rest on the pavement about 3 feet from me. It was an old rubber ball that looked like it had been chewed up by a pack of famished dingoes. It was in pitiful shape, and no one wanted it. I stood up, picked up the tattered rubber ball, and tossed it back across the street in Sammy's direction. I pivoted to retake my seat on the hard curb when a black, two-door Plymouth had turned the corner of Route 155, onto the end of Juniata St., just in time for its occupants to see me, a presumed mannerless Black boy, throw an object at a well known, harmless White boy, just riding his bike on the sidewalk. And that is what she thought she saw.

Before I had time to sit back down, the Plymouth had come to an abrupt stop close to our curb roost, with Anthony and Mike still sitting. The woman was in her 40s, with dark brown hair bobbed and the increasingly familiar look of misplaced White people's outrage on her face. The man driving the car sat impassively without joining in the woman's wrath. I didn't know why she was so exercised or what it was that set her off. She was so upset that she could barely speak coherently, but that didn't stop her.

> I saw what you did, boy. You should be ashamed of yourself for doing something like that to Sammy. What did he do to you?
> What's your name, boy? Where do you live?

That's what she said that I could hear. I was familiar with certain White adults confronting Negro children aggressively like it was a right of theirs. It seemed to be their duty to set little colored kids straight whenever it was needed or called for, considering how badly we must have been raised. I tried to tell her what happened, but she had seen all she wanted. Why should she talk to a lying little colored boy anyway? As far as she was concerned, I threw a ball across the street, trying to hit harmless Sammy from the Alley, which is tantamount to abusing a ladybug or disturbing a praying mantis. Nobody ever bothered Sammy, but the woman saw what she saw, and no degree of parallax reality was going to change her mind.

At one point, I turned to Anthony and Mike, in an appeal for them to tell this lady what had happened. They both shrugged their shoulders and hung their heads, to indicate they had nothing to say on the issue. They hadn't seen anything that would have produced an opinion that they wanted to share. I saw what the deal was with my two curb mates. I was disappointed but not surprised by what they did not witness and, now, had nothing to say about.

Sammy was still across the street on his bike, looking at what he had started. I am not sure how much he got of the details or nuance of the part he played in the present discussion. But he was still a peripheral part of the show on Juniata Street. Allowing a little Negro kid to get a word in countering her take on the situation was not going to take place. The lady in the black Plymouth was a compact, self-contained judge and all-White jury. Court was over, and she only needed to find a bailiff to take me away to start my sentence. That's when I noticed an Havre de Grace Police car coming down the last rise on Erie Street. The lady noticed it too, and she probably felt lucky and blessed that a fortuitous patrol car had suddenly appeared in her hour of great personal need for instantaneous justice and Christian satisfaction.

When the police show up on the scene with a Negro person present, anything can happen. I wasn't extremely worried because I hadn't done anything bad except being a Negro, which some could interpret as a borderline unlawful state of being. As the police car rolled down the street closer to the intersection, I saw that I could finally breathe a sigh of relief. The Officer driving the car was Sgt. Pauli Bungori, Danny's father. Danny was the quarterback of our undefeated football team, and his father had been to many of our games, including the league championship. Sgt. Bungori had seen me play a lot. He had seen me compete against able-bodied boys on the football field regularly. Also, I had been to his house once for the football championship party. He knew the kind of person I was and that I didn't have to bother Sammy from the Alley, or anybody else, to feel good about myself.

The Plymouth lady likely felt that the timely deliverance, bringing Sgt. Bungori, to her at the intersection, was a divine occurrence. Fortunately, Sgt. Bungori knew he came in a Chevrolet patrol car, not a drawn chariot, and with no direct help or guidance from any deity. After hearing a few words from the agitated, irked woman, then looking at unblemished Sammy standing safely across the street on the sidewalk, the Sergeant looked at me, stuck his arm out the driver's side window, and pointed up Erie Street to my house. Without a word, he ordered me to go there immediately. The look on his face indicated he understood the situation, and he wanted me out of the area before handling the Plymouth lady's problems, and anxieties, concerning me, her boogeyman of the day.

I was lucky it was Sergeant Bungori who showed up and not some unknown cop who may have wanted to placate the anxieties of the White woman more at my expense. It does not take much to get in trouble if you were a boy like me outside of your home. Even if you didn't do anything, you make a good suspect for just about everything for certain people. Nothing else came of the incident. I never tried hanging out with the boys in the neighborhood again. It could be dangerous in a couple of ways. Making friends had never been important to me, and it was even less so now.

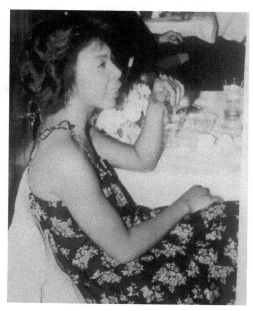

My very intelligent big sister, Pat, who set the
standards for scholarship in our family.

LJF/FORD/GRIFFIN COLLECTION!!!

My lovely daughter, Leslie Vanessa, always loved spending
time with her cool Uncle Wayne.

LJF/FORD/GRIFFIN COLLECTION!!!

CHAPTER 14

Coatesville and Mr. Bill Taylor

The second year of my enrollment at the whilom White school began with a reunion. Having realized they did not have the funds to continue paying for separate school systems divided by race, the county Board of Education had suddenly, reluctantly, and unexpectedly announced the system's overdue demise in the spring of 1964. The announcement was all the more curious because Dr. Willis, and the Board, had again prevailed in the Christmas versus Harford County Board of Education lawsuit. My sister, brother, and I were plaintiffs in the suit, which asked for the immediate closure of the two colored schools and the transferral of all Negro students and teachers to integrated county schools. Of course, they beat us one more time in the lawsuit, to the taunting and mocking delight of many White citizens of the county, as evidenced by articles in the Bel Air Aegis newspaper. Evil and whiteness had once again triumphed right before it sort of surrendered.

All of the county's Negro students, who had decided to remain in the moribund Central and Havre de Grace Consolidated Schools, now had no option but to attend the once-forbidden white school. I could not understand why some of my Consolidated School classmates refused to integrate the previous year, but they did, and time was now up for them too. I had some sympathy for them not wanting to jump at the chance to go to the school and be around White people in a way they had never experienced, especially the adults. Some of the students may have had a personal or family history that made it difficult to be comfortable in this environment.

It wasn't so much a hatred of them, in general it was more a cumulative, grinding nausea and disgust that many Negroes had for the unsavory goings-on between the races in Harford County before, and since the Civil War. Occasionally, you would hear snippets of a conversation from an adult or at the barbershop, referring to lynch mobs in Aberdeen, or an actual lynching in Bel Air, in the early 1900s. There were other stories not spoken about frequently or loudly. Many Negro citizens and families, had been personally touched by the savagery, perversion, and cruelty that interactions with whites could bring. There were whispers, or quiet conversations, between adults that touched on subjects they would hesitate to voice aloud.

My Uncle Walter was the family historian, information person, and portal to thinking about unusual and scary things. When we first moved from Georgia in 1956, he told me about living through the winds of Hurricane Hazel and the last occurrence of the 17-year locusts in 1953. I was warned by Uncle Walter never to put a penny in my mouth because that's the coin undertakers use to close dead people's eyes. He only had to tell me that once. He always gave me something new to be afraid of for a few days.

He rarely made mention of a horrible act committed against a Negro man in Coatesville, Pennsylvania, in 1911. The town was a bit north of Harford County and across the Mason-Dixon line but suffered from similar social maladies, despite technically being scarcely in the North. Uncle Walter was a teenager of about 14. What happened was something that practically every Negro person would have heard about at least once. My Uncle didn't reveal much of the details of the case. He would say a Negro man was killed by White people. I never heard talk of a White policeman being killed on a bridge in Coatesville.

His name was Zachariah Walker, and he had been drinking, by some accounts. Both men had guns during the confrontation. Walker shot first, killing the policeman. The Negro man went on the run for a day and sustained significant wounds after an unsuccessful suicide attempt before his capture. He was taken to the hospital for treatment by police after his arrest. Word of the incident had spread in the small town, upsetting and enraging many people. Walker was taken from his hospital bed, by a group of incensed White men, to the outside grounds of the hospital, where he was severely beaten. The mayhem was watched and encouraged by a sizable group of onlookers, who had previously, angrily surrounded the hospital. After the public, communal beating, Walker was put upon a hastily prepared funeral pyre of wood and paper and set alight in the matrix of death. His burning body briefly escaped the inferno, but he was soon recaptured and returned to the fire to finish being burned to death.

The crowd approvingly observed the obscene acts of abomination and sadistic ritual meted upon the victim in lieu of his deserved day in court. No degree of White culpability would have elicited such a violent, extrajudicial response; such treatment was reserved overwhelmingly for Negroes. When the fire died down, scavengers, disguised as human beings, picked through the man's residue for souvenirs. The rest of Zaharia Walker's human remains were collected by the mob's participants, put in a small box labeled "To his friends," and dropped off at the hospital. Six White men were later indicted for the murder and were acquitted at trial shortly thereafter. The town of Coatesville was condemned as a disgrace by the Governor, and that was the end of it. The terror and inhumanity were the points and the message; the impunity was the reality and the stinging insult delivered to Negroes.

The pettiness, brutality, and remorselessness of Whites, which had touched many Negro families over the years, seemed innate and natural in them, ingrained and constant over time. It was a small wonder that a few Negro students, and their families, did not want anything to do with attending a white school or attaining the education that was in it. They had no like of, or trust in, Caucasians or the institutions built for themselves and their children. Some Negro families did not want to entrust their children's education and safety to the purveyors of white pedagogy, who were likely the enablers and beneficiaries of Jim Crow America. Time was up for everybody, including my few friends who had chosen to stay at the Consolidated School until they couldn't stay any longer. Time was also up for the forces in the county who could have never imagined their children being taught by a Negro teacher, standing in the front of a classroom in their school, in charge.

On the first day of school, I went to my assigned homeroom. Much to my delight and joy, sitting there at the teacher's desk was the legendary, no-nonsense, poker-faced Mr. William "Big Bill" Taylor. He was a beautiful sight to see sitting at his desk, large and definitely, in charge. He looked as friendly and prickly as an annoyed porcupine, as usual. I could bet on what was going on in his mind that morning. After 15 years as a science teacher, this was Mr. Taylor's first day in an integrated classroom, at the quondam white school.

Last year at this time, the County still had not decided if Mr. Taylor, or any of the other teachers from the Consolidated Schools, were qualified to teach White children. Of the Negro teachers, school superintendent Dr. Charles Willis said this in the Bel Air Aegis newspaper in December 1963:

> "They have been teaching their own race for so many years that it is difficult to deal with children and parents of both races."

I would bet anything that Mr. Taylor read that Christmas edition of the Aegis newspaper, as did many other Negroes in the county. Mom read it, of course, and didn't think much of it. Then Willis tried to clarify things a bit later with this:

> "However, this reference was made to both white and Negro teachers, who must be trained to meet the new situation".....

So, Dr. Charles Willis, Superintendent of Harford County Schools, was not specifically talking about the previously untransferable, apparently "inferior" Negro teachers from the Colored Schools. No. He was talking about everybody, which was not how these things usually worked. I learned early on that with some of them, it appeared reality was fluid, relative, malleable, and optional whenever they wanted. Dealing with Negroes was mainly an ostentatious, transactional, fixed political power game whose existence was generally denied.

Since no Black teachers were allowed to transfer with us last year, the White students were going to get their first exposure to a non-White classroom teacher. I was pretty sure they had never met anyone so apparently detached, and, seemingly, just not into people, as Mr. Bill Taylor. It was reassuring to see a protective adult Black face in the school, who was not doing custodial work.

In my homeroom, there was one student who had stayed at the Consolidated School for the final year. I think he just didn't want to go to school with White people, ever. He was sitting at his desk head down and quiet, dealing with his new, unwanted situation. He was having a difficult time on his first morning of integration. His eyes were moist and he appeared to be mumbling a few words of encouragement to himself. I wasn't too worried about him, and I was sure he would regroup by the afternoon, which he did. By gym class, he seemed resigned to his fate, if not accepting of his victory.

Still, I was bothered by his physical reaction to being here in the school and around White people for the first time in his education. Whites would probably be confounded by the degree to which some Negroes disliked them, and being in their presence voluntarily was never a desire, or a goal. Finally getting inside their building for a better education and a chance to compete was a major part of what the fight was about, and now we had won. It was our victory, like it or not.

CHAPTER 15

Glossy White Rocks

The 9th grade was mostly enjoyable, except for earth science and football. The class that was the hardest and also the most useful was Latin. At the Consolidated School, the only foreign language offered was French, but at the High School, in addition to Latin, French and Spanish could be taken. Latin was quite difficult, but it had roots that spread and reached deeply into English, science, and math to a surprising degree. I found out how important a language, long dead, could be in learning and everyday life. Latin was logical enough, but you had to focus intently on the changing nouns, verbs, and declensions, which could be confusing.

The stories, the parables, and the adventures kept my interest throughout the tedious hours of translation. I never did understand what, or who, the Oracle of Delphi was. The language was thick, demanding, enchanting, and mystical, with heroes, villains, sirens, and minotaurs. Magical beings that I had never heard of were always appearing in the stories and doing extraordinary things. Mainly though, Latin gave me the keys to understanding how to use the big, powerful, intimidating, and dangerous 50-cent words of the English language by knowing their roots. It was empowering, and it made reading the opinion pages of the newspapers considerably easier.

I didn't think anything, or anyone could make me not want to play football. Football practice had started a couple of weeks before classes. Meeting Robert Rudolph quickly changed my desire to play. I am sure I was spoiled by having Mr. Lisby as coach last year. Rudolph was young and not much of a teacher of the game or anything else. He had a goofy and sadistic streak, to boot. But it was football, so he wasn't alone in having those characteristics. What set him apart from anyone else was his complete lack of empathy and helpfulness. He seemed to enjoy seeing certain people fail at their tasks on the field. He was not so much interested in correcting your mistakes as he was in assaulting you with them constantly. I did not like him as a coach, and even less as a person or teacher.

Mercifully, my ex-Consolidated teammate, Jerry "Apples" Waters, tore up my right knee in a practice drill early in the season. We called him "Apples" because he was always eating one since he lived by Brayan's apple orchard, up Chapel Road. My injury allowed me to separate from Mr. Rudolph and football. I missed football, but I had decided I would never again play at the school, as long as Rudolph, or someone like him, was coach. It was only a temporary joy that I didn't have him as a teacher that year.

My Latin teacher, Mrs. Kemp, was in her late 50s and from Indiana. Her accent was different from most of the Maryland/Pennsylvania teachers at the school. Her speech was plain, free of excess verbiage, and a bit nasal, with a touch of mid-western twang. For some reason, Indiana was a hotbed for the dead language of Latin. They even had celebrations in the state on the Ides of March, the 15th, the day Julius Caesar was killed. She would relay these latter-day Latin curiosities to us and how defunct Latin still lives on in our daily lives. Mrs. Kemp also taught English. It was interesting seeing the same teacher twice a day, for two different languages, and realizing more and more how related they were.

Geography was easy for a couple of reasons; I loved anything having to do with maps, and I had a good memory. The course showed that my long-term encyclopedia reading was sticking in ways that surprised me once or twice a week. Something would come up in class, and often I could see the very page it was on in the encyclopedia. Or, I would clearly see the map of a region we were discussing, rivers, cities, mountains, and all. Sometimes, we would talk about a subject I had just read about the night before.

Mrs. Ruth Burkins was the geography teacher. She reminded me of the caring teachers of the Consolidated School in many ways. She was always delighted to see how much I enjoyed her class and blew up her tests. Once I missed an answer on a test, and she comically let me have it. Lake Baikal was the only missed answer, and she made a little joke about it with the class. —Larry, how could you have possibly done something as simple as that? Everybody knows Lake Baikal is the obvious answer.... The class laughed at the upside-down humor of our teacher. I made a pretty good, seemingly confused straight man for the class too. There was no condescension in Mrs. Burkins. She just wanted me to learn as much as possible and having some fun doing it was fine with her.

It seemed, with me anyway, if something notably off, or weird, was going to happen during the school day, it was usually going to be the 6th period, the end of the day. Miss Beatty was the first-year art teacher. She was from Texas, and she sounded like you would hope a Texan would sound, twang and all. My ability in art was limited, but I worked hard on my projects, with little success.

One day early in the school year, she was about to dismiss the class, when she said, "The class can go, except for Larry Ford." I did not have any inkling as to what she wanted to say to me, and I was very surprised when she said it. She was friendly and smiling as if she had a joke to tell me; something she thought was very funny. She was tall with a post-athletic frame like she could have played competitive basketball at some point.

"You know, Larry....I saw you sitting in class, and I thought of something funny from my past. And I thought you would get a kick out of it too." I managed a forced, lukewarm smile and said, "Okay."

She continued, "I grew up in Texas, and we went to school with the colored kids for a long time, unlike this school." She was still smiling, and I was still trying. "So, I had a friend, a colored girl, ... She was in my class in high school. She had the most unusual name, which I always thought was really funny. She was a very dark-skinned girl, but very nice..... What do you think her name was?"

I was lost, with no easy exit, and I never learned to smile just to make other people comfortable. After a few seconds of thought, I managed a soft, "I don't know." She was smiling, like I was going to be surprised by what she was going to say. She was right.

"Well, this very dark skin girl had the name of.... get this...her name was Glossy White." Miss Beatty was pleased with her delivery, timing and she smiled even more until she realized that my amusement of learning the girl's name did not track with hers. My initial feeling was one of embarrassment for Miss Beatty. I looked up at her face which had gone from playful to perplexed, and a bit red, by my lack of positive reaction to her musing.

Most of the time, I had a fair understanding of why some people at the school did particular things, in particular ways. But this was not one of those times. Miss Beatty wasn't being mean, or anything. When White people are being mean to you, they want you to know it right then. Otherwise, what's the fun, and what's the point? She was well-meaning but misinformed. I let it slide, not giving much thought to it, or holding anything against Miss Beatty. It was just weird. I asked her if I could leave, and she said yes.

Come; Over; Some; Day; Maybe; Play; Poker. That was the mnemonic Mr. Carl Bissett taught in his earth science classes. It helped in remembering the Latin sounding names of the geologic periods of earth's history; Cambrian, Ordovician, Silurian, Devonian, Mesozoic, Paleozoic, and Permian. We would study what was happening on the earth in a particular period and consider the climate and the changes in weather that would have affected the species of flora and fauna. Some of it was interesting, but most of it was not to me. Trying to pay attention and, perhaps, to get a little excited about the boring subject of rocks, and the uninspiring presentation of the teacher was difficult. I had finally found a part of science that did nothing for me, and I hadn't thought that was possible.

When the earth was just another pinball in the cosmic shooting gallery, and the tremendous forces of volcanoes and tectonics chiseled out the continents, I was much more interested in the pressures, temperatures, and time that it would take to make a physical revolution happen. Science, to me, was most interesting when things were about to explode, transform in some elegant way, or escape the inescapable, especially on a molecular level. You could squeeze your imagination into spaces among the sub-particles, bonds, and magnetic forces that hold everything together. I was just tapping my toe to keep time in earth science with Mr. Bissett until I could get to biology and chemistry, where I wanted to be. Latin was coming in handy in breaking down the difficult scientific words. I tried to get something out of the agonizing hours in class, but I had never encountered a person like Bissett in the classroom. He couldn't imagine that I could ever do well in his class, and I was helping him in that endeavor.

He was a simple man from rural West Virginia, who brought all his personal history and particular proclivities from the hills of Appalachia to the Chesapeake, to teach the unsuspecting students of Harford County. One morning in the hall before the start of school, I was looking for Mr. Taylor to ask him something. Bissett was standing by his classroom door. I asked him if he had seen Mr. Taylor. He looked at me with an angry, smart assed smirk, and told me, "I didn't know it was my turn to watch him this morning, Ford." That was the kind of inspiring, sparkling, effervescent teacher he was.

He had a hilly accent and had a difficult time saying words like Washington; it came out as Wersh-shing-ton. (As in, go "wersh" your hands before supper.) I was uncomfortable in his classroom, even before I first sat down. After being there a week, I knew two things; I didn't like earth science as a subject or the teacher as a person —and it was going to be a long year. It was the first science class in which I had problems paying attention. Bissett gave me a "C" for the first grading period. I didn't make too much of it since early in the year, I was still playing football. I believed my disinterest was affecting my preparedness and performance in the class, but I was hardly a "C" student. I had forgotten to bring a homework assignment on a Friday, near the end of the first grading quarter. He used that transgression to mark the ok "B," which I assumed I was getting, down to an unexpected "C." He was a petty man who would regularly look for excuses to be even more so.

That "C" was partly on me. But there was something about Bissett that was repellent and a little disturbing. He was the kind of person I would try to avoid being around. You always had to be on full attention around some White adult males, with their penchant for condescension, aggression, or playing verbal games with you, like you can't understand English or what they are meaning. He liked giving me and other students a hard, sarcastic time when less passive aggression, or no aggression, would have done fine. He seemed to enjoy being himself, and it appeared he thought he was in possession of a modicum of cool. Through his hill haze, he was convinced I was just another average colored kid in his class that he had to teach by contract. He was hoping to convince me of my lack of distinction and worth, as he had already convinced himself. He was still going to give me a "C" to fit in with his understanding of the world and how things should work, and because he could.

Earth science wasn't difficult, but it was a science without much magnetic appeal. Most of the wonder in it happened 10s of millions of years ago. The volcanoes, tremendous pressures, and temperatures accompanying the violent transition of the Earth were a terror on a splendid scale. The rain of rocks, flowing magma, toxic gasses spewing, and things falling from the sky sounded downright hellish. That was frightening and cool to imagine, but we didn't spend much time on apocalyptic issues like that in class. It was mostly about rocks. We had to define many terms, learn the periods in order, plain rote memorization of everything, and learning the difficult spellings of the related scientific words. There was not much conceptualization or deep thinking needed. You didn't need much imagination, either. Just being able to regurgitate facts, as Bissett saw them, generally got you by.

At the beginning of the 4th quarter, and three colored "C's" later, I'd had enough of Mr. Bissett and myself too. Bissett needed a belated message sent to him. I decided the next test he gave the class would be crushed and annihilated by me, a "C" student. He was never going to grade me fairly, and I was never going to be into the science of the earth enough to enjoy the class or worry about excelling in it. The next big test was a week away. I had decided that on that test, Bissett would not be able to ask any question that I could not answer correctly. The two chapters were outlined, and I used my barely explainable keyword connection method to remember as much text from the lesson as possible. I wanted to mess up his test and mess with him too.

The day of the test came, and I was confident. The exam was about earthquakes and tidal waves and a couple of other subjects. I finished it fairly quickly, then went over it again, looking for any obvious bad brain mistakes, and turned the test in. The next day in earth science, Bissett had graded the papers and was ready to return them. He took his time walking around the room, going from the lowest grade to the highest, dropping a few comments as he went. He only had three tests left in his hands. He returned two test papers to the students, leaving him with one in his hand, a smirk from the hills on his face, and superiority deep in his nature.

He took a couple of steps in my direction and said, "And, Larry Ford. You got a 100% on the test." His eyes brightened like he'd been planning for this since last night. I looked at him straight on with a stare that let him know I hadn't smiled all day, and I wasn't going to start right now. He continued, "But, you misspelled two words .....So, I gave you a 98%," and with that, he tossed the test paper in my general direction and onto my desk. No congratulations, as expected. I looked at him directly in his eyes and not at the paper just contemptuously flung towards me. I let my silence do the talking. After a second or two, he pivoted to return to the front of the class. He was satisfied in not giving me completely what my knowledge had earned. I was satisfied that I made him do it right in front of the class, just in case any of them thought I was a "C" student too.

But I was sure the students in the class didn't understand what they had just witnessed. I knew there were more Bissetts in the world who were likely to be in my way. I needed to be more mindful of my spelling, which seemed to be a feature of whatever was going on in my brain..... Tsunami!! I wanted him to accuse me of cheating, which would have fit nicely with his view of my very pedestrian abilities. How else could a colored "C" student have done it?

Outside of school, the country was getting worse and worse, with Vietnam taking up the national spotlight, along with race relations. The issues intersected when MLK gave a speech on the war in New York at Riverside Church. Dr. King described the war as being deleterious in its effects "on poor people in America, as well as the peasants in Vietnam."

The year before, he stated that the country could spend "millions of dollars to hold troops in Vietnam, and our country cannot protect the rights of Negroes in Selma." The speech was sharply criticized by much of White America and the major newspapers, including the Washington Post and the New York Times. It wasn't that it was an untrue statement; the papers, and the country, did not want to deal with it in any deep, thoughtful, or logical way. So, it was dismissed. The Post said of Dr. King's speech, it had "diminished his usefulness to his cause, to his country and to his people" through his simplistic view of the war. Usefulness for what and for whom? — were my questions of the Post and like-minded Americans.

George Lincoln Rockwell, the president of the American Nazi Party, viewed Adolph Hitler as the "White savior of the 20th century." Rockwell was all over the news, and the country, denying the Holocaust, spewing his hate against Jews, fearing creeping miscegenation, "primitive Black" people and democracy in general. His fervent wish was to have all Negroes in America forcibly expelled to Africa at government expense. It was difficult to know what to make of the presence of Nazis in America's streets in 1966. I thought World War II had taken care of them, but I was wrong. Nazism had appealed to White people, just like the Klan and racism in general; they liked the feeling and the power. They thought there had to be a place in America for them too. What kind of people, in this country would think being like Hitler was desirable? - One guess.

James Meredith was the first Negro to enroll at Ole Miss, the University of Mississippi. His enrollment in 1962 was greeted by a riot on campus, multiple gunshots, and the death of two students. In the late spring of 1966, while on his one-man "March Against Fear" to highlight the continued White barbarism in the interactions with Black people in the Mississippi Delta, he was the victim of an attempted murder. He was also calling for Negroes to register to vote, despite the intimidation and threats by whites.

He was shot on a highway in Mississippi by a White man in broad daylight. It was done in front of law enforcement officers and the FBI, who did nothing to stop the attack. James Meredith was shot in the head, neck, and back with a 16 gauge shotgun, loaded with birdshot. The sniper had been hiding in the woods with his weapon. He called out for bystanders to move out of the way from Meredith before he pulled the trigger. He called him out by name and shot multiple times in rapid succession. Meredith survived being hit. The shooter served 18 months after pleading guilty to attempted murder and was released.

The one righteously invigorating happening in early 1966, late in the school year, was the NCAA basketball finals. Five Black boys from Texas Western College beat the eternally all-White team from the University of Kentucky. The Kentucky coach, Adolph Rupp, was an inveterate, recalcitrant racist who vowed never to have a Negro player at Kentucky, as the game and times passed him by. In the first few minutes of the game, "Big Daddy," David Latin, the center for Texas Western, arose from the floor under his basket, like a magnificent 6'8" muscled missile, and dunked on Pat Riley and the entire commonwealth of Kentucky. I set my homework aside to concentrate on what was looking like a historic and special game.

The game was on the radio, and I was listening to it on my transistor in the kitchen by myself. When the Kentucky Wildcats were down at halftime 34-31, the ever-illiberal Rupp reportedly told his team, "You've got to beat those coons," and "you got to get the big coon," referring to "Big Daddy." I cried a little when the fairytale game was over. Through a little tang and taste of brine, I rejoiced in Adolf Rupp finally getting what he had needed for a while, a sincere butt kicking on the court by superior, and better coached, Black basketball players. If he choked on his large meal of national humble pie, I hoped someone offered him water. Final score 71-65. According to one of his players, Pat Riley, Rupp did not possess any racism in him, which would have made him an extraordinary human being, in that or any other era.

School ended. Bissett gave me another "C." I was glad to get rid of him, and so was my Mom. She was sick of hearing about him. If I needed something to fight against, I had it now. I was ready for the summer and getting away from the people in school for a little while.

Report to Parents

Harford County Public Schools

HAVRE DE GRACE — High School
FORD, LARRY — 9-F — 1965-66
Pupil's Name — Grade — School Year

Dear Parents:

This report of your child's progress will be sent to you four times during the school year. The letter grades will inform you of the quality of his achievement in each subject.

If you would like to discuss this report or any aspect of your child's program, we will be happy to have you visit the school. Please contact the principal in advance of your visit so that he can arrange the conference.

We are anxious to secure any information from you which will help your child attain success in his school work. Any comments or suggestions which you may wish to write in the space designated for that purpose will be appreciated.

Sincerely yours,

William L. Taylor
Home Room Teacher

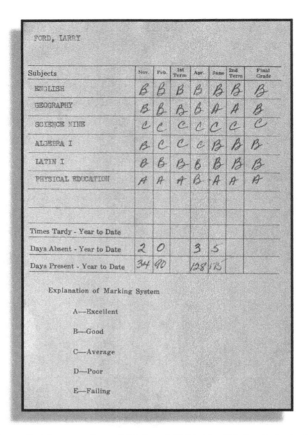

D This is what four quarters of "Colored C's" in the 9th Grade looks like.

LJF/FORD/GRIFFIN COLLECTION!!!

CHAPTER 16

The Pinning

I had a nice, slow Maryland summer, full of family backyard cookouts, eating blue crab cooked in Old Bay, dodging sudden thunderstorms, and enjoying another small-town 4th of July. The Baltimore Orioles had a very good team in 1966, and they were hoping to go to the World Series. It was hot and peaceful uptown in my neighborhood, Little Italy. Every Sunday, older, dapper Italian men would play bocce ball, speaking their native language and gesticulating in a way that made translation a waste of time. The old men never talked to me, but I was tolerated at a respectful distance, trying to figure out their simple game.

At the end of Erie Street the Susquehanna River emptied into the Chesapeake Bay, making a large brackish flat, perfect for hydrofoil racing. It was part of a regular Havre de Grace summer to wake up to the roar of the exhaust manifolds of speed boats and follow that sound a half mile down Erie Street, to the old canal Lock House. There, you could find a seat on the river bank and watch the hydrofoils racing, with their rooster tails arcing gracefully over the glassen flat. I loved growing up in Havre de Grace, and I rode my bike around town a lot that summer by myself, and nobody bothered me. I was ready to start my third year at the High School, and things were about to get competitive.

The first PTA meeting of the school year was in October. Mom went to it, as usual. She liked to know who my teachers were and what their personalities were like. She had seen enough of Mr. Bissett from the previous year and was not looking to have a conversation with him again if she could help it. I guess Bissett must have forgotten about last year. Mom didn't. Bissett saw Mom walking in the hall at the meeting and tried to strike up a friendly little talk with her. It was a short one.

"Hello, Mrs. Ford. How are you doing? How is Larry doing this year," he asked with all the insincerity available to him on such short notice. Mom replied," I'm doing fine. And Larry is doing just fine again, once he got out of your class, which evidently was all he needed," and she kept walking. We were both relieved that I would never have to sit in a class with him again. He likely wouldn't try to speak to Mom again unless he wanted to get face-planted a second time.

My new biology teacher was a tall, soft-spoken man with broad shoulders from eastern Pennsylvania, Mr. Levkulic. He had an easy, honking laugh and didn't take himself too seriously. We called him Mr. Levee. He was many things that Mr. Bissett, my 9th grade science teacher, was not; friendly, not absorbed with himself, from a different set of hills (not in West Virginia), and teaching an interesting subject. I never liked the thought of touching a frog, a fetal pig, or any previously living specimens. My interest was how their cells worked and what the chemicals inside were doing. Mr. Levee had an appreciation of teacher showmanship. He would get our attention with his desktop experiments, which usually went fine, but sometimes didn't. We teased him about always being seen eating dinner by the window of Vigna's Italian restaurant in downtown Havre de Grace, right next to Butch's dad's Tonsorial Parlor.

Biology was easy as long as you kept up. Unlike earth science, it did have a lot of "oh, that's how that works" moments for me. I usually stayed ahead by a week or so if the subject was very interesting. It did not require a lot of slow, deep reading or the heavy outlining that I had to use when I needed to know everything about a subject. I was aware that not everybody in the class had my love of science or an aptitude for it. Some of the students probably didn't have the time to devote to study, had to work, or had something in their environment that made it difficult to keep up in class. My only duty was to do well in school. I didn't have to work, and the only stress at home was fighting over the television. Not everyone in class was in the same circumstance as me, Black or White.

The tests given in biology were mostly fill in the blank, true/false, and a couple of questions requiring a written answer and, perhaps, some matching. They were not particularly rigorous exams, especially the quizzes. My seat was near the back of the room. The desks were arranged in two long lines against the walls, from front to back, leaving the center of the room clear. Most students were seated between two other students. I was between a White girl, who I didn't know well, and Bootsy's cousin, Kenny.

The girl was not a good student, and she didn't pretend to be. She was a nice enough person but seemed a little sad to me overall. During test time, she made no effort to hide the fact she was looking at my paper for a little help or just the answers. I tolerated it some, depending on how I was feeling that day. I humored myself by wondering if the White girl ever thought she would find herself cheating in biology off the test of a kid from the Colored School. That's desperation, and it was probably a situation Dr. Willis of the Board of Education had never considered possible in his world, not in his ossified way of thinking. Or, you might say that a White girl cribbing off a Black boy's test was a definite sign of progress and recognition of a difficult reality for some of them to grasp. She was appreciative, in an entitled sort of way. She seemed to think I should take it as a compliment that she chose to cheat off of me, and that should be my solace in the affair. The girl was able to pass the course, and I didn't get in any trouble in class. It was something I tolerated in small doses.

The most interesting and somewhat intimidating class, was English with Miss Spencer, a new teacher. It was a small class, held in a small former book closet. But the prime reason this class was different was who was in it. I had always wondered how smart the top section 8-1 kids really were. When I started at the High School, I had heard that my 8th grade class was considered special by many because of some of the students in the 8-1 section. It was now my time to find out how bright they were. I was put into the English class with the smart White kids and Karen from the Consolidated. I guess the administration didn't think I was going to hold them back. I was happy to see my ex-Consolidated School friend, Karen, in the class. She had already taken several classes with the old section 8-1 kids, especially in math. She was very smart in a quiet, non-threatening way, and nobody ever seemed to bother her.

For me, the hardest part of English was the reading and trying not to get lost in the traffic of my busy brain. It was a time consuming, intense struggle much of the time. I did not have a solution for it, but it was getting better. It was a bit intimidating speaking in class. I tried to keep what I had to say short and organized so that it would not give my brain enough time to misfire to the point of embarrassment. My writing was mistake filled frequently if I didn't pay triple attention to what flowed on the page. Most of that improved during the year, as I became more accustomed to how the smart old 8-1 kids, and smart Karen, did it. I knew I was endowed with imagination, but I needed to better express it verbally and in writing.

During the year, we had to give several presentations in front of the class in that very small cigar box of a room. Each student got about 3 minutes to speak on whatever subject they wanted. I watched closely the words they chose to use. Most of all, I watched their delivery, diction, and the overall comfort they had with the English language. Some of the subjects that were spoken about were not the kind of things I could have come up with on my own or would hear at my home. They spoke of their culture, concerns, and history in some ways that were new to me. I sat in the front row and had a bird's eye view of all the proceedings.

One of the students gave a talk that got my attention. She talked about the German World War II concentration camp known as Dachau. She was controlled and commanding in her delivery of many painful facts on a difficult subject that she felt we should know about. I had heard of Auschwitz before from watching Walter Cronkite on TV on Sundays, but I was not familiar with Dachau. I was taken by what Arlene said and the way she said it, with certitude and conviction. I wondered what went into her decision to talk to the class about Dachau. Arlene, and a couple of the other students, were very impressive and informed. They were confident in themselves and had no questions regarding their abilities. I don't remember what I talked about. In that class, I was the most nervous I ever had been in high school. But this was why I wanted to get out of Consolidated, and I had my wish of being in class with and competing against some of the smartest kids in the county.

The section 8-1 smart kids were different. They were serious about almost everything and did not mind expressing their opinions in beautiful correct English. One day our regular teacher was out sick, so we had a substitute teacher for the day, Colonel Maloney. He was a jocular, solid, compact figure of about 65 years. Everybody seemed to know him, except for Karen and me. My classmates were excited to have him for the day. The Colonel was just that, now retired and doing substitute teaching occasionally.

The Colonel never sat at the teacher's desk. He preferred to patrol the narrow path between the front row of students and his desk against the wall. He liked to talk about various topics having nothing to do with English. He was encouraged in this by the questions, comments, and reactions coming from the adoring class. One day he was walking his usual beat when he stopped just to my left and looked down at me. We made eye contact, and he shot me a little smile like your mischievous uncle might when he was up to something. He looked at me for a bit, then raised his head and let the class, and me, know what was on his mind.

He went into it military straight, no chaser, saying clearly, "I want to tell you white guys something right now," in a slightly gravelly authoritative voice. He got my attention. I had no idea what was coming next or how I was going to be involved in it. I was just hoping it was not going to be another Glossy White moment, like with the art teacher last year. At least that was in private. This was in front of the whole class.

"Black boys in this school dress quite a bit better than you white boys." The Colonel flashed a little wink my way and waited for the incoming. I guessed he liked my outfit. "I'm just telling you what I see," he added. A quick retort came from the back row. One of the boys shot back and disagreed with the Colonel's assessment. "I don't think that's true. Just because Jerry Waters wears that military jacket a lot doesn't mean they dress better."

I was hoping that the Colonel did not look my way again because I had no intention of getting involved in this discussion. I was not one to take notice of what the other boys were wearing or fashion in general. The discussion on the table didn't last too long, and we moved on to English. It was always interesting to know what your classmates are thinking from their view of life or what their take is on a particular circumstance. I didn't make much of the kerfuffle.

The flip side of my experience in English class would be my experience in the general business class taught by Mrs. Griffin. I had no business in that class. My sister had told me the teacher was very good, and it was a fairly easy "A" It was definitely an easy "A," and a rare chance for me to see what was going on in the business curriculum in school. The students in the class were the polar opposite of the students in my English class. Mrs. Griffin liked me right away when she found out Patricia was my sister. She may have liked Pat even more than Pat liked her, and that was a lot.

The main problem in the class was that only a couple of students seemed prepared for the lessons, and most students were not particularly interested in engaging in discussions about the class assignments. This was a new experience for me in a classroom. There was a lot of chatter and other activities, including note exchanges, signaling, and whispering about some important, urgent piece of high school life that could not wait.

Mrs. Griffin made life a little worse for me a few times. She would ask a question of the class, and if no one answered for a while, she would look in my direction and say, "Larry.....can you help us out?" I was hesitant to answer too many questions, not wanting to appear to show off in a class like this. One day the teacher did ask for help in answering a simple question about the last reading assignment. I gave her the obvious answer to her light query. My mastery of the assigned material was not appreciated by everyone in the class. In particular, one of the ex-Consolidated School students, who I did not consider a friend, had something to say directly to me. He lived on the north side of town, but across the highway from my house. I didn't run into him too often, which was a good thing. My mother always told me, "Do not hang around with people you cannot learn anything from." I think she had this boy in mind.

When I answered Mrs. Griffin's undemanding question, the boy's reaction was quick and sincere in his own way. He turned a side glare at me, and then out of a sneering mouth came, "If you are so damn smart, then why ain't you rich?" I didn't respond to him since Mom had previously inoculated me to this kind of thick, benighted behavior from any quarter.

Mom also told me, just a few times, "Remember, son, crumbs come in all flavors, and some of the worst may be your own." It took a special effort to stay away from that boy for years.

I didn't have any semblance of a social life in 10th grade, and I was unaware I was missing anything. Bootsy thought not only was I missing something, but in addition, I was clueless when it came to girls and dancing, which was true. Boots would come over, get me out of the house occasionally, and we would walk a piece and chew the fat. He would tell me about his latest girlfriend, basketball, driving his mom's car, or getting his driver's license. Once, he asked me why I never went to the Duck Inn, which was a club for Black teens in downtown Havre de Grace. He knew the answer already because I didn't have much in common with many of the more social kids in school and never had. But it wasn't their fault. What would we talk about? And I got the feeling that a couple of them may have a problem with me or my family. I had been there once and stayed for a short time.

I told Bootsy that I had only one goal for this year, to make the National Honor Society and get my pin. He looked at me as if he had heard something truly novel and off kilter from his, or anybody else's usual thoughts. Bootsy added, "Man! You are serious.... You aren't stiffin', are you?" I told him I was very serious and had been in a slow, running skirmish with a few teachers over the years, and I wasn't sure about the administration either. This was how to get back at them, among other things. I was going to take something they didn't want to give up. It was a small but important war.

He was interested in what I was saying. Bootsy always supported me, even if he thought what moved me was different from what moved him or anybody else in school. Boots was smart but not very serious about his studies. Any time he wanted to do well in class, he could have done it. But most times, he was okay with just getting by. Being his friend gave me a little cover from the couple of hardheads in school that I had to watch out for. Unlike several of the ex-Consolidated students, Bootsy was happy with what I was doing, and he had my back. It helped balance being called an "Uncle Tom" for doing well in school, by a few people who should have known better. That didn't matter much to me, either.

The National Honor Society induction ceremony was in late May, near the end of the school year. Like Mom said, my grades were fine once I got away from 9th grade science and Mr. Bissett. But, it seemed like grades alone weren't enough to get my pin. Pat, who was already an Honor Society member, had discovered something important several days before the induction ceremony; I did not exist. Or, more accurately, my record was not looked at for induction for unknown reasons. Pat was aware that the list of new inductees did not include me. So, she asked Mrs. Lampson, the guidance counselor, and head administrator of the

National Honor Society, if I was going to be inducted. She appeared not to know who I was. Our question was not answered the day before the ceremony, and I was worried, but Pat said she would take care of it.

It turned out that Mrs. Lampson had not calculated my GPA, grade point average, to determine eligibility for induction into the National Honor Society. At least, that's what she said to Pat. On the morning of the ceremony, neither of us knew what Lampson was going to do or why she hadn't done it before this time. Pat said she would try to get the word to me before the proceedings started. But by the time of the ceremony, I still hadn't heard from her, and the classes were starting to file into the auditorium. I was craning my neck, looking around for my sister on the stage. It was empty except for chairs, a lectern, and microphone. No Patricia. I was seated toward the end of the aisle, eight rows from the front, still looking for my sister and the answer to the question.

The auditorium was filling up quickly. The seat next to me was finally taken by a girl from the 8th grade, who I didn't know personally. Her father was a teacher at the school, which may have accounted for some of her upcoming impertinence. She was a very plain looking round child with oval glasses. That's all I had peripherally noticed at first until she insisted on conversing with me, and I was forced to take a direct look at her. She said, "Hello." I acknowledged her, but my attention was still on the stage, looking for Pat. The round girl continued, "Do you think you will make it?"

What she said finally hit me. A random White 8th grader had just sat beside me and asked if I thought my work in the school, over the last two years, in classes she had yet to take, entitled me to membership in this very exclusive high school organization full of the smartest kids in school. I looked through her impudence, baffling misplaced 8th grade superiority, and suppressed what I wanted to tell her at that point in my day. I maintained enough composure to just to tell her, "No," and thought it was the end of the conversation.

By that time, the Society members had taken their seats on stage. Pat found me, smiled, and gave me the signal. That was about the same time the round child sitting next to me said, "No. I don't think you are going to make it either." That from an 8th grader…I wondered what she had based her confident and unsolicited evaluation on. I also wondered what kind of things she had possibly heard at home to give her such enlightenment at her age, especially considering her father was a teacher. It couldn't have been anything too well-reasoned. But I had no desire to have any further words with her. I was going to try not to do anything unbecoming when my name was called to get my pin. I would just settle for a little shock and embarrassment on her part if she was capable of that. She was remarkably comfortable on her 8th grade perch, passing on her evaluation of a total stranger, two grades ahead of her. She seemed possessed of the right to say whatever was on her mind at the time to certain people whenever she wanted. That was a recurring theme with several people in some of my interactions at the High School.

Mrs. Lampson had finished the official notes and started announcing, alphabetically, the new inductees sitting in the audience. I was called early in the order, and I guessed they must have had an extra pin. When Lampson called my name, it took all the comportment I could muster to keep from looking straight into the face of the round 8th grader and give her a look that would stay with her for a while. But her having to look at me on stage getting my pin after saying that to me would have to do this time.

My name was called. I got up from my seat to proudly walk to the stage. I knew Mr. Bissett was in the audience somewhere, and I wished I could see his face and read his backward backwoods mind for a few seconds. Lampson knew who I was now and awarded me my National Honor Society pin. My Consolidated School friend, Karen, was also inducted that day. After Pat's class of scholars graduated, Karen and I were the only Black members of the Honor Society in school, and it would remain that way until our commencement.

Pat and I still had questions about what actually had almost happened. I knew I was going to need to pay close attention to Mrs. Lampson from that day forward. It was asking a lot to believe she didn't know my GPA, which was her job as head of the Honor Society. I did not have the luxury of thinking it was an understandable mistake; not at this school and not with me. We just caught her in time, this time.

The National Honor Society inductees of the Havre de Grace High
School class of 1969, after the pinning ceremony, in 1967.

LJF/FORD/GRIFFIN COLLECTION

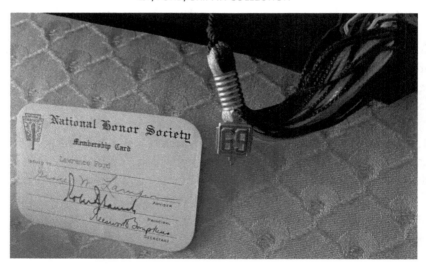

National Honor Society member card/Tapping Ceremony Program.

LJF/FORD/GRIFFIN COLLECTION!!!

CHAPTER 17

Breathing Again

It was clear that I was an afterthought to Mrs. Lampson if that. I had my National Honor Society pin and gave it to Mom in its cellophane wrapper. She kept it on her dresser, beside some of her favorite books and family pictures. It was never opened or worn. The point was I had it despite the obstacles and wishes of some at the school. I didn't need to show it off. It was going to be harder for the school teachers to bother me academically next year, at least that was my plan, and hope. I was correct, up to a point.

Thinking about those four colored "C" from 9th grade earth science was an irritating distraction the entire year, courtesy of Carl Bissett. His feelings about things, and people, were pretty transparent if you knew what to look and listen for. He was just a hill guy from West Virginia. Adding something positive to my school experience in his class was not one of his primary concerns. That pregnant smirk on his face said it all, contempt topped off with superiority, encased in gilded alabaster, that I could not un-remember. I was sorry I couldn't see his unconvinced face, as I walked to the stage to get my pin.

Pat had to practically tackle Mrs. Lampson to get her to admit that I was, indeed, extant. She could have merely calculated all student GPAs and seen who qualified. That sounded sensible enough, but she didn't do it in this case for some reason. This was the kind of situation the Consolidated School teachers had quietly tried to prepare us for, when curious things happened, for no good reason, other than the obvious one. Lampson was going to be my guidance counselor for the next two years. I couldn't imagine how her ostensible guidance would benefit me, given what she had already done. I was probably going to end up guiding myself, who I trusted much more than Miss Grace.

The first guidance meeting with Mr. Miller this school year, didn't go all that well either. I knocked on the door of his windowless office for the scheduled meeting. He looked up at me from his busy desk and said, "Well, hello there, Jim. Come on in." I told him who I was and that my given name was Larry. Some of the adults in the building seemed to be uncomfortable in their interactions with us, but we weren't all that comfortable with them, not that it mattered. It seemed they didn't know how to act concerned about us without it appearing to be an act.

In the early summer, there was always a daily fight with the allergenic state of Maryland and its legions of wild plants and shedding pollen attacking my respiratory tract. It is difficult to do anything if you can't breathe. I envied people who were able to use their noses to inspire, which was almost unknown to me. The medications weren't helping much; Dristan, Contac, and Coricidin. All of them had mind-dulling side effects, as well as lethargy, and they generally made things worse without helping the congestion.

Aside from the allergies, though, I just did not feel well. I should have been happy with my Honor Society pin, and I was. I suspected that what I had gone through in school had taken a toll and was, in part, responsible for how I now felt. Being slightly sick, to one degree or another, was almost normal for me. It was hard to know if something was making me sicker than I was going to be anyway. I didn't want to add to my perennial illnesses. If the breathing problems didn't stop me from doing anything important, it was considered a pretty fair day. It was certain that the final days of school had bothered me more than I was allowing myself to feel. I was always on guard at school and was feeling some of the long-term effects of that. It was what Mrs. Turner was trying to prepare me for in 5th grade. This was the time she was talking about, and I had to be ready to face it.

I started having that dream again. The one I sometimes got when I was bothered deeply by something going on or if I had recently seen a dead person. It was infrequent but recurrent for several years. It was the same every time - a feeling of presence, without the feeling of a body, in a blank, expanding, soundless, dark void, somewhere.

A sound started with an innocent, low-pitched hum from all directions that became a deep, imposing, choral, atonal arpeggio over time. A barely perceptible amount of nascent matter would start collecting across the opaque void piecing molecules together, one magnetic atom at a time.

The matter containing all things that did not belong together grew, rapidly filling the void as the mass of incompatible contents sped toward my awareness. It was an expanding, massive, dirty comet from a cosmic dump, coming at the speed of light.

The sounds changed from soft white noise into an aggressive, mechanized glissando of various clanks, screeches, and the grinding of metal on itself. The matter sped at my being at impossible speeds, getting closer and closer, like a threatening asymptote, but never quite reaching my position. Shortly after the jarring crescendo, I would awake a bit shaken and sweaty. It was over until the next time, and it was always interesting.

In the world outside of my head and Havre de Grace, discontent was brewing in the country in a very large cauldron. Lester Maddox, the axe handle wheeling segregationist from Georgia, had been elected governor of his "Cracker State," that was the proud, self-given state nickname for Georgia. Californians had decided to elevate Ronald Reagan, a B-grade actor from the 1950s, to the same office in their state. The ongoing saga of the Vietnam War played out nightly, now in color, in our living rooms. The grandfatherly, soothing voice of Walter Cronkite was a balmy counterpoint to the troublesome images shown on the screen and the sometimes macabre insinuations of what was not being seen or directly referenced. Many American soldiers were dying, with no end in sight. Several local Havre de Grace Consolidated and Central Consolidated School graduates had been killed in battles in Vietnam, which made it more urgent and personal for everybody.

The long, hot summer of 1967 had begun with urban riots in Newark, New Jersey, and Detroit. Eventually, over 150 riots spread across the east and midwest, from hamlets like Plainfield, New Jersey, to the big industrial towns of Milwaukee and Buffalo. There was even a riot in little Cambridge, Maryland, on the eastern shore, after a visit from the Black nationalist H. "Rap" Brown. He was a constant irritant to White people all over the country. He was threateningly Black, without apology. He even shocked some of the older Black people, who didn't want the boat rocked too much while they were still alive.

With all the tumult, acrimony, and teargas in the air, I was happy not to be in school with my classmates and teachers interacting, or not interacting, on the day's events. Negroes from all over the country were collectively tired of the never-ending pressure and the often feigned cluelessness exerted, and exuded, by the people in charge. Their unrecognized paternalism, cruelty, and pernicious ways were tools of purpose handed down to them over the generations. They had no problem using them and had no intention of giving them up while usually denying their existence.

Having conversations with White people about what kind of folks they appeared to be to us was not going to happen for a while, if ever. To them, my reality was a mere opinion, perception, delusional fantasy, or a lie and readily dismissed. It was hard to know whether they truly believed the empty verbiage from their own political or religious mouths. Maybe some of them were hopelessly thick and impervious to facts, just like Mr. Lisby had said. But some of them were in charge and were calling the shots, sporting their new Robert Hall suits and loafers, carrying briefcases, and a few even toting bono fide Ivy League degrees. They influenced the local press, the government, the school board, and the law. The White citizens of the county were not all uniformly scared, gullible country people. A few were a lot more dangerous than that.

My Mom's home was a place of refuge from the school wars I was fighting. After 9th grade, I didn't tell her much about the academic goings on in school. I never wanted Mom to have to go out to the school office in person to handle any affairs. Mom had no tolerance for nonsense directed toward her children, and she had no problem looking people directly in the eye and letting them know exactly how she felt. Mom was always the doomsday option that you did not want to use. Pat was more like Mom than me, which is why she didn't have a problem getting in the face of Miss Grace Lampson. I wished I was more like her in that way. But as a Black boy, you had to be more circumspect in dealing with White people, who already irrationally feared you and were ready to call the police at the drop of a dime for any minor issue that made them uncomfortable.

Like many of my old Consolidated schoolmates, some of my new schoolmates must have found me a bit different compared to the other Black boys in school. I didn't try to be different I just was, and always had been, even at the Consolidated School. I would hear, from time to time, about problems some of the Black students had with some of the boys at the High School, including my brother, Wayne. Other than the irate, aggrieved boy in 8th grade, none of the White boys in my class bothered me, but I didn't spend much time in the shop building, and I wasn't on the baseball team.

I was mostly quiet, a bit aloof, and not looking to start a conversation with anyone in school except for Bootsy or Jeff Christy, my old friends from the Consolidated. I had low-key confidence, sprinkled with enough arrogance and wariness to radiate a space for myself in the school. One of my classmates told me that I walked around school with an "edge" about me that was apparent to her. I didn't really have a place in this school or a group to which I comfortably belonged. But I wasn't looking for a place either. All my mother's children were like that. We thought we were normal. Not everyone appreciated our manner or upbringing. But we knew we had won the cool Mom lottery, hands down. Mom always made sure we had enough space to be and to do, whatever we wanted, within reason.

The music that summer was just okay. I didn't have a favorite summer song that year; there was no "My Girl" or other great tune. The white radio station, from York, Pennsylvania, was playing the Beatles and the Association. The Black kids were listening to Aretha Franklin singing" Respect" on WANN or WEBB, from Baltimore. And everybody was listening to" A Whiter Shade of Pale" and trying to figure out what Procol Harum meant. Even WANN, the Black radio station from Annapolis, was playing 'Whiter Shade of Pale." The station hardly played any white music, except for some Timi Yuro.

I assumed that Procol Harum were Black since they blew very soulful. But the group was very White and from England. Often at that time, the English groups would repackage Black American music, soften it up, put a respectability stamp on it, throw a serious major 13th jazz chord in and some borrowed syncopation, and send it back across the Atlantic to a more accepting, primarily young White American audience. That was a little disappointing, but at least they weren't Pat Boone trying to be Little

Richard or Fats Domino, or The Beach Boys' "Surfing USA," shamelessly ripping off Chuck Berry's "Sweet Little Sixteen."

My sister, Pat, was preparing to leave for college in September. She was gone a lot that summer, either traveling places with her friends or going down to Baltimore getting ready for college at Morgan State. Morgan was a Black state college, and it seemed like it was the choice of most of the Black college bound students that I knew. It was the alma mater of many of the teachers at the county's old Colored and later Consolidated Schools. Pat was going to be in college with many familiar faces from Central and Consolidated and unfamiliar faces from the rest of Maryland and the middle east coast. She was going to enjoy herself at Morgan, which also had a very good football team and a completely outrageous college band. I couldn't wait to go to their Homecoming in the fall, which was always a very big event in Baltimore. That's how it was mostly if you were a Black student. You graduated from high school, and then you went to college at Morgan, Princess Anne, Bowie, or maybe Coppin, in Baltimore. Occasionally a student might go to Lincoln University in Pennsylvania, or rarely Howard, in D.C. I had never known a Black student from Harford County going to any white college, not even the University of Maryland.

I was just beginning to think about college, and I hadn't considered any of the Black colleges. I couldn't see why I would want to go through all the integration dislocation and everything that came with it to go to the same college I would have gone to before integration unless that was where I wanted to go in the first place. I don't think Mom would consider that progress for me. But Miss Lampson might consider my going to a Black college a win for her and whatever side she was on.

I thought Patricia and her classmates were always the tip of the spear. Her class had a lot of very strong and smart Black girls in it. They came to the High School for only two years and graduated. Linda Erby, Pat's classmate at Consolidated, was valedictorian of her class of 1967. I was very proud of all of them. Last year, Pat, and some of her high school girl posse, helped Mayor Vancherie to see the light and integrate his long standing, softly segregated restaurant in the center of Havre de Grace. Pat had a lot of nerve, little fear, and a love of danger that I, fortunately, did not have. She could always get out of, or away with, a lot of things, being a girl.

The previous year, Pat had won a national scholarship to attend an Encampment for Citizenship for high school students. She spent the summer at the prestigious Fieldston School in the Bronx. There were kids from all over the country with beliefs from all over the map. We got to visit her, and her unusually liberated friends, one weekend on family day in the Bronx. I wished that I could have been there to see my big sister take on the John Birchers in the program that she had told me about. I would have paid for that ticket to the show. Pat was leaving me for college, but she had set the standards for the siblings to follow, the courses to take, and the people to avoid.

Later that summer, I saw Teddy Walke by the high school in his dream of a car, a 1967 maroon Pontiac GTO, with the tachometer on the hood and four on the floor. He was a senior and a mainstay on the football team. The car was nice, and so was Teddy. He was so cool that even my big sister had a little crush on him. I walked over to his machine, and we said hello. We talked about his car a little, but he had something else on his mind. Teddy told me that football practice was starting soon. I nodded that I knew. He asked me, "Are you going to come out this year?"

The question caught me flat because playing football again wasn't something I ever thought about, especially with Rupprecht still being the coach. I supposed that a lot of the other town Black boys at school felt the same way since there had been only one or two of us on the football team for the past few years. The downtown boys never said anything to me about why they were not playing, and I never asked. The fact that several of my downtown friends were playing soccer instead of football, said a lot.

"Come on out this year. I'll be your personal protector out there," Teddy told me. He wasn't just talking, either. Teddy had the body of a full-grown man at 6'1" and about 190. He had the neck of a stevedore, but the face and voice, of a choir boy. I would feel safer with him around, in general. We both laughed, but he did want me to play. We had been in the same gym class a couple of times. So, he knew I was pretty fast for a bookworm, and I had a fair idea of what to do with a football. Gym was the only class I would try to show off in sometimes. Of course, I was not the only teenage boy doing that. I thanked Teddy but let him know that football was not on the schedule this year. I told him that someone had asked me to be the student announcer at the home football games, and I was surprised the school asked me to do it. Teddy said he wasn't surprised at all and hoped I had a good time doing it. We waved, and he took off down the street, in that boss 1967 Pontiac GTO, with a throaty surge from the 400 cubic inches in that engine.

By the end of summer, I was ready to return to the school wars, and I was determined to try to enjoy myself more while remaining in good health. I still needed to crush this year academically and deliver a final coup 'd grace to those insulting colored "C's" from 9th grade earth science class. And I was ready.

CHAPTER 18

1968: A Very Bad Year

The 11th grade suited me fine. It was "Pax Gratia"; my Latin, for my peaceful year at "The Grace." The Honor Society induction gave me credibility as soon as I sat down in the classroom, just in case a teacher had questions about how average I was. My standing academically eclipsed my Blackness much of the time, except with Lampson. It was hard for them to give me anything lower than an "A" that year, so they didn't. My brain was much better, and I felt mostly together for the first time in my school life.

I was at home in the chemistry class that I had been looking forward to getting into for the last 2 years. I already knew a lot about chemistry, since I did most of Pat's home lab crystal growing experiments, and such. I was still a bit shaky on the stoichiometry, which was math in disguise. Mr. Harry Hoovermill was my teacher. He was a funny little man in a bow tie, who drove a funny little European car that stood out in a town of Fords, Buicks, and Chevys. He held an open chemistry lab every Thursday night for 2 hours, which I never missed. It was my social life.

My actual math course that year was geometry, with the gentle, graying Mrs. Davis, who had been teaching for many years at the High School. Geometry, to me, was lots of spatial imagination, interpreted by numbers and measurements. I was in love with a math course for the first time in my life, and it seemed to mesh well with my brain, without causing a fight. Often, students would have to go up in front of the class, and recite theorems and proofs, which was very old-fashioned and absolutely logical. Other than the math work, the main feature of the class was watching Mrs. Davis' daily fight with her falling, rogue bra strap, and telling Ellen to stop chewing gum, which she never did. Even after going to school with white kids for 3 years, I was still amazed at how unafraid of authority they were. They probably thought they were the authority themselves, or personally knew who was. They were always fascinating in that respect and unlike the students from the Consolidated School.

That year, I got a note passed to me from a girl who was not in the geometry class, and it was not about angles or theorems. The writer, who I knew a little from 8th grade, invited me to meet her after school sometime, for a cherry Coke. I thought it was a joke at first. Then I got a little embarrassed when the girl's friend, who had delivered the note, told me it was not a joke at all. I wasn't sure how to react, other than being surprised. I wrote a few words back to the girl thanking her, but I knew I wasn't clued in enough to socialize yet. I was starting to appreciate what my very social classmates were up to all this time, while I was at home reading, or chasing molecules. Bootsy got a big laugh about my communication when I told him of it later in the day. He agreed that I was out of my class on this one, and he was glad I knew it.

I had English with Mrs. Gladys Allison. She was every bit the coal miner's daughter from the eastern hills of Kentucky. Her accent fully gave her heritage away with very few words. It was a sweet drawl, riding a musical twang, and was pleasing to the ear. Her reading of passages from Shakespeare, a la Kentucky, added a wholesome universality to the ancient words. The thing about Mrs. Allison and "The Bard" was this; she wanted to make sure that everyone in the class got the dirty parts of what was being said — like Hamlet talking about "country matters." We got it!

Mrs. Allison liked some of the "out there" things I would occasionally write and turn in to her. She encouraged my offbeat thinking and wanted to see more of what I could produce in my compositions. So, I wrote what I needed in the assignments with an added twist of words, creativity, or irony. It was enjoyable thinking about all things, catching surprising inspiration coming in gushes or drips, backward or forward, with flotsam and pearls floating together. I liked writing with a point of view claiming my own space and style, which Mrs. Allison liked. I tried to give her something a bit different every time.

The plan for the year was to handle my school business better than the previous year and avoid getting any sicker than I had to be. I was trying to have fun and enjoy myself, which was never easy, and to try to be open to new experiences and people with Mom's blessings. After football season and my football announcer gig ended, there was the annual Powder Puff Game between the junior class and the senior class.

The seniors were whooping us pretty good, and our sideline was feeling down. That's when I saw the coach of our junior team, Lee (the same Long Leg Lee who initiated the music class caper in the 8th grade) walking and looking into the stands, searching for somebody. He saw me sitting with a group down in the first row of the stands. He quickened his steps towards me and then waved for me to join him. I knew he was up to something that probably included me.

We met at the wire fence separating the seats from the field, and Lee told me what skullduggery he was up to. He wanted me to help our girls by going into the game. It wasn't the first shady thing that had come out of Lee's brain over the years. "Come on, Ford! Just get it and score, then hide. You know they can't catch you. So do it!" I at first refused, but Lee wasn't having any of it. He finally talked me into agreeing to go into the Girl's Powder Puff Game for just one play. He put a jersey on me with small socks for boobs and told me to keep my head down on the way to the huddle to conceal my faint, post-pubescent mustache. First, the girls would hide me in the huddle, then Lynn would toss me the ball, and I would run the 70 yards the end zone, to the darkest part of the field. The girls would run down to the far end zone and cover me as I slipped out of the jersey and disappeared into the night.

It almost went like that. I sneaked onto the field and into the center of the huddle. I looked up at the ladies and their giggling faces looking down, trying to conceal me with their bodies. It was a very different view of the girls I had known for the past three years. They were having a good time. Lynn called the play to be run on the count of 2. The huddle broke, and the smiling ladies lined up in formation, waiting for the count, trying not to laugh and blow the surprise. Lynn got the snap and tossed the ball back to me, running around the left end. My eyes briefly met up with those of a blonde-haired, unsuspecting senior girl on defense, playing end. She looked at me and my facial hair before reaching her hand for the flag on my waist. She missed but continued to run after me, and my mustache all the way to the end zone. It was close for a couple of steps.

I couldn't see Lee on the sideline, but I knew he was splitting his sides and congratulating himself for scheming up the play. I scored, but no one ran down into the darkness to cloak the crime. The ball was returned to the line of scrimmage after the laughter died down. I went back to my seat in the stands to enjoy the rest of the game. We lost, of course. The juniors always lost.

The 11th grade was an easy year in school, finally. My head was much better now, and I could work around or through most problems. I wasn't sure, (but I sincerely) hoped that everyone's brain did not work like mine. It would be an interesting but inefficient world. I wondered if my classmates could tell I was silently fighting with myself or trying to be extra careful with my words most of the time.

I was less conscious about my delivery when speaking in class, which was a great relief. The reading speed was still not fast enough, but it was improving. It was always going to be a problem and always a work in progress. Having a sharp, clear, reliable brain, like some of my classmates probably had, was never going to be in my possession. I was always going to have to reteach myself many things in a way that worked for me. But every so often, I would have unpredictable periods of remarkable clarity on one specific subject for an hour or so. I would briefly feel what my smart classmates were probably feeling all the time, and I was a little envious of that.

For the first time in school, I had the time, and the desire, to do non-study activities out of the house. Last year was dedicated to cleansing those four colored "Cs" from the 9th grade. It was a delight not carrying that burden around anymore, but their instructive memory was permanent. The most entertaining, non-study part of the first semester was announcing and scorekeeping for the boys' basketball team. One day before a home game, I walked down to the record store in town, The Music Box, and bought, with my own money, the popular instrumental record "Soulful Strut" and used the record as the warm up song for the basketball team. It was uplifting and spirited, with a beat that you could sway to. The boys, and even Mr. Rudolph, liked the tune. The team used it for several years until people got sick of it and wanted to know whose idea it was to begin with.

It was fun keeping score and being in control of the clock and the mic. I felt pretty high school powerful for a couple of hours. I tried to help the boys out a little whenever I thought I could get away with it. The referee caught me red-handed once, being a little slow to start the clock since the boys were down late in a home game. The ref was cool. He just gave me that "I know what you're doing and cut that stuff out" look. And I did for the rest of that game.

Bootsy and several other old Consolidated friends were on the team too; Shelley, Herman, Robert, Cruzy, and Bobby Harris. We got to talk some and enjoy the bus trips on the away games. I managed to mostly stay clear of Rudolph, which was always my goal and difficult to do on a bus. The basketball team was good, entertaining to watch, and getting better with every game.

Another good part of school was getting to know Miss Marie McGreevy, who taught 11th and 12th grade English. She was young, very smart, and perceptive in a way I had not seen before from other teachers at Havre de Grace High School. She could have been your slightly older, very hip sister. She was only 26 or so. I never had her as a teacher, but I enjoyed talking to her; she was an antidote and balm to "The German Twins," Rudolph, and Rupprecht. She was a drama coach of the upper grades, along with the equally young and cool Mr. David Johnson.

Her homeroom was a magnet for the more theatrical, artsy elements of our class. Miss McGreevy was much more interesting than the other teachers and didn't mind interacting with us, closer to our level. Basically, she just got it, and she was "too cool for school," in my eyes. We sometimes called her Miss McGroovy, for obvious reasons. She was great, and knowing her got me out of the house occasionally.

The day after Dr. Martin Luther King was assassinated in Memphis, Tennessee, was Wednesday, the 5th of April, a school day. I didn't feel like talking much, but I went to Miss McGreevy's room to say good morning before the start of school. When Martin Luther King was killed, he was one of the most disliked men in America, mostly by scared White people. At the time of his murder, his disapproval rating with the American public was 75% by poll for the man awarded the Nobel Peace Prize in 1964.

Dr. King had company in the scary Black boogeyman category. Much of the country didn't have much use for heavyweight champion Muhammad Ali either. I wondered, what are they so afraid of when it came to a man like Dr. King? It was easier to understand why White Americans were frightened by Ali and his disquieting Blackness and Muslim associates. In his own way, Dr. King threatened White Christian America more than Ali, the athlete. So, they killed him.

If they were going to create an acceptable Black man for themselves, what personal qualities would he need? How educated or deferential would he have to be to register comfort with them? Would it be better if he were not a true Christian and man of God who held a mirror up to their own personal and spiritual imperfections? How big, small, or dark would he have to be to avoid inciting some shady primal fear in them? It seemed to me that White people spent a lot of time being afraid of one thing or another. It appeared to be some sort of need of theirs to be afraid, and that justified their reactions to their boogeymen.

I learned something that day that stayed with me. I said to Miss McGreevy," Your guys got one of our guys." She let me know straight away that I needed to think about what I had just said. As sad as the day was, it obviously was not as simple as I had distilled it. There were some White people with open eyes who saw much of the world as I did. She understood the origin of my distress, and she shared it. Whatever she said to me usually gave me something to think about and chew on, sometimes for days. I told her that I appreciated being able to talk to her and that I would think about what she said to me. I stayed to myself the whole day. I imagined that some in the school were not as distraught as I was.

Unexpected thespian fever hit me towards the end of the year. I liked hanging out with Miss McGreevy so much that I tried out for the junior class play. That's when I finally started getting to know a fair number of White students in my class, more than just saying hello. It was the first time most of them had been around me too. A lot of the popular students in the class tried out for the play. Also, I got to meet the new Black student in class, Buddy.

Buddy hadn't gone to the Consolidated or any other segregated school. His take on life was distinctly different in many ways, and he could be friends with anyone. He was different because he was an Army brat, well-traveled, and relatively worldly. His early schooling had been in Germany, both elementary and junior high. Now, he was living with his grandmother in town. Buddy had Miss McGreevy for English, and he had been a regular morning visitor to her classroom for much longer than I.

He knew many of my classmates much better than I did after being at the school less than a year. Buddy even introduced me to several of my classmates for the first time. I couldn't believe that it took this long to meet people like Eddie Mays, who was just a naturally fun, smart, guitar playing guy. I was sorry I hadn't met him earlier in school. We would be in a play together the following year that made up for some of that.

The junior class play was a farce in two acts called "The Perfect Idiot." Paul and Dahlia, well-known and popular classmates, had the lead roles. Also, the other Lee, the Beatles lover, who I didn't know well, had a major comic role, which he played over the top. You never knew what was going to happen in practice with Lee around. He was good friends with Buddy, who really did know everybody in the class, but he wasn't in the play. The farce was about a football player trying to pass a test to maintain eligibility to play in the big game.

I had a very small part at the end of the second act in the two-act play, which I still managed to ham up, according to Mr. Johnson, our English and drama teacher. I was a spat-wearing, bearded dandy of a German psychiatrist, Dr. Hockhorst von Barf. The doctor had the answer to the football eligibility problem, but no one would listen to him. So, stage right at the front, I got to silence the hoard by yelling, "QUIII... ETTT!!!" in the auditorium, at the very top register of my voice and the capacity of my lungs, for about 6 seconds. The audience was shocked to be suddenly assaulted by all those decibels. The play was the purest dumb fun I ever had in high school. And it was good to finally meet some of my classmates after almost four years of sitting in class with them or passing by in the halls. They were very interesting people, and my new friends were interested in me too.

The 11th grade was my best time in school, even as the country continued to try to disintegrate. I did very well with everything they put in front of me without much of a sweat. My disruptive brain was becoming easier to control when it wasn't trying to Sashay off in a direction it had chosen. And I didn't have a classroom teacher bother me all year, but Mrs. Lampson, the guidance counselor, was another story entirely.

The school year was ending with another world-shaking assassination; this time, it was Senator Robert Kennedy, the brother of the assassinated President John F. Kennedy. The date was June 4, 1968. It was the second killing of a major liberal democratic figure in 61 days. We were getting used to being the class of 1969, which had always lived in interesting, confounding, and dangerous times. We started school by learning to hide under our desks to avoid personal, instant nuclear liquefaction, and we bore witness to the continuing cruelty, savagery, sadism, and sometimes murderous hate, from deep in the American soul over and over again. We were seeing our third killing of a major, liberal political figure, including the President of the United States of America, within the last four years. Who's next?

The train, pulled by engine 4901, was four hours late. I was watching with Mom as the body of Senator Robert Kennedy was taken from St. Patrick's Cathedral, on 5th Avenue, to Pennsylvania Station, and placed in the ceremonial funeral car for the final journey to Washington. The crowds along the track, on the television, were large, quiet, respectful, and truly looked like middle Atlantic, working class, union America. When the slowly rolling train passed Wilmington, I left the house to walk to the small railroad station in town to watch the funeral train pass. It was the same walk, that I had taken the first day going to the white school and every day thereafter. There was a lot to think about then and even more now.

What a completely messed up, violent country this was and had been forever. There was no reason to think I would ever really feel comfortable in the United States. I hadn't been comfortable so far, and the prospects for evolving tranquility, considering the present state, were not good. It was hard to imagine what this country was going to be like in another 50 years. Why is it that our leaders keep getting assassinated? The killing of Dr. King was easy for me to understand; he was hated by too many White people to continue being alive in the presently constituted United States. I was still puzzled by why a person from Syria would come here and kill Senator Kennedy, the last good hope for us to get a measure of justice in our historically unjust land.

Two blocks from my house, I could see other people walking to the train station. There was a good size crowd standing on the platform by the time I arrived. It was mostly familiar town faces, quietly standing two and three deep along the old, dim, musty station platform. A horn blast from the north side of the open station indicated the funeral train had crossed the Susquehanna River bridge and was plodding its way towards us. Not long after the horn sounded, you could hear and see the hulking black engine, getting larger and louder every few seconds, swaying gently on the track. Its progress had been slowed to a mechanical amble as it prepared to pass through the station, with its silent, stunned gathering of townspeople on the platform.

The engine came into the station at a crawl to allow the observers several seconds of proximity to the history and pain of the moment. There was little human sound on the platform, only the heavy hum of the powerful locomotives and the metallic grinding of the slowing wheels on the tracks. The train had two large engines, as black as this day was sad, in tandem, pulling several Pennsylvania Railroad cars full of important people. They were mourning his death and accompanying the Senator back to the Capital for the final time. The last car on the train entered the station at a walking pace. The length of the casket, draped by the American flag, went by for what seemed to be a drawn, slow several seconds.

Sounds of low sobbing could be heard from some of the men and women on the platform, as well as some scattered clapping of hands from a few. The funeral car had progressed to the spot where I stood amongst the mourners. Several members of the Kennedy family were standing on the small landing extending from the train carriage. On the back of the car were Senator Theodore Kennedy and Ethel, the wife of the slain Sen. Robert Francis Kennedy. There were several younger family members with them, all waving back, acknowledging the large respectful crowd, while trying to manage the discomfort of a smile, knowing how cruel history had been to their family once again. All of us on the station platform watched the unrushed egress of the train down the tracks south to Washington and left the station with our private prayers and meditations for our wounded country.

CHAPTER 19

Dry Corn Bread

The greatest waste of time in the last two years of school was anything having to do with my guidance counselor, Grace Lampson. My first encounter with her was during the National Honor Society induction in 10th grade. Lampson hadn't bothered to calculate my GPA until Pat alerted her to my existence, possession of a pulse, as well as ambitions. We never did get an explanation of what happened, and I'm sure she didn't think she owed us one. Lampson hadn't shown much awareness, or interest, in my academic pursuits to that point, but her neglect was just getting started.

The scheduled meeting with her in 11th grade was strange and borderline perplexing. Lampson was short, about 60, with purplish gray hair frequently worn in a slightly messy French roll. She wore glasses that were a bit cat-eyed, and they slid low on her nose as she perused my school records on her desk. All in all, she was a frumpy, southern White lady with strong feelings about things that, to me, approximated an agenda. Some people probably would have found her soft North Carolina drawl quaint, pleasing, or appealing. It struck me as a grating, aristocratic anachronism that was as appealing as a forced viewing of a statue of Confederate General Nathan Bedford Forrest, the post-Civil War founder of the Knights of the Ku Klux Klan.

Mrs. Lampson could have been cast in the movies as the Ole Miss of some well-kept Southern plantation with arching oak trees, cool mint juleps on the table, spittoons on the floor, and everyone is being served by very happily enslaved people. And that voice of hers— it was sticky and sweet like sugar cane, but dry and dangerous, like three-day-old cornbread. All our conversations were limited by the mere sound of her voice and knowing where it came from, its implied power, and the pretense of culture and civility.

Mrs. Lampson started her crabwise attack on my academic plans and desires by being equally dismissive and paternalistic. I thought this was supposed to be a meeting about me and my future. Grace Lampson had other ideas. It was actually a meeting about what she thought were my limitations, without telling them to me, and how they should affect my post-secondary education. I still told her that I wanted to be a chemist and go to the University of Delaware, which had a respected program. My chemistry teacher, Mr. Hovermill, had gotten me interested in the school because several of his past students had gone there.

I mentioned several other schools, including Bucknell and the Air Force Academy. But she wasn't about hearing anything I wanted for myself. The Ole Miss knew the best for me in her way of thinking. Her feet seemed affixed in concrete, on my needing to go to a nice "colored college."

She never said why that was her feeling or how much my wishes should count in this matter of my life. For some reason, she felt qualified to make that call for me. I wasn't too serious about the Air Force Academy but had always wanted to fly, and the application was free. The possibility that I could fly was powerful and intoxicating. But I had to get all my teeth fixed before they would even review my application. Emerson, my stepfather, had been in the Air Force, and he was overjoyed by the fact the Academy would send an application to a young Black man. That is something that would have never happened when he was my age. He was proud of me in a way I had never seen. Mom had other thoughts about the subject, which weren't so positive.

After hearing my desires, Lampson first used a bit of butter on me before resuming the old Okie-doke. "Well, Larry, you are a fine student. The schools you like are very fine." Then she showed her hand and part of her agenda. She had appeared attentive enough when I was talking, but I didn't understand that I had just engaged in a one-way chat with myself, and she hadn't actually heard a word of it. She went on with, "But have you thought about Morgan State College? It is a fine school too. It might fit you better."

Morgan State is a Black college in Baltimore that my sister attended. Most people I knew who had gone to college went to Morgan, which was a fine school. But I didn't want to go there, and I was disturbed by her persistence and intentional deafness to that fact. It appeared all she needed to know was what she knew when I walked through her door; I was Black. Or, more likely, in her case, I was "colored." My early and frequent misgivings about the Ole Miss were coming true. She was a fairly dangerous and powerful person to be a factor at this stage of my life. I thought integration was about being free to chase some of those wondrous thoughts in my head and advance where my talents took me. Something she saw shook her enough to want to limit or slow my advancement if she could.

At that point, I could only conclude that she was running a game on me, and I wasn't supposed to be bright enough to notice what she was doing. She had no intention of providing me with any advice that would help in getting into the college that I wanted. My guidance counselor was a con artist without any true interest in my further education, not to mention my advancement in her world. She was most interested in getting me to voluntarily resegregate since Negroes had failed to agree with continued voluntary segregation, as some White people had wanted in the 50s. She was taking a second bite at that apple.

Mrs. Lampson had displayed an unusual interest in advocating and pushing for my education to continue at a "colored school," a "fine" one, voluntarily. Did she tell other Black students going to college the same, or was there something peculiar, disturbing, or negatively special about me? Did she tell Karen, who was the only other Black student in the Honor Society, the same thing? What did she tell the other Black students going to college who were not in the Honor Society?

I was going to have to make some guesses about her motives in the matter. But, in the words of "Bard" Bootsy Joyner, Jr., Lampson was trying to shoot me with a "shitgun" the whole time. I wasn't expected to notice her disingenuousness, the odor left behind by her weapon of choice, or that I might have a concern hearing a message from her mouth, delivered in a plantation tone, tenor, and cadence familiar to my ancestors. I did not pay much attention to the rest of the meeting. I just wanted to go back to class and get away from the "Ole Miss."

That was last year. Now, the final year was about to start, and I could count on dealing with the "Ole Miss" again. At the start of summer, I briefly thought about getting a job. Mom never encouraged us to look outside for work because she didn't particularly like who or what was outside. As Black kids go, we were fairly pampered, and some said spoiled. I did have one job growing up as a newspaper delivery boy for Mr. McElhenny, for one Sunday. But then again, what boy in Havre de Grace didn't deliver papers for Mr. McElhenny at least once? The only other option available would have been washing dishes somewhere or working at the Bata Shoe Company, the local employer of last resort.

Fortunately, I received a job offer right at the end of school in chemistry class. One of the students in the class, Penny, made me an unexpected offer of employment. She wanted me to tutor her and Patty, another classmate, twice a week. I was more than a little bit surprised but very appreciative of her offer. She had already talked it over with her father, who agreed. They wanted to pay me for what I knew, but I would have done it for free because it was chemistry. So, the only thing left for me was to say yes, which I did.

At the first tutoring session, I drove out to her house in my old Ford Falcon with the manual choke. I met Penny's father, Dr. Norment, and her mother too. Shortly after I went into the house, her dad had one, and only one, question for me; how to make sulfuric acid? I told him how to do it, and it was to his satisfaction. So, the tutoring began.

I had been in class with Penny, but I didn't know the problems she might be having. There were certainly plenty of places in chemistry to get perplexed, mystified, confused, or just plain lost. It wasn't long before I saw how I could help her make sense of things you could not see or feel but had to imagine in whichever way you could. Penny was a very good student, and I enjoyed figuring out different ways to make what was happening to the molecules easier for her to understand. When he was around, I always enjoyed talking to Dr. Norment, who was Canadian and a very easy conversationalist.

By the end of the summer, Penny had become a pretty fair chemistry student. She wanted to go to nursing school, and having an understanding of chemistry was going to help her greatly. She was happy about her progress, and so was I. I had gotten to know my section 8-2 friend in an unexpected and meaningful way that benefited both of us. It surpassed the usual transient relationships in high school into a deeper, lasting friendship. She was a friend, and I was happy to say so to anybody. And it was a good feeling being paid for what I know.

CHAPTER 20

Senior Year

The senior year had begun early with the start of football practice in mid-August. It was hot, humid, and horrible, but I wanted to play one more time. I got my chance when the high school changed head coaches from Mr. Rupprecht to Mr. Marron, our new physical education teacher. There was no way I was ever going to risk hurting my knee again playing for Rudolph or Rupprecht in any sport. Football practice in August in Maryland was barely survivable, and it gave you a new appreciation for the quenching, vital properties of water. Football was still fun, but the boys had grown since I had last played. So, I needed a new approach to football physics to remain in one piece.

Coach Marron arranged a special treat for our team three weeks into practice. We crossed over the Susquehanna River bridge to Cecil County, home of the Bainbridge Naval Station, where we scrimmaged the U.S. Naval Academy Prep School team. The players on the Navy team were older, bigger, stronger, faster, meaner, and some had probably been to Vietnam since they were all in the service. We held our own in spots, but basically, we got a beating on the field at the hands of grown men. In spite of that experience, I liked Mr. Marron a lot, and I was hoping for a good year for the team.

When actual school began, I was ready to get my year started and see what surprises came in the final act. I was even looking forward to trigonometry and reteaching it to myself, as usual. But the fun was going to be doing independent study in biochemistry with Mr. Hovermill. I was his classroom teaching assistant and got to help the smart 10th grade students understand what was going on with chasing molecules. I warned them that hot glass looked just like cold glass, don't ever pour distilled water into strong acids, know the importance of the periodic table, and what all the numbers meant. They were very eager and had no problem absorbing the material. Mr. Hovermill appreciated my fascination and love of chemistry, and he saw that I could teach it too. Otherwise, I did pretty much whatever I wanted for 55 minutes, with Mr. Hovermill's blessings.

At that moment, I knew this was exactly why I had wanted to leave the Consolidated School; to get all this equipment and opportunity. And, we had enough Bunsen burners for all the students, instead of one per classroom. I was thrilled to be in the chemistry lab, and so was my brain.

Mom told me in the summer that I should try to enjoy my last year in high school. She wanted me to have some new friends I could learn from and do new things with. Emerson had given up on me having any social life that we could connect on, but he was satisfied knowing that I did like girls.

Before the start of school, he did give me what amounted to an order for my own good. He told me that when elections for the Class of 1969 officers were held, I was to accept any position to which I was nominated, even if it was dog catcher. Emerson knew it was my natural inclination to avoid doing highly visible things like that, but he didn't understand why, or anything about my adventurous brain. I didn't understand it well either, but I knew it was something for which I was constantly compensating. Emerson was right, I needed to expose myself more, and do different things, especially if it made me uncomfortable. He wanted me to do more than play football and live in the chemistry lab.

When school opened, it was good seeing people again and realizing that as the senior class, the school was ours, more or less, for a year. The first week was normally busy, checking out the teachers, getting books, supplies, and catching up on news with friends you hadn't seen for a while. The song "Grazing in the Grass" seemed to be everywhere, along with "Aquarius" and other songs from the rock opera "Hair." The class, as a group, was upbeat and positive. We liked each other and had always gotten along well over the years. The end of the first week would be a special day with class elections, a pep rally, and the first home football game against Elkton with our new coach, Mr. Tom Marron.

On the big Friday, the class assembled in the auditorium for our scheduled Problems of Democracy—POD— class, taught by Misters Rupprecht and Rudolph, of the social studies department. The entire senior class took POD, so it was the natural time to hold the class elections. There were no speeches given, pledges made, signs posted, or balloons released, just nominations and votes for president, vice president, treasurer, and secretary.

Ralph was nominated for class president in the first election in short order and to no one's surprise. He was well respected, capable, very smart and organized, and we all knew it. I was sitting toward the front near the stage, with my back to most of my classmates. Ralph was elected and installed, then the nominations for vice president were opened. I heard the voice of one of my classmates in the back of the room. I could hear her, but I couldn't see her from where I was sitting. She put my name in nomination for the office, along with two other students also running. The instructions Emerson gave me at home were still fresh, but I still had an instant of hesitation and doubt after hearing my name called.

There had never been a Black senior officer in the Havre de Grace High School, but that didn't factor into my mixed feelings. I was thinking about myself and my comfort level, before remembering what Mrs. Turner, my 5th grade teacher, had told me long ago; the struggle was more than just about me and those that can do must do. I accepted the nomination and election to the class office. My gracious classmates of four years had elected me their vice president for the Class of 1969. Naturally, I was glad I didn't have to give an acceptance speech.

However, I knew with my new office, my visibility in the school increased even more. I could be called on, at any time, to represent my class if President Ralph was not available. I was sure not everyone in the auditorium, or the school, would find my election something to cheer about. But my classmates liked me, and I liked them too, which was all that mattered that morning. We finished the elections with the installment of Julia as treasurer, and Joan, as secretary. The elections concluded, and we resumed the Problems of Democracy class.

That was the morning, but my interesting day was just getting started. We had a pep rally scheduled for the afternoon for the entire school, with cheerleaders, pompoms, band music, and all. Coach Marron, who had given me his old jersey number to wear earlier, was going to be in charge of the assembly, introducing himself and the team to the High School. All of the school's students and teachers walked across Congress Avenue to the gymnasium and filled the bleachers for the coming show. After the sundry official announcements about the game, the mic was turned over to the coach to make comments about the team, then introduce the starting lineup for the offense. My old Pop Warner teammate, Robert Ware, was playing quarterback this year, and he was to be the first Black student to play that position at the school, which I figured was noticed. It was naturally going to be a problem for a few, or maybe a lot. It was 1968, below the Mason-Dixon Line, and old habits die hard.

When Coach Marron got the microphone, he told the school who he was and his goals for the football team this year. Coach Marron was from Pennsylvania, just like the "German Twins" in the social studies department, but the similarities ended there. He played football at Michigan State and Arizona State, and not the east or south of the country. His college coaches were Duffy Dougherty and Frank Kush, who he talked about with reverence and fear. Coach Kush would take his team into the Arizona desert to practice for mental and physical conditioning.

Mr. Marron had lived in areas of the country that attempted to treat people equally, as a general human rule, which had never been a serious concern in the South. When he evaluated the team and assigned positions, he was depending on his eyes and stopwatch. It didn't matter what you looked like, what your last name was, who your big brother was, or what position you played last year. Many of my Black friends, who had played soccer last year, came back to football that fall because of the new coach.

Mr. Marron called out each player and introduced him by position, starting with the linemen, proceeding to the ends, and then the backfield. The coach would call his number and then say a little something about each player. When he got to me, he said," And at flanker, we have senior Larry Ford, #40, who, pound for pound, is one of the toughest guys I know." That was flattering and a little embarrassing but appreciated at this school. He took a shine to how I played, like being 130 pounds didn't matter in football physics. However, the plaudits were slightly misplaced, because everybody on the team knew this; pound for pound the team's toughest guy was Jerry Waters, hands down. Nobody ever wanted to run into him head-on, and some of us had paid the price, including me. However, any appreciation I got from the teachers and staff of the school was welcomed and balanced out some of the other nonsense that came my way. But this was my day and I was still feeling like a "Big Dog," as Bootsy would say.

School was out after the rally, so I went back home to eat and tell Mom about my day. She was happy to hear about it, but she didn't seem particularly surprised. Her expectations of us were always high, but she kept them to herself unless she thought we needed to hear them. After eating, I went to my room to get off my legs and think about my sublime day, and the upcoming game under the lights.

After the respite, I got up to get ready to go to the gym for our 7:30 game. In the kitchen, I downed some juice, two salt pills, and a couple of glasses of cold water. It was going to be a warm, humid night, and you didn't want to catch a cramp somewhere. The last thing I grabbed before being driven to the gym was a handful of tissues and my irreplaceable Vicks Inhaler, which were always stuffed between the foam ridges in my helmet. I was hoping they wouldn't be needed tonight.

When I got to the locker room, most of the team was already there, preparing and primping like bantam roosters before a cockfight. We greeted each other and did the locker room butt slap to anyone excited or yelling about the Warriors winning the game tonight. I participated in the Ra-Ra some, but what I wanted was to find an empty classroom so I could be by myself for a few minutes. I found a darkened room in the front of the gym and took a seat near the back. I just needed to focus the rowdy squash in my head on this one thing now and find a temporary chip to put on my shoulder to get completely ready to play.

I was thinking about Elkton and trying to find a reason to dislike them for a little while. I landed on how I felt seeing all those "Impeach Earl Warren" signs that used to dot the small yards of the little bungalows along the highway across the river from Havre de Grace. That was bad enough if you know the importance of Supreme Court Chief Justice Earl Warren and his monumental role in ending school segregation in America. The good God-fearing folk of Cecil County never forgave the Justice for it, and they hosted a KKK rally a couple of years ago to prove it. That was enough to think about before playing the big farm boys. I rejoined my teammates for the meeting with Coach Marron, and our traditional cleated team march from the gym, across Juniata Street, to Tomahawk Field.

We started doing our warmups and sizing up our opponents on the other side of the field. It was a pretty large crowd for our school, filling the stands on both sides. The team was going through passing and defensive drills, and so was Elkton. They looked like big-ish country boys who didn't look all that fast. Maybe it was the high-top cleats some of the players were wearing, which could make any runner look slow.

Before the kickoff, I scanned the crowd and found Mom sitting beside Aunt Sue, who had come to visit us from Chicago. It was going to be her first time seeing me play anything, but Aunt Sue was a sports fan and knew a lot about her hometown teams. The night was beautiful, and, more importantly, there wasn't even a zephyr puffing in from the Bay. Now, it was kickoff time to the last part of my extraordinary school day, and I was still feeling just like a "Big Dog," rolling in the shade.

They won the coin toss, which put us on defense first. On defense, I played mostly linebacker and some defensive back. Elkton was primarily a ground game team because their big boys weren't going to outrun you too often. They were grinding it out, forcing us to tackle their good-sized running backs head on. They couldn't sweep us, but they were plodding ahead 3 or 4 yards at a time, eating up the clock. Elkton mixed in a couple of short passes with their runs, putting together a nice, slow scoring drive of 60 yards. They capped it off with an inside dive play from the 2-yard line. It was 7-0 Elkton in the first quarter, and we needed to keep them from getting into 3rd and short. Otherwise, it would be a long night.

We were a bit down after Elkton had scored. But we had a lot of time and speed that the Elks hadn't seen yet. We started from our 35-yard line and ran a couple of running plays, and then hit a short pass to Billy Ryan, our end, that put us inside the 50-yard line, in Elkton territory. I had been playing around with the boy defending me but not showing him how fast I could run, sandbagging him. The play Coach Marron called was the 125-trap pass. Bobby Ware called the play on 3, and we broke the huddle and went to the line of scrimmage. The Elks defensive back, #27, was about ten yards off the line, just as he had been playing the previous downs. My eyes got big looking at all the empty space between #27 and the end zone. A nasty move wasn't needed because the boy wasn't that fast. I could save the old dead-leg move for later in the game.

On the count of three, I drove hard at the defensive player, causing a quick retreat, but not quick enough. A little sideline hip fake froze him, then I took off for the goal post. Crossing the 25-yard line, I was all by myself and was sure #27 was surprised by the streak that had just breezed past him. The ball was falling out of the black sky and the tall bank of field lights. Bobby had thrown a tight, perfectly spiraling pass that was going to be easy to catch. It was just me and the ball, which I had no intention of dropping. I caught it at the 15, squeezed the rotations out of it, smiled, and darted to the end zone, almost running completely through it. Game tied, 7-up. I took a deep breath, listened to the distant, delayed crowd noise, and realized that my dreamy school day was still in progress.

Coach Marron was pleased on the sidelines, along with the team and the fans. We were into the 2nd quarter, and our defense was doing better against the Elks' big backs. I had made a couple of tackles that made me appreciate how much bigger the players were now. Head on tackles were out, and I was looking for angles to attack the running backs. We held them on downs and got the ball back on their 45-yard line, near the same spot as the touchdown in the first quarter.

The Elks were not double-teaming me, so #27 was all by his lonesome on the edge. We called the same play with 10 seconds left in the quarter, and it looked like deja vu. On the count, I did the same thing as last time, a little fake and gone. I gave him a parting look as I blew by him again on what I thought was going to be another touchdown. The pass from Bobby was a bit late, forcing me to slow up to catch the ball. I met up with the ball at the 10, but #27 had thawed out and had time to recover on the slow pass. He caught me at the 2-yard line, making the tackle just short of the goal line. The ref's whistle sounded, ending the first half of a good 7-7 game.

At halftime, we were confident that we could win a home opener, for a change, and we couldn't wait to get the second half started. After the halftime festivities, the Warriors received the kickoff, bringing it out to our 30-yard line. When I went to line up for the snap, I saw there was some extra company on my side of the field. The Elks had decided one man couldn't cover me, so they double-teamed me. It was an admission that I was pretty fast dangerous, and I could catch the ball downfield. I smiled about it and felt a little more honored by the Elks on my excellent day in school.

Coach Marron called a skinny curl play that went right into the strength of the double-team. I didn't think I was going to see the ball on the play. On the count of 2, I ran down 15 yards and slanted in, looking for some space away from the two players in the front and back of me. But the ball was thrown to me again, now sandwiched between two defensive backs. The ball came fast, hard, and with enough mustard on it to clear #27 in front of me. I put my hands up, trying to get a touch on the ball. In an instant, and to my great surprise, I found a motionless football stuck between my hands as the tackle came from behind.

We three landed on the ground, all with the same thought in mind; how did that ball get caught? But, it was my day, and, naturally, I was going to make an impossible catch at least once. They double-teamed me for most of the rest of the night. I didn't catch more passes, but it freed up Billy and Pam on the other side.

Neither team scored in the third quarter, and we were pounding each other equally. I was hoping we could get in position to throw that 125 trap pass once more. Before that, the coach called a wingback reverse to me. I loved the play but usually our linemen weren't fast enough to get to the edge first, leaving me to take on the linebacker and whoever else was on that side. I started the play and was able to turn the corner for about three steps when I got hit hard from the side. The hit felt like it was from someone who had been waiting to do it for the whole night. It was a fair, hard hit, but it wasn't the reason my night was over.

I was thinking I should have taken another salt pill before I hit the ground. Both of my calf muscles were gripped with severe cramps and turned instantly into stone. I wasn't hurt, just in a lot of pain. Coach Marron came on the field, bent over me, and asked if I was hurt. I told him no, and that it was just cramps. So, he threw me over his shoulder, carried me to the sideline, and deposited me on the ground next to the wire fence.

I was lying on the grass face down and trying not to move when I looked up to see Mom and Aunt Sue leaning over the fence. Mom had a look of sheer panic on her face, but not Aunt Sue. I told Mom I was fine, and it was just leg cramps, nothing else. That is when Aunt Sue bent over the fence, got close to my head, and gave me some advice: "Boy, get your face out of that dirt before you get pimples." I looked at her, smiled, and tried to laugh through the pain. Eventually, I was able to stand up and watch the rest of the game. The game ended with Bobby throwing a last minute, 20-yard sideline touchdown to Pam Malloy, and the place went crazy! Game over; Warriors 14 and Elkton 7.

The locker room was loud and happy after our rare season opening win. The sweaty room was filled with all kinds of people, from teachers to gym coaches from last year and even a newspaper photographer. The newsman wanted to take a picture of Bobby, Pam, and me, the "Erie Street, uptown mob." The Havre de Grace Record used the picture and wrote a nice account of the game, saying that "Havre de Grace hadn't seen an aerial attack like that in many years." It would turn out that not everybody would like that picture. But that's Havre de Grace.

I had a couple of people come over and talk to me as I was carefully taking the tape off my ankles, and paying the price for not shaving my legs before the game. To my amazement, I was visited by Mr. Rupprecht, who congratulated me on a good game. I thanked him, then he said, "Ford, you should have played last year," which sounded to me more like an order than a wish. I just smiled and kept my thoughts to myself on that one.

I had one memorable, marvelous, excellent day in school, and it was one of the best days of my life. I went home, put some Ben-Gay on my calves, and went to bed. I was thinking in my next dream, I might finally score that winning touchdown.

I was able to play football my senior year, after the
school changed coaches to Mr. Tom Marron

Images: Courtesy of Harford County Board of Education.

The "Uptown Erie Street Boys" celebrate victory of their
first senior year football game.

Photo: Havre de Grace Record

I played wingback on offense and linebacker on defense

Images: Courtesy of Harford County Board of Education.

CHAPTER 21

After the Game

The morning after the football game, it took a minute to remember what had happened the previous night. Then I recalled that we had won! The pain, still present in my calves, reminded me of that. I was sorry that I couldn't play the end of the game. I knew the Elkton players thought they hurt me after I burned them all night long. I should have taken more salt pills and drank more water. It may have helped. Mom and Aunt Sue were in the kitchen having breakfast. Mom asked how I was, and Aunt Sue checked me for any new pimples. I told Mom that I was okay and that I'd had worse cramps to wake me up from the dead of sleep. She gave me a couple of chores to do after I ate and stretched my legs.

I drove to the cleaners on Otsego Street to pick up some clothes for Mom. When I limped in the door, a pair of young, smiling eyes greeted me with, "Well… hello, Larry. Wow, that was some game last night. You guys played really good!" I didn't know the girl working there, but I thought she was a friend of Bootsy and was probably in our class. I had just never seen her before, and I was surprised she knew me.

"I didn't know you played football. You didn't hurt your legs too bad, did you?" I thanked her for her nice words. I told her I hadn't played football since 9th grade but decided to play this year. I assured her my legs were going to be okay, and I was going to play next week. She gave me my clothes and flashed her lovely smile again all the way to the door, saying, "Bye-Bye. That was a really good game."

That set the stage for how interesting school would be on Monday. There was a light and cheery air in the building that morning. We had won the first game of the year, which was a big deal, in our traditionally bad little football school. People were very nice to the players, with congratulations all around. In the late morning, I went to my trigonometry class with Miss Scibeck. She was a brand-new math teacher in her late 20s, with no discernible accent. I became a fan of hers right away because on the first day of school, she styled the place all day long in her long, satin kitty cat skirt.

She greeted me as I walked into the class and gave out some plaudits for a good game. She also told me how surprised she was to see me playing football. Then she said, "Well, if you need any extra help with your trig, let me know. We've got to make sure you stay on the team." I smiled and told her I was glad she enjoyed the game, and I appreciated her offer for help in trig, but I thought I would be okay.

The morning was buzzing with all the talk about weekend fun, parties, and the game. It was delightful seeing the school so thrilled to have won the opening game. But I was not used to all the attention coming my way. It was funny to see students, and teachers, being nearly stunned that I even knew what a football was, not to mention how to play with one.

The expected attempt to sabotage and rain on my good day would come at lunchtime, from the usual suspect. Bothering Black males, for no particular reason, was a time-honored blood sport for some White men and was self-affirming of their superior masculinity, I supposed. I knew the attack was coming from the self-appointed torturer for my senior year. He could not pass up an opportunity like this to release some of the built-up stress and stomach acid my mere presence gave him. I liked giving him new things to grouse about, but he did a good job finding those on his own. My peripheral vision was kept at the ready, scanning for the appearance of a meaty dolt with glasses and loafers, all attached to a crew cut.

At lunch, I ran into Bootsy for the first time. Being the silver-tongued lad from Hill Town, I knew he would have the right words to top off the morning. Boots was smiling slyly as he came to sit at my table. He said, "Ford, Ford, Ford!! My Boy! You are definitely what is happening in this world today — you understand what I'm sayin'." He was both joking and a little serious in the effusive, ultra-treatment he bestowed upon me at our table. I feigned embarrassment, and we laughed out loud. Boots was on a roll, and I was eating up the show like a Deacon in the front row. "As you know brother Ford you will always be my main Boy, even if you don't get no bigga'! When you was out there snagging all of them passes at the game, I told everybody sitting around me in the bleachers, he learned all that shit from me, y'all!"

We were getting ready to do some serious social talk when the expected, loathsome squall line blew in. The unwelcome rain man was Robert Rudolph, of course. He slithered over to the table to dampen everything and gulley washed the conversation right down the slough. He had placed his cartoonish chassis in front of the lunch table, and he appeared to be in full idiotic mocking mode. Rudolph would never actually joke with the likes of me, though he may condescendingly pretend to do so. It was all about condescension and maybe a spot of jealousy with him. So, anything he did came from the deepest recesses of his small, dark heart or whatever a man like him carries in his chest.

He pretended to hoist a heavy, old style hand-cranked newsreel camera onto his shoulder as he commenced a make believe, sarcastic interview laced with his special misplaced distaste for me.

"How are you doing today... Superstar?" He did not possess a low voice or anything approximating class or grace. So, he bellowed on, "You have a half-decent game and...Well... you're a big important man now. Right?"

Rudolph twisted his imaginary camera lens, repositioned its heavy nonexistent body on his shoulder on the left side of the ample, dense block he called a head, and he asked the question again. He saw that I was neither amused nor intimidated by his adolescent behavior. In his boorish, churlish dreams, this was a big moment for him. It was disturbing, and a little creepy, to think how long this had been fermenting in an adult like him, who would bother an intelligent, athletic, popular student, primarily because he was not White? And what else might he try to do before the year was over? I showed no reaction to him other than looking him straight in his eyes and wishing for him to disappear or self-immolate immediately. And he did leave, after venting more venom and spleen, to deliver whatever kind of message it was.

Bootsy gave me that "Hey man, don't waste your time worrying about it" look. But I did think about it; the everyday racism that was all over the place, masquerading as a joke, something innocuous or at least deniable. Racism was insidious, pernicious, and irrational on its own to all except the racist. It was also conveniently invisible if you didn't care to see it. Throwing a few dozen ex-colored school students into a previously white school was not going to magically fix the bestowed majesty of whiteness in this country, enjoyed for the last 350 years. They don't even know there's anything wrong that needs fixing.

There was nothing to converse about with a person like Robert Rudolph. Even the white kids didn't like him. So, it wasn't my imagination. He seemed to enjoy trying to break me down and elevate himself in the process. He didn't know it, but my mother didn't raise low self-esteem, easily breakable children, and he was wasting his time. I just needed to keep away from him, Lampson, and probably Banick, the principal, as much as possible until graduation.

There were things bigger than football going on; after all, it was 1968, a very bad year. Earlier in the year, Lyndon Johnson had stated he would not accept the Democratic nomination to run for President. This put the Democrats in a free fall, especially considering their violent, police riot-infused summer convention in Chicago. Richard Nixon was easily scaring White people all over the country on multiple topics. His "southern strategy," for winning elections without needing Black votes, was humming in fourth gear to very receptive audiences in the South, North, West, and East.

Martin Luther King had panicked many White Americans before his murder earlier in the year. His approval rating in America at the end of his life was 25% for a man who had won the Nobel Peace Prize 4 years earlier. But there were still lots of other convenient Black boogeymen around to instill the fear that White people needed right before an election; Stokley Carmichael, the hated Muhammad Ali, John Lewis, and H.Rap Brown, to name a few. And just to make sure the racist underbelly of America was fully and democratically, represented in the 1968 election, George Corley Wallace, the populist, segregationist, opportunistic governor of Alabama, was on the ballot as a third-party candidate.

The entire senior class took the Problems of Democracy course taught by "the Pennsylvania German" twins, Mr. Rupprecht and, the ubiquitous, Mr. Rudolph. The class held a mock convention, minus George Wallace, to learn how the democratic process of elections worked or did not work. The class was divided into Republican and Democratic camps, which then selected their candidates. There was wheeling, dealing, rumors flying, and backbiting going on to a comical degree. My old 8-2 classmate, Alex, had transformed himself from class history buff to convention kingmaker with cunning and enthusiasm. Most students were getting into the show.

When the dust settled, the Democratic nominee was Bobby Miller, previously from section 8-1 (the 8th grade class with the smart White kids), and the Republican nominee was I, from lowly 8-2 and C1. I surprised myself by allowing it to happen. I think Alex, my history loving old 8-2 friend, talked me into being a candidate. Being publicly exposed on stage still wasn't something I was comfortable doing. It was also something I knew I had to overcome and get familiar with what it took to pull off something like this. I knew there wasn't another Black student in the class who was either able or willing to do something political and "very White" like this. I was a little scared. Since I put myself in this position, it was very important to come through well for the other Black students in the class, even if they didn't completely get, or appreciate, what I was up to.

This was one of those times my 5th grade teacher, Mrs. J.P. Turner, at the Consolidated School, must have had in mind when she told me, "Those who can do must do for us all to advance." I always thought it was important for Black students to be part of every aspect of school life. I may have been the only Black student in my class willing, or crazy enough, to do something about it. Of course, the added benefit of running for President in the mock election, was knowing how much it was going to bother Rudolph, watching, grading, and grinding his teeth. I was going to give him something to grade, alright. Additionally, I was sure Mr. Rupprecht hadn't forgotten about last year in history class when I told him what a "sinologist" actually was. He didn't like it, and I couldn't help it.

After all the machinations, graft, vote buying, innuendo, and Machiavellian high school intrigue, the scene was this; the whole senior class in the auditorium, the teachers in the back grading, and Bobby Miller, from 8-1, and me, from lowly 8-2, debating each other on stage.

I was trying not to look at my seated classmates until I got used to what I was doing. I thought about how much I had changed from starting this school in 8-2 and wondering how smart the 8-1 kids were. Now, I'm going to verbally grapple with 8-1. Boy, do I have nerve, I thought to myself. Are you ready, Rudolph? I wanted to badger him by showing my ability and confidence to do this in front of the class and him. Yep me a kid from the Colored School, not asking for your permission, for your respect, or anything else.

It was a good debate. Bobby was the Democrat, Hubert H. Humphrey and I was John Lindsay, the young, charismatic Republican mayor of New York City. Bobby was up on his current events and pretty good about mud-slinging when he had the chance. Alex had come up with our strategy to surprise the opponent, and we had a few zingers and some mud handy to throw back Bobby's way. The class enjoyed and appreciated the effort both sides were giving. Bobby was showing why the 8-1 kids were respected for being very smart and capable, and Alex and I were showing them what 8-2 grit, guile, and determination looked like.

My brain had not misfired, locked up, or gone into any paroxysms of embarrassing stutters. I could see what I wanted to say, where I wanted to go with it, and then get to a logical end in my speech. I was in control of myself, so far, and using everything I could remember from watching the news every night or what I had read in the newspapers to thrust and parry with Bobby. I hoped Rudolph was having a fine time watching and hoping that I was just another average Black "Super Star," waiting for my crashing and burning that never came. Put down an "A" for me in the grading book for "The Super Star," as you derisively referred to me after the first football game. It was just between me and Rudolph at that point. He probably knew I was thinking about him and that I was taking a victory lap right in his Neanderthal mug.

When the class voting was over, John Lindsay and I had won. I had survived and learned from my encounter with stage fright and politics. My guerrilla skirmishes with the school powers were taking on a different flavor this year. But now, I had a few weapons of my own. I didn't want to annoy them to the point they would go off and do something horrible to me. But I couldn't help rubbing it in their faces whenever the opportunity presented itself. You should not taunt people like them too much, but don't let them think they can roll you over, either. I had never spent much time thinking about social popularity in school, but I had been elected vice president of my class and President of the United States, all within six weeks, by my accepting classmates. There were forces in the school not happy with that, of course.

Richard Nixon was a backward thinker on race, and he didn't seem to respect, covet, or need the Black vote or Black people. His "Southern strategy" helped him win the Presidency in 1968. A truly horrible year in America ended with an awful man in the White House. It was a small relief for Black people in Maryland that Nixon's win swept up Spiro Agnew, the Governor of Maryland, out of Annapolis, and into the Vice Presidency, down the road 30 miles to Washington.

We were ecstatic to see him go but perplexed as to why Republicans would think having a classless man like Agnew, one heartbeat away from the presidency, was a good idea. But they did it. In the final national election result, George Wallace, the proudly racist governor of Alabama, won five states; the solid Dixie block of Alabama, Georgia, Mississippi, Louisiana, and Arkansas. He also got 13% of the national popular vote, in a nod to the southern politician's mother's milk, race, and what is at the historical, social core of this country, rot.

Beyond Football

The rest of the fall passed by quickly and smoothly in my classes, but football was another matter. We had won the first two games of the season without much esprit de corps on the team. Then something happened, and things got a lot chillier. Some of the suppressed hard feelings, caused by who the new coach was playing this year were re-surfacing. Undeniably, there were many more Black players now, including Bobby Ware at quarterback. Bobby said he never had a direct talk with coach Marron about it, but he did feel some subtle pressure being the first non-White player in the school at his position. But it wasn't like it was something new to Bobby. He had played in the same town Little League with me in elementary school when many of the White coaches called any of the Black players Tasby and laughed about it. He knew what athletics in the town looked like and had known for a very long time.

On the less subtle side was what Emerson had told me occurred at a parent's booster meeting early in the season. A White parent complained about the team having "too many stars," which was language intentionally barely in code. Emerson was insulted but not surprised. He was used to some White people speaking of us, in our presence, as if we were not in the room or couldn't understand plainly spoken English. The opinion of the White parent was clear and he was not a fan of the Black players, or "stars." I was pretty sure that he or other powerful parents had made their feelings known to the school.

I had been told directly that some of the White players had no plans to block for the Black players anymore. I don't know how serious the rumor was. Maybe it was because they just couldn't block very well that was causing our problems on offense. I never heard a word or saw anything in practice that would give a hint anything was amiss. I was expecting something to happen one day, but it never did. Marron would not have stood for that on his team. He was all about playing the best player at a given position. He came in new to the school and the area, with its particular views on race that he did not agree with. But, he could read a stopwatch and knew who wanted to play, regardless of what they looked like.

I went to Homecoming because I had to. We had lost to Cambridge in a game we could have won. I had an okay game, despite fighting the Cambridge pulling guard most of the day. But my old Consolidated School friend, Jerry "Apples" Waters, had a monster game. Jerry was plain old country strong, fearless, humble, and gracious. His body seemed to be made from something harder than granite and not from this world; you could hit Jerry all day and bounce off without making him move. He played over center on defense but was only a tad bigger than me. He was smacking the opposing center back into his quarterback the whole game. Jerry was our lone bright spot in an otherwise disappointing game. Coach Marron selected Jerry to be the MVP, most valuable player, for Homecoming 1969 because he deserved it.

Homecoming was the first and last school dance I ever attended since I did not go to the Prom. Barbara Dorsey, who I had known since first grade at the Consolidated School, was our classy, beautiful homecoming queen. She was smiling and radiating her charm all through the gym that night. Seeing her reign was the best part of the night.

At one point in the evening, I was near the entrance to the gym, standing at the trophy case along with several other players. The homecoming trophy was there, along with a paper stating that the name of Jerry Waters would be engraved on the piece, in recognition of his outstanding play throughout the game. This was my first social interaction with my teammates, and I was mostly watching and listening to their comments about the game, and the trophy. It was hard to listen to the words that were spoken next. One of the linemen said of Jerry's winning the homecoming game award, "Well, Jerry never had much and probably won't have much in his life. So, it's probably a good thing he got this award now."

After hearing that, I was ready to go home, but I had one more thing to do. I had helped to decorate the gym for homecoming with a lot of my classmates, whom I had never seen outside of school before. It was an interesting experience going to the Ames Department store to get or liberate some decorating supplies with the ladies. The girls were fearless, having a real good time and acting like laws concerning the liberation of decorating supplies were mere suggestions if you were really cute. I was a bit sweaty at times shopping with the young ladies. After going to school with them for almost five years, I finally got to know what they were like in one night. Before I went home, I went by the tables and said good night to all my classmates and new friends, who were helping to make school a little fun, finally.

CHAPTER 22

The Road to Colquitt

My family spent Christmas vacation of my senior year in Albany, Georgia, my birth town. We drove to Georgia, and much to my surprise, Emerson ceded most of the driving to me in a 1967 Buick Electra 225, a deuce and a quarter. The car seemed to have enough horsepower to leave the ground and fly. It took an hour to get the smile off my face after driving it and passing a few trucks after stamping on the accelerator into the passing gear. I had a good time motoring on the open road and advancing toward Georgia, a hundred miles at a time.

We were going to see Mom's family for the first time since my grandmother, Addie, passed away three years ago. Going back to Georgia was always a shock to my body, as well as my mind. I was hoping that being there in the winter would be healthier than trying to survive the oven that is summer. When you are in Albany, there is not much left of the United States or the North American continent, since 120 miles due south would put you in the Gulf of Mexico. You couldn't go much deeper into the Deep South than Albany. It was a hot, flat, sandy, hardscrabble town, famous mostly for pecans, cotton, southern decadence, and being the birthplace of Ray Charles Robinson— Ray Charles.

I could remember, as a small child, being uncomfortable most of the time we lived there. I seemed to be reactive to many things in the environment, especially dust, which was abundant. Breathing was hardly automatic, but generally a labored chore, especially after running around. My grandmother finally took me to her church to see if Elder Lippman could shake out or, in the name of Jesus, heal me from the insides and take the illness away forever. The young Elder stood in the well of the church, with sweat on his brow and his eyes clenched tight, to summon all of his powers and focused them on my ill little soul. My grandmother was holding me in front of the whole church as the Elder put the heel of his hand upon my forehead and his fingers on my crown. He shook me firmly several times as he called on Jesus Christ to heal Mother Johnson's grandson. "In Jesus name, heal this child!" He repeated this several times.

The packed church joined in with more vocal praise and rhythmic hand clapping from the front row, where the Mothers sat fanning themselves, and from the pews, filled with believers of the faith. An occasional "Hallelujah" was added by the Deacons in the Amen Corner as Grandma Addie smiled and carried me back to the pew. She sat me down and gave me a stick of Juicy Fruit Gum to keep me quiet. Being a Mother of the Church, my grandmother had other duties to perform, so she left me with a church friend. I sat quietly on the hard wooden pew, surrounded by tall, standing, singing people and being rocked by the joyous, thunderous noise shaking the Lord's House. The next morning at home, I awoke to find chewing gum stuck in my hair again, and my breathing was still bad. Grandma Addie fixed the hair problem with a washcloth and a little kerosene. It always worked.

But culturally, Georgia was always a world away from Maryland, even with Jim Crow and segregation being practiced in both places. Georgia was a hard and grinding existence that wore you down and robbed your soul and dignity in a way Maryland didn't do to Negroes in such an openly hostile manner. Maryland did it more with double-talk, double-dealing, and mendacious delusions peddled as Gospel; it was a more gentlemanly, Christian take on racism. A few years ago, during a visit, one of my cousins called me a Yankee, which was funny and ironic. It begged the question; well, if I am a Yankee, what does that make you? She never gave me an answer to that and I never told her about the confusing adventures of living Black, just 20 miles south of the Mason-Dixon Line.

The accents of my relatives were typical for South Georgia, and the terms my grandmother used at times were difficult to understand. She told me once to go to the store and get some "roasting ears," which was a term I hadn't heard before. I went down to the Piggly Wiggly, and the store lady told me what roasting ears were, in Southern speak. So, I brought my grandmother eight ears of corn, and she was tickled and delighted by my embellished story of getting to know what she had originally ordered. I guess my cousins thought we were very different, too, aside from being Yankees. I enjoyed Wendy introducing me to her school friends and talking about topics in their lives. I asked her if one of the guys in the group was her boyfriend? She said yes, but he was just an "all-day boyfriend." I pretended like I knew what that meant. And, of course, there was always the joy of meeting more cousins and putting on that I understood all the complicated genetics of our relationships.

I have a large family full of lots of aunts, uncles, and cousins galore. It was such a difference from our small family unit in Maryland. Mom had 2 brothers and 3 sisters, and they truly loved each other. When I got to see my mother at a family party in Georgia interacting with her cousins, it was like watching a younger, very hip, amplified version of her that she seldom showed. She was Mom alright, but even more so.

Our large family had a couple of dinners together at my uncle's home in Albany. Christmas Day was exciting watching the grownups and the cousins enjoying their kin. There was more food on the table than I had ever seen, and a few of the victuals in place were not familiar to my eye, or my stomach. One of the foods was Brunswick stew, which Mom always raved about. She was rather vague about what exactly was in it, which made me suspicious about the origins of the organic content. There were chicken, beef, and pork dishes done up several different ways from Haley, Robinson, Cheek, and Johnson family recipes.

The grownups had their Christmas and blues music rocking and drinks running all around. They were even playfully talking stuff to each other, especially the women to the men. But women ran my family, and everyone knew it. With their dancing and partying, they seemed to have temporarily reverted to their 20s and forgot their children were in the room. They were enjoying each other, and it was a little scary to think what they were like when they were 20. I just closed my eyes to some of it, laughing all the time.

During dinner, I talked to my Uncle EB, Mom's baby brother, about what I wanted to do the following day. He wasn't sure what kind of request was going to come out of my mouth. He always thought I was a little different right from birth, so he was ready for anything. I was his shadow from shortly after I learned to walk. He liked to show off my special skills to his friends or just enjoy me all by himself. Sometimes, we would sit on the porch, and I would name all the cars coming down dusty, unpaved Cherry Street. He told me I got to the point that I could tell the difference between a Ford, Chevy, DeSoto, or Cadillac by the sound of the engine, before seeing the car. I hoped he made some money off of me, as well as being entertained. Uncle EB was magical to me, and when he was around, things happened, or we went places.

So, he was not all that surprised when he heard what I wanted to do the following day. I told him that I wanted to see a cotton field. He thought about it for a bit, then he nodded and said, "Okay. We'll go to Colquitt in the morning." My Uncle didn't ask why I wanted to do such a thing. Any of my Georgia relatives could see a cotton or sugar cane field several times a day if they needed to. Many of my relatives may not have taken my request as calmly or seriously as my Uncle. Like — Boy, why in Sam Hill would you want to do something like that at Christmas? — My Uncle had his plan for the day too.

Colquitt was about 50 miles from Albany, stuck deeply in the state's southwest corner, which made a near perpendicular union with Alabama and Florida in the middle of the Chattahoochee River. The land was flat as a table, without a mound or hillock in sight. It was full of huge farms side to side, which was surely just a small historic step, or two, from old slave plantations. Where there wasn't sandy red dirt and tall skinny pines encased in swaying Spanish moss, there were more swamplands dotting the landscape as we drove southward, ever closer to Florida.

I was struck most by the sheer, relative numbers of Black people in the small towns and forks in the road that we passed. There were many places no White people were to be seen, unless behind a register at a country store. For someone on vacation, asking to go to Colquitt would mean you had already seen everything you wanted, and now you were ready to see something else. The remote area sat out the Civil War because of its extreme southern position. It was much closer to Tallahassee than it was to Atlanta and the front lines of the war. The little town was more than 100 miles south of the infamous Civil War prison, Andersonville, and was of no strategic value to the North.

Uncle EB was the baby of his family. He got to do some things his older siblings could not have dreamed of doing. He was the first person in our family to go to college, at Albany State. He would send me football programs of the Albany State Rams and their star quarterback, Art Gamble. When he was in college EB was involved with the local Civil Rights movement to increase voter registration and force an end to the intractable, baked-in segregation he had grown up with. He, and his friends, marched with Dr. Martin Luther King against the Jim Crow oppression that negatively pervaded the life of everyone in the South who wasn't White. He also marched in the streets of Albany with Ralph Abernathy and George Foreman, the heavyweight prizefighter.

My Grandma Addie told me about things the protesters did to get ready for what they could expect at the hands of the police and their chief, Laurie Pritchett. My uncle, and his college friends, would gather at a local Black church with other marchers and learn what getting hit was going to feel like. The young men and women exchanged punches to various body parts, slaps to the face, verbal abuse, and unfriendly holds on each other to get prepared for the coming assault by law enforcement. My Uncle was arrested and put in jail, as were many of his friends.

Dr. King's goal was to fill up the Albany jails to the point that Laurie Pritchett would run out of room to put in any more of them. But, the police chief decided to send the arrested demonstrators to several cities around Albany. Uncle EB was sent to jail in Camilla, 30 miles away. The chief of police's ploy worked, and Dr. King could never fill up the jails or conquer Albany. Many whites felt Albany was a win for them, and it bolstered their hope for eternal segregation. It was a rare defeat for Dr. King and the setback in Albany caused substantial consternation throughout the Civil Rights movement for a while. Dr. King was undeterred and moved on to Birmingham.

We had a nice slow ride to Colquitt. I took in as much as I could of the difference between what I was seeing here and what I was used to seeing in Havre de Grace. A lot of the rural scenery did not seem all that far removed from slavery and pre-Civil War times. It was easy to imagine this area 110 years ago filled with slave plantations and, likely, with some of my relatives tending them as implements of agriculture.

Arriving at Colquitt only amplified my assessment; by any standard, this was poverty and hopelessness on scale that I had never seen before.

It looked like everyone I saw in the neighborhood was living a life that I wouldn't want, but they went about it displaying quiet, uncomplaining dignity. I was trying not to be a voyeur, but I felt overwhelmed and angry with the connection between what I knew of American history and the intentionally failed Reconstruction period that helped to make the South the bedeviled, wicked, morally compromised place it had always been.

The roads were narrow and rutted in spots, but the few passing cars did not produce choking plumes of brown dust like in Albany. Uncle EB parked the car in front of an old, weathered shotgun house elevated on cinder blocks. A shotgun house was a rectangular one-story edifice. Most of the houses were similar to the one we parked near; basic functional shelter, and that was all. You could fire a gun from the front door, through the house to the back door, without causing any damage, thus the name shotgun house.

After my Uncle got out of the Army, he did some teaching in Colquitt and met many local people, including relatives of my grandfather, Joe Outland. The shotgun house we were parked in front of was that of my grandfather's relatives. Uncle EB and I got out of the car, walked a few steps to the front door, and knocked. An older woman answered the door and was glad to see my Uncle and me standing before her. We walked into the small front room where two other people, an older man, and a middle-aged woman, were sitting on the couch. Uncle EB introduced me to all as Joe Outland's grandson. They were surprised that I would appear suddenly on that day but were happy to meet a previously unknown, but fairly close family relative.

My relatives inspected me closely. I said hello and answered a few questions they had, like where I lived, if I was in school, and my age. The room was neat but small, and it was a bit crowded with chairs for people to sit. There was a wood coffee table by the couch, with the Bible and several other books sitting on it. The floor was made of wood planks, elevated from the ground on cinder blocks, and covered over with rugs. The room was drafty and a bit cool in December. If chickens wandered under the house, you would surely hear them clucking just a few inches beneath your feet. The kitchen was small, functional, and crowded, as well.

We stood for the short time we were there. Listening to older southern people talking is a lesson in itself. Their cadences, deep accents, and use of words sometimes left me a bit lost as to the meaning of certain of their phrases. They had a calm, rather divine air about them, like the children of Job. They had seen, felt, and lived through extraordinarily vicious, evil, and dangerous times in America, with only faint visibility to the country at large and no political power to speak of. No person should expect at birth that they would live a life full of senseless cruelty, deprivation, violence, and ignorance at the hands of Bible-quoting charlatans.

But we survived and were more Christ-like than our tormentors. The idea that their low station in life was natural, and part of God's plan, never did take hold in southern Black people, as some Whites had wished. All that, and still, Negro people exhibited inextinguishable and confounding hope. It was a mirror in the face of irrational, southern White Christianity. Many Negroes loved the idea of America without particularly caring for certain of its people.

As my Uncle continued to talk to the Outlands, I was thinking about what growing up here would be like. Pondering your future here must have been an exercise in masochism or like playing a joke on yourself every day. You may have to lie to yourself to get through the day as you keep going forth, back into the past. My last thought in the house was how fortunate my family was to get out of Georgia when I was young. I felt bad for some of my relatives still living here. It was painful to think that these were good, smart people caught in a system with nothing for them by design, and it was functioning well before they were born.

We said goodbye and got back into the car to drive the short distance to our last stop. Finally getting to the cotton field was an anticlimax to all I had seen, heard, and thought about in a short time. I just wanted to stand on the land of bondage and pain that conveyed perspectives and sorrows to people for hundreds of years. I wanted to stand in the sadness of the soil and absorb whatever strength, knowledge, and wisdom that still lay locked in the brown, sandy loam. I picked a couple of the small, left behind bolls of cotton, as well as a piece of sugar cane from an adjacent field. I was ready to leave, having seen, heard, and felt much more than I could have ever expected.

On the way back to Albany, my Uncle and I talked about several things, like his being in the Army and the places he had traveled outside of Georgia. But the best part was talking about interesting departed relatives that I never knew. Mom talked about her grandmother, Susie

Haley, often and with unabashed reverence. I always thought Mom got her personality and her wide ranging love of reading and knowledge from her. Susie was born in Dalton, Georgia, in 1880 and was a Cherokee medicine woman. She could read and write without any schooling, and she read to her brothers every night after they came home from the fields. My Uncle confirmed Susie's love of reading saying "She would read every last word on the page. If the dog barked three times, she'd go Bark! Bark! Bark!" I asked what she was like. He paused a bit, smiled with all his dimples showing, and said," Well, she was a fiery, pipe-smoking, temperamental, little, Black Cherokee Indian woman."

He went on to say that she was skilled at many things, including the art of cussing, and she used it occasionally, to good effect on my great-grandfather. And, she wouldn't back down from anyone, as in nobody. She thoroughly disliked White people without apology. Being a Black Cherokee, she got to hate them twice as much as she was part of both of the country's original sins; slavery and the Trail of Tears, the forced march of Indians to the Oklahoma territory.

Great-grandpa was the opposite, quiet, humble, and just looking for a safe spot to play "Catfish Blues" on his dobro and wait until the storm passed over or great-grandma calmed down. His family was from Barbados. I had little doubt that our family was different in large part because of Susie, her lineage, literacy, tenacity, and tough, temperamental Cherokee Indian ways.

I had one last question for my Uncle; did he know any other people like great-grandma Susie? He hummed, gave it some extra thought, and then said, "No....Just her sister." We both had a hardy, delayed laugh when the full implications of that statement to our family sank in, and it was fully appreciated.

Later on, I found out that Susie's grandfather was, the somewhat infamous, Jack Dean, my 3rd great-grandfather. He was born in 1810 on Goochland Plantation, northwest of Richmond, Virginia. In 1858, three years before the start of the Civil War, he was in jail in Virginia for forgery. That suggested that Jack Dean was a free man since they did not put slaves in jail when killing them would suffice. Also, he was quite literate and enterprising, since he was jailed for the crime of forgery (most likely against White people). Sometime after 1858, he relocated to Dalton, Georgia, 400 miles to the South. I supposed the Confederates didn't want an obviously dangerous Negro, like Jack Dean, to be too close to the Northern lines. There was no telling what an unshackled, literate Negro man with a criminal record and an obvious attitude problem was capable of doing.

My family loaded up the car and drove back to Maryland the following day. We all had an unexpectedly good time in Georgia, except for Mom. She expected to have a good time with her family, and that is exactly what she had.

CHAPTER 23

Mach I and Mom

A little before the Christmas vacation of my senior year, Elroy Christy, my ex-Consolidated School classmate, had driven down to Fort Meade Army Base with me to get my required physical exam for the United States Air Force Academy. It was good to have Elroy along to help steady me in my first drive through the Harbor Tunnel under the port of Baltimore. The road was narrow and scary at times for a novice driver, but the drive through the tunnel was short. During the summer, I received a letter from the Academy asking me to apply, and there was no application fee. I had been getting brochures from a fair number of colleges, but I never expected theirs.

Emerson, my stepfather, grew up loving the Military Academy football teams, then he joined the Air Force for four years. I cut my teeth listening to tales of Doc Blanchard and Glenn Davis, otherwise known in college football lore as "Mr. Inside" and "Mr. Outside," for their particular running talents on the field. The two made the cover of Time Magazine in 1945. Emerson adored them as a teen. He thought going into the military was good for any young man's development and that every able-bodied boy should serve the country for at least two years. After graduation from West Point, Doc Blanchard was commissioned into the US Air Force as a fighter pilot.

Emerson would talk of the few Black Generals that he knew of while he was in the service. The one that stood out to me was General Benjamin

O. Davis. He was a magnificently unusual man. His father, James O. Davis, Sr., was made a brigadier general in the Army in 1940 after serving 41 years as a junior officer. His son entered West Point Military Academy in 1932. Benjamin Davis was nominated to the Academy by Representative Oscar De Priest, who was the only Black member of the United States Congress at the time. Emerson told me several times about Davis being silenced for the entirety of his four years at "The Point." His White classmates had planned and executed, not speaking to him, other than on official school business. He never had a roommate, and for four years, he always dined alone.

Every time I heard the story, I had the same reaction; what kind of human could put up with that treatment, and what kind of human would do something so sadistic to another person for that length of time? I already knew the answer to the second question.

Beneath Davis's yearbook picture was a class confession of sorts:

> The courage, tenacity and intelligence with which he conquered a problem, incomparably more difficult than plebe year, won for him the sincere admiration of his classmates.

Sincere admiration? They admired him only after he made the decision not to be bowed or broken by them under any circumstances. His classmates appreciated his ability to excel at West Point, despite every obstacle they gladly threw at him. General Davis went on to join the Army Air Corps and served as a pilot with the Tuskegee Airmen, among many other achievements.

Emerson was as proud of me as I had ever seen him. The idea that his son could get to fly was so much to grasp, considering how he had grown up and the things he knew about the Air Force. I had come a long way from being told by the next-door neighbor in Aberdeen at the age of six, that my desire to be a B&O train engineer was impossible. Now, I was at the point where it was a possibility the United States Government would educate me and teach me to fly for free. I wasn't completely sold on this as my future, given the history of military academies. But it would be a very different experience going through the application process for a country boy like me.

The physical was thorough, but I soft-shoed and sidestepped my way through the questions about my breathing, which was good that day.

The morning finished with an eye exam that gave me no confidence the specialist administering it knew what he was doing. That was confirmed after lunch during the official ophthalmologic exam. Your eyesight in the Air Force is a very big deal, and so are your teeth. The Generals didn't want you running into other planes at 40,000 feet, and Mach 1 or to have your fillings pop out from severe G force turns.

I checked in with Elroy, and we went to the cafeteria to get something to eat. I told him I had just one more big exam in the afternoon then we could go home. It was a school day and I greatly appreciated Elroy coming with me. The ophthalmologist was a Major in his late 30s. He was snappy and to the point, almost to a fault. "Are you Ford?" he demanded, to which I affirmed. He looked at me, back to the papers on his desk, and up at me again. "Did you walk over here by yourself?" I thought he was joking. However, the numbers he was reading from my earlier exam were horrible, and the Major did not believe them.

He redid the eye chart exam and looked into my eyes with various instruments for about 10 minutes. At the end of his evaluation, he told me that the first exam results were wrong and that I was not legally blind. But I had astigmatism, needed glasses....and, no.... I was not going to be able to fly a US Air Force plane. I had a decision to make. Did I want to go to the Academy, get a good education, and put up with all the other nonsense surely coming along with it if I could not fly? Still, I was amazed that I was even getting to ask myself the question at all.

I was given another appointment for late February to come in for the second part of the physical evaluation at Andrews Air Force Base outside of Washington, D.C. I was going to have to stay there for three days all by myself. This was going to be new for me, and I was a bit anxious but excited by the upcoming adventure out of Havre de Grace. I never mentioned this in school. As far as I knew, Miss Lampson, in her southern wisdom, still thought I would be more comfortable at a "fine colored school." Since they had to send the transcripts, the school had some idea what I was up to, trying to surreptitiously get an education on my own. I did not trust anyone at the High School who had an office, especially Lampson and Banick, who had never spoken a single word to me in almost five years. I had only been on the receiving end of some of his chilly stares in the halls. Since there had never been a reason to discipline me, Banick never had a reason to talk to me. It seemed discipline was his only job, as far as many of the Black students were concerned.

My parents drove me to Andrews Air Force Base on a Friday afternoon for registration and other paperwork. Mom gave me a hug, and Emerson patted my back, wishing me good luck before they drove back to Havre de Grace. During registration, I noticed four other young Black candidates, and it happened that we were all billeted near each other. We had single, small rooms, without bathrooms, in the officer's barracks.

It wasn't long before a couple of the guys were figuring out what to do with our free evening before the exam tomorrow. We all decided to meet at the shuttle stop by the barracks and take a lap around the base by bus. I was pleasantly surprised at how quickly and easily we got along. They were from the East and Midwest. We talked about where we went to school, our towns, other colleges we had applied to, sports we played, what the physical exam was going to be like tomorrow, and all things not related to grades or girls.

They were all low-key and confident boys who had traveled around some, and they all seemed a bit older and worldlier than me. Never had I been around Black boys my age who reminded me of myself or who I found so engaging in conversation. But we had a lot in common and recognized we were in a few of the same wars. It was comforting to know them and affirming in some ways. You don't have to display cool, to be a smart, confident Black boy. They were probably good church boys, too, unlike me.

We went to the Rathskeller, as suggested by the bus driver, to get some food, drink some soda and talk some more. It was apparent that two of the boys in the group were military and had thought about going to the Academy for years. None of them had accents, but that revealed some of their upbringing and experiences. At first, I wanted to make sure I was making sense when I talked and I was very aware of every word. Then, I got comfortable with my new friends, and we all melded into the flowing, meandering conversations. After we ate, we took the bus back to our billets, to get ready for the morning.

The next morning, all the candidates met in the main gymnasium to break out into smaller groups to get started. We warmed up individually before commencing the morning program of pushups, sit-ups, leg lifts, and standing broad jumps. I still had the decent muscle tone leftovers of my fall football body to get me through the challenging day. The gym was filled with hope, noise, sweat, testosterone, and competition. We were sizing each other up and trying to keep a strong outward profile. The candidates were heterogeneous in their size, musculature, attitude, and past exposure to the military. All the boys were White, except for me and my friends. Most of the White boys were strutting jock types, but a few were surprisingly less projecting of masculinity than the others. In general, they were mostly cookie-cutter, All-American-looking boys, and they knew it.

It was obvious a lot of the boys had gone to military schools. The giveaway was their crew cuts, square shoulders, military speak, and the large devices on their wrists that they referred to as chronometers. Some of them were very gung-ho in their approach to the physical tasks we were performing and probably to life in general. They were running the obstacle course, stopping, starting, cutting, jumping, and tumbling like their lives depended on it. One of the boys topped them all; he showed everybody up with a one arm chin press on the horizontal bar, with a cast on the arm he was using to press. The boy looked hill tough and sounded very country.

After the first day, I had a moderately strained low back muscle and some things to think about. I had never been in a group like the Academy candidates. I guessed this was where war heroes and Medal of Honor recipients got their start. Maybe they just loved America or wanted to fly so much that they would run through walls if directed. I liked the Black candidates I had met very much. The White candidates were like guys you would see in a beach movie. They had a visible sameness on the surface anyway.

In the military, it was important to be part of the group and move within its uniform motion. That would pose a major problem for me since I never voluntarily wanted to be part of any group that wasn't playing sports or marching in the streets. There was little Ra-Ra or Gung Ho in me. The country needed people who would run through walls on command, but I probably wasn't one of them. I thought about General Davis' experience being silenced at West Point and how that would compare to my living and communicating daily with people so different in upbringing and outlook than me for four years. I would likely get to the point where I would appreciate some silence from my classmates.

On the second day of the exam, I was only slightly physically affected by the back muscle strain, but my head was another matter. The day was only 4 hours of tests of strength, agility, and reflexes, with another obstacle course thrown in. The morning went by fast, and I didn't have much time to observe the other candidates or contemplate their motivations for doing something like this. At the very least for me it was a valuable and enlightening experience meeting people in a novel environment. It was another rare opportunity to get out of the cocoon of Havre de Grace and get a peek at the world. After the last task, we signed out, said goodbye, and good luck to all the future pilots.

My parents picked me up, and I went back home a little wiser and less conflicted about going to the Academy. It only took a short, hushed conversation in the hall, by the kitchen with Mom, to know where she squarely stood on the matter. She told me, "It was nice that Emerson was so happy that you might go to Colorado, to school at the Academy. But you have to do what is best for you. And besides that, you are my child, and I know you don't like taking orders from people anyway. Do you?" She had a point, but I was leaning heavily in her direction anyway.

About a week later, I was in my homeroom listening to the morning program and thinking about college, like many in the senior class. That's when the morning was shaken with an unexpected acknowledgement over the PA system. After she had finished the official school announcements, Mrs. Gorsuch went on for one more:

> The school office has received this notice from the office of United States Senator Joseph D. Tydings.
>
> We would like to congratulate Larry Ford, of the senior class, of Havre de Grace High School, for being named a finalist for nomination to the United States Air Force Academy.
>
> Good luck to Larry.

I was not the only one in the room who was surprised to hear the announcement. There were gaped mouth stares at me from a few people. My homeroom teacher, Mr. Bill Taylor, from the Consolidated, looked a bit puzzled but didn't say anything. I had not mentioned this to any students in school except for Elroy, who had gone down to Fort Meade with me for the physical exam. I did not want anything from the school when it came to getting into college. The last thing I needed was a halfhearted congratulations from the office to start my day. But that's what I got.

I thanked some of the people who gave me congratulations. For the one who expressed concern, I let her know that I hadn't lost my mind and I would talk to her about it later. Anyway, the point was moot since my last talk with Mom. All in all, the minor commotion wasn't too bad, but I hadn't seen Mr. Rudolph yet. It surely would bother him that his US government was thinking about giving an undeserving, lowly, un-American type of person like me a supersonic airplane with missiles. I was looking forward to what he was going to say today and seeing how much it bothered him that I was on the verge of doing something he never could do. Besides, he couldn't get into a flight suit if his life depended on it, and they likely didn't make helmets in his size.

The rest of the morning was uneventful, and lunch was just about over without a challenge so far. I was at the cafeteria door, holding it open and looking for Bootsy. Instead of "my Boy" showing up, a six- foot tall, overweight ex-jock with a midriff and the look of moderate dyspepsia was headed in my direction. He slowed as he approached and then stopped next to the door that I was holding open. Then without turning his body, he swiveled his cranial block and aimed his unpleasant face down at me. It was apparent that what he'd heard over the PA system about my good fortune had gotten to him, again, in a particularly acidic way. It looked like he had eaten a very bad oyster and needed a Bromo- Seltzer.

Rudolph didn't even feign a smile; he was all about evil in a whisper, with a little jealousy mixed in. In a voice that only I could hear, he decompressed before he quietly exploded. "You will never make it, Ford. Never." He looked down at me as if I were dross in the hallway. Then he finished with, "Look at you. You don't even know what a military line is." He heaped a little more scorn upon me, before he slithered away like a corpulent serpent on two feet. He was right, I had no idea what a military line was, and I didn't care about it or anything else coming from him.

I was thinking—boy, I got to Rudolph today. His unprovoked reactions were extreme but quiet this time. It bordered on a weird, masculine jealousy mixed in with his everyday superior White man's attitude, all in a Saturday morning cartoon Baby Huey body. He felt I could never be at his level, which I already knew was true. I felt compelled to bother him from time to time, because I could do that better than any other Black boy in school.

But there was something else bothering him and some other people in the school. Whatever I was doing or projecting was offensive to some of them, to the point where they had to say, or do, things to help their mental states. I thought all teachers were supposed to be helpful, guiding mentors who shepherded us through the tough parts of school life. But that was at the Consolidated, not here.

Some of the high school teachers could occasionally say inappropriate things to Black students, sometimes in quiet and other times shamelessly out loud. That kind of stuff had happened to me and even more often to other Black students at the school. I was tired of having to deal with it and tired of dealing with a few teachers too. They were going to have to use more than Rudolph's kind of intimidation to bother me. That they were willing to do other things I was sure of and was just waiting to see what came next. I did not know what their limits were or if they had any. These people were potentially dangerous so close to graduation. Annoying them too much was not a good idea, but I probably had done that already with my counter-punching, and general bad attitude toward them. I didn't have to give them another poke to get their notice. Being a sitting target, like in the old days at the school, was not an option for me now. I was not the kind of anodyne little "Colored Boy" that made them comfortable, and I was never going to be. They seemed to fear me in some very White ways, to which I said, "GOOD!"

STUDENT NOMINATED TO THE UNITED STATES AIR FORCE ACEDEMY

Larry Ford, a member of the senior class at H.H.S. was recently notified by the office of Senator Joseph Tydings, of his nomination to the United States Air Force Academy, in Colorado.

Larry plans to major in chemical engineering. He has always been interested in chemistry. He said he's been playing with chemistry sets and reading books on the subject since he was 10 years old.

Larry is vice-president of his class, and was selected as the "Best All 'Round" by his classmates. He is a member of the National Honor Society and spends most of his time in -- where else ? -- the chemistry

The local newspaper, the Havre de Record, wrote a story about the Nomination to the United States Air force Academy, by Senator Joseph Tydings.

DEPARTMENT OF THE AIR FORCE
HEADQUARTERS, 1001ST COMPOSITE WING (HQ COMD USAF)
ANDREWS AIR FORCE BASE, WASHINGTON, D.C. 20331

REPLY TO
ATTN OF: CBPO-CC   6 Feb 69

SUBJECT: Qualifying Examination for the United States Air Force Academy

TO: MR. LARRY J. FORD
      816 Erie Street
      Havre De Grace, Maryland 21078

Dear Mr. Ford:

As Commander of Andrews Air Force Base, I extend my personal congratulations on your selection to compete for appointment to the United States Air Force Academy.

You are to report to Building 3615, Room 20, Andrews Air Force Base, Maryland, to complete your physical aptitude examination, and Class I Medical Examination not later than 8:00 AM Monday, 17 February 1969. Provided you have not previously taken your Class I Medical Examination, be prepared to spend two days here. Civilian applicants will be billeted in the Visiting Officer Quarters (VOQ). Military applicants will be billeted in the Visiting Airman Quarters (VAQ). A reservation has been made for you for Monday night only. In the event you arrive at Andrews on Sunday and require overnight accommodations, please notify the Testing Center (981-5135 or 981-2448) upon receipt of this letter.

You must bring athletic shorts, high top basketball shoes (for protection of your ankles) white sweat socks, athletic supporter, and a T-Shirt to wear during the physical aptitude examination. A suit (or sport coat and slacks), shirt, and tie are required for wear at some of the activities you may desire to attend during the evenings. You will need at least $10.00 to cover expenses during your stay. If you wear contact lenses, you must remove them on the Friday prior to your arrival (3 days before your physical examination).

Upon arrival at Andrews Air Force Base, present this letter to the Air Policeman at the gate, and he will give you further instructions. In the meantime, if you desire additional information, write to the Air Force Academy and Aircrew Examining Center, Andrews Air Force Base, or call 981-5135 or 981-2448, Monday through Friday.

02/06/69 - The qualifying examination was held at Andrews Air Force Base. The candidates were instructed to bring high-top basketball shoes, white socks, athletic supporter, and at least ten dollars for the weekend.

LJF/FORD/GRIFFIN COLLECTION!!!

Dr. Larry James Ford

DEPARTMENT OF THE AIR FORCE
THE REGISTRAR
USAF ACADEMY, COLORADO 80840

REPLY TO
ATTN. OF: CRA

28 JAN 69

SUBJECT: Notice of Candidacy

TO:

FORD, LARRY JAMES
816 ERIE STREET
HAVRE DE GRACE MD 21078

BERNARD A ENIS JR
MAJOR <RES>
416 MAPLE ROCK DR
ELLICOTT CITY MD 21043

PHONE 301-465-2798

Your name has been recorded as an official candidate for admission to the United States Air Force Academy's next class under the category indicated below. You have been assigned the candidate number indicated and must include it in all future correspondence.

The attached "Instructions to Candidates" booklet should be read thoroughly and followed explicitly. To insure full consideration of your candidacy absolute compliance with these instructions is mandatory.

This letter will serve as authorization to take those tests shown under remarks at the Air Force Academy and Aircrew Examining Center indicated below and must be presented for identification upon arrival. If you have completed an Air Force Academy Qualifying Medical Examination since 1 July refer to that section of the instruction booklet concerning examinations administered at an Air Force Base.

Please accept my best wishes for your success as an Academy candidate.

REMARKS:

SCHEDULED FOR PHYSICAL APTITUDE AND MEDICAL EXAMINATIONS.

A. CANDIDATE NUMBER	B. NOMINATING CATEGORY		COMPETITIVE
512290	SEN J D TYDINGS MD		
C. LOCATION OF EXAMINING CENTER		D. EXAMINING DATE	
ANDREWS AFB, WASHINGTON, D.C.		17 FEB 69	

13 Atch
1. Instructions to Candidates
2. Acknowledgement Card
3. Candidate Identification Labels
4. Change of Address Cards
5. Withdrawal Card
6. Report of Medical History
7. Physical Aptitude Examination Card
8. Liaison Officer Reply Card
9. Candidate Personal Data Record
10. Candidate Activities Record
11. Secondary School Record Form
12. Instructors' Statement Cards
13. CEEB Bulletin of Information

DIRECTOR OF ADMISSIONS

01/28/69 – Official notification that I was a candidate to the United States Air Force

AcademyLJF/FORD/GRIFFIN COLLECTION!!!

215

CHAPTER 24

Hello Out There

Senior year had been okay so far. Most people were still holding their breath and checking the mail daily for college news. I hoped to hear from the University of Delaware in the next couple of weeks when Norman Franklin Joyner, Jr., Bootsy, gave me some unwanted and curious information after his scheduled visit with Mrs. Lampson about college. Bootsy never talked much to me about school or academic things. He was smart but not moved too often to show it off. He always assumed he would go to Morgan State or Princess Anne, Maryland State. Bootsy was a lady's man, basketballer, and generally into enjoying himself as much as possible; he fancied himself a rather "rakish lad" after hearing that term in English class one day. So, when he came back to the Problems of Democracy class after seeing Miss Grace, he gave me a lot to chew on for the rest of the day.

Bootsy returned to the auditorium midway through the class, took his seat on my row, and gave me a serious looking nod before scribbling a quick note on paper and passing it my way. The folded paper arrived after three touches and I figured it must be important because nobody ever passed me notes. I unfolded it, read it and read it again:

Hey Ford, just back from Lampson's office. Something seriously funky is going down. She offered me a 4-year scholarship to the University of Delaware and told me

Don't tell you about it. So, I am telling You!

I nodded to Bootsy and flashed him a wide-eyed look of interest and a little nod of gratitude for my friend. I read the note once more before tucking it into my tablet for later consideration. I talked to Bootsy at lunch about the details of the meeting. He said Lampson knew he wanted to go to Morgan State, but she asked if Bootsy had ever considered Delaware for college. He was surprised by the offer, and he knew Delaware was my first choice. It bothered him what Lampson had asked him to do and enter into a conspiracy with her against me. Bootsy said, "She couldn't have been seriously thinking I wasn't going to tell you.....I guess I was supposed to be a "good little boy," doing Miss Grace a favor, or something."

For much of the afternoon, I didn't spend time looking to find a cogent reason why Lampson would do that because there wasn't one. Even Bootsy thought it was crazy. Lampson didn't have the problem with Bootsy's pedestrian "C+" GPA that she had with my "colored" 4.0 from 11th grade; colored pedestrian trumped just plain colored, in my case. I knew she was up to some righteous funk like Boots said, but I didn't know what it was yet. I was impressed by her deviousness and deceit and very interested in why Bootsy might not need resegregation, like me. I had witnessed or heard about some White adults doing many questionable things in this school. The evolving saga with Lampson was blowing the doors off of any other mystifying thing that ever happened to me at the High School. It was not a good feeling.

I knew something big was brewing because too many pieces were in motion for nothing to happen. I didn't trust one thought from Lampson's body or the sneaky, half-Confederate sneer she tried to hide while talking to me. It was a treacherous game to her, and I needed to be very watchful for the rest of the year, front, sides, and back. The school wars had taken a very hard turn, and whatever was driving her was deep and ugly. I had a cold fear that Lampson may feel her actions were something closer to a Christian calling and her otherwise questionable acts were justified for a greater good. It made me wonder if this was something peculiar to Havre de Grace High School or was it a more widespread practice in Harford County? Did they go after the Black girls too? All I really knew for sure was that the office people had a major problem with who I was, and not my grades. The gatekeepers were willing to let a selected Black boy pass through, just not me.

I needed a break from my forever school wars, and I was open to something different to do. I was in Miss McGreevy's room one morning before school when she asked if I would be interested in doing another play. There was a Harford County drama competition at the junior college in early May, with all the high schools in the county participating. She hadn't decided what play to do yet, but she was close. I told her I would do it, without knowing exactly what it was. With Miss McGreevy, I knew it would have some point or twist to it. She said it would be a serious play be a serious play, unlike our junior class farce last year. I still didn't like being in front of the public, but I was learning to handle the spotlight occasionally for short periods without embarrassing myself. And it was something I needed to be able to do comfortably.

A couple of days later, Miss McGreevy told me she had decided we would perform a one-act play with only five people. It was titled "Hello Out There" by William Saroyan, an Armenian-American writer from the San Joaquin Valley in California. Upon hearing of the choice, Mr. David Johnson, another English teacher and sometimes co- conspirator to Miss McGreevy, stated he wasn't aware that Saroyan ever wrote anything worth producing. She had decided to cast Arlene, from 10th grade English class, and me in the lead roles. I would have to be on stage the whole time, which was going to be interesting in a county like Harford, doing the play this way.

The play was about a young man, my character, in jail in a small town for rape. His guilt, or innocence, was not definitely known in the play. The sheriff, who jailed him, was trying to keep an angry mob from lynching him. Arlene played a slow but sweet young town girl who brought food to the jail daily, and she had a set of keys to my cell. I was using everything I could think of to con the key from Arlene before another classmate, Eddie Mays, came in and killed me. So, the little kiss scene was key to the flow of the story.

I had gotten to know Arlene a little for the first time in my four years at the highschool. We decorated the gym for homecoming. She was popular, and I knew it would be fun doing the play with her. Arlene was sharp and had qualities I had never seen in anyone my age at the Consolidated, or anywhere else. She was well-read, had traveled some, was a quick thinker, and definitely an intellectual, but not showy about it. You had to stay awake around her, and I enjoyed getting her take on things that I may not have considered. So, when I read the play through the first time and got to the kiss scene, the first thing I did was read it again. Then I thought, Miss McGreevy was crazy, to which she may have agreed to a point. And I wondered what Arlene thought about it too. We had the first reading the next day with the Sheriff, Arlene, and me, but we didn't make it to the kiss scene. I was on stage for a long time by myself, and it would be a relief to finally have some company out there.

Before the end of the first week of practice, our drama coach gave us some disappointing but not surprising news. Mr. Banick, the principal, had told Miss McGreevy that we couldn't do the little kiss scene, which we hadn't even had a chance to practice. I didn't know about Arlene, but I was very disappointed we would not going to see how rural Harford County reacted to two very different people in a tender moment. After being disappointed, the next question was, why? Why did Banick do it? The answer was too easy because that is who Robert Banick was; a chip right off of Dr. Willis' old bigoted block, and they both would turn back time if they could. Other than that, the reason was certainly the usual one. I wasn't happy about Banick being involved. I was sure he would pay close attention to both the student kisser and kissee and make a strong mental note of it.

In the middle of practice for the play, Miss McGreevy treated me and a few other classmates to an exceptional event. On a school night, she took us to see Duke Ellington in concert at Westminster High School. It was always nice to get out of Havre de Grace for a while, even if that meant going to more rural Carroll County to see "The Duke." It was always interesting going to another school just to see how different the students looked and how many Black students they had. Westminster was in the sticks, so I didn't expect to see many Black students. Duke's coming to the town must have been the biggest happening in a very long time.

Miss McGreevy drove the group of students, in her little Rambler, the 55 miles to the concert in Westminster. The school had a nice auditorium that was nearly full by the time we got there. We walked up to the mezzanine level of the hall and found our seats as the music was starting. My stepfather, Emerson, loved jazz and played it all the time, especially on Sundays, after Mom's gospel music had finished. I grew up with Duke, Byrd, Stitt, McGriff, and Ahmed Jamal, right alongside Mahalia Jackson, Edwin Hawkins, James Cleveland, and Clara Ward. It was all great music to me.

Getting to see a Black legend that everyone knew was, indeed, a legend without argument was extra special and very rare; like, a few years ago, getting to see Dr. Benjamin Mays, the president of Morehouse College, speaking at a White church in Aberdeen. There were White people sitting in their otherwise segregated church, listening to a Black man speak on a Sunday. It was hard to know what to make of that or how happy I should be about it. Dr. Mays and the "Duke" were both magnificent Black men, and most White people could agree on that fact without finding something to fear

The band warmed up the large, overwhelmingly White crowd that had come to hear American music in one of its purest forms, jazz. After playing a jump tune to get the audience riled, The Duke graced the stage, and with baton in hand, he counted down and the band came in solid on the one, going into a great song from the 40s, "Let's Fall in Love." The audience was enjoying the show as Duke went through his opus. He followed the opening offering with "Creole Love Song," "Don't Get Around Much Anymore," and "I'm Gonna Sit Right Down and Write Myself a Letter." The band was adding in some great tunes from Cole Porter, Gershwin, and Kerns, and the place was rocking, with dancing on the main floor and up in the aisles of the mezzanine.

Miss McGreevy was grooving, like your very cool older sister, and I enjoyed watching her sway and sing to the music. The concert was winding down when I had a thought; it would be cool to meet Duke Ellington, and I would never have a better chance than this. I came up with a workable plan, but needed some company, to make me appear less suspicious carrying it out.

Sitting next to me was the perfect classmate, Dahlia, who was not afraid of anything. We were in the junior class play together last year. We had hung out a little at her house a couple of times, talking at length about everything we could think of. Her dad was a physician, and her mom was an architect. Dahlia thought my asthma may be psychosomatic like it said in her father's medical magazines. When her dad was about our age, he and his family were in Germany, doing everything possible to get out at the start of World War ll. I always learned a lot from her, and I sometimes thought about some things differently after we talked.

I whispered my plan into her ear as the music played on with melodic urgency, riding blues - infused syncopated riffs up to the ceiling and back. Dahlia's eyes opened wider, and she nodded in agreement with the scheme. We got up and wriggled our way through the shaking dancers in the aisle and on the stairs of the mezzanine. We made it to a landing and then down another set of stairs to a level below the stage. This being a pretty standard looking high school auditorium, we figured Duke's dressing room was probably a normal classroom near the stage area. We found ourselves in a long hall in the basement as the music was wrapping up in the auditorium.

The last classic strains of "Take the A Train" could be heard as applause, whistles, and clapping started signaling that the concert was ending. We walked down the hall toward a door area and more light when we noticed two men walking through the opening and towards us. It was immediately clear our plan had worked, as Mr. Edward Kennedy "Duke" Ellington and his valet were walking toward Dahlia and me, by ourselves in the hall. I was stunned being in his presence, but Dahlia was handling it better. I barely got out an excited hello, but that was it. I was speechless.

Mr. Ellington was extremely gracious, elegant, and handsome. He looked a little older than I had pictured him, but he stood straight and regal like the jazz royalty he truly was. Dahlia was smiling, wide-eyed, and very comfortable talking to him as I remained tongue-tied and star-struck. In a short time, the three of them, Duke, the valet, and Dahlia, went into the classroom, turned dressing room, closed the door, and left me alone in the hall with my thoughts. I was disappointed a little with myself, but not surprised. I was still just a little South Georgia boy at heart and by temperament, and I still acted like it much of the time. The next time something like this happens, I told myself, I'm going to remember how Dahlia handled it while I was standing in the hall, waiting for an invitation. Okay—Next time.

Dahlia emerged from the room with Duke's autograph and a story for the ages. I had a story too, often embellished some, depending on the audience. But it was fine because I had learned something that I wouldn't soon forget. We found Miss McGreevy and the crew and headed back to Havre de Grace with some pretty good memories of our visit to Westminster.

After the concert, it was back to the reality of my senior year and the war against the Confederates and Rebels in the office. I was tired of the weighty situation on me when I was supposed to be having fun in my last days, like my classmates. The stress was starting to distract me, tax my concentration, and sap my energy.

The play would be in another week, and I didn't feel that great. But I knew my lines, and Arlene and I had already decided what to do about the non-kiss. We were looking forward to springing it on Harford County and getting back at our principal. Arlene was almost as bad as I was in some ways but from an interesting Jewish perspective. We seemed to have arrived at the same conclusions about a lot of things, coming from very different paths. However, any plan or scheme the two of us could come up with would likely be seditious on its face; at least, that's what we were hoping.

Practice was demanding because I knew everything depended on my character being on top of things the entire time. It would be disastrous if I were off with my timing, line delivery, or movements, even a little, in such a short play. Miss McGreevy knew something was bothering me as we were getting closer to the time of the festival. I told her that I would be fine. I was going to use my personal melancholy and transfer it to my stage character, to get something useful from the feeling.

Personally, the best benefit from the play was Miss McGreevy pointing out a characteristic of my speech and articulation. She relieved me of my last shibboleth of Southern speech that possibly said too much about me. She pointed out that I pronounced my th's as f's. So, earth became "earff", which would not sound good on stage. I was happy she pointed it out to me. If she had noticed it, others had too.

On the day of the play, we met at the junior college on Saturday morning. Our small crew was ready to go and excited about being in a new place with new people from all the schools in the county. This was kind of a big deal, as Harford County goes. We watch several presentations by the other county high schools, especially Bel Air. They were quite brave and ambitious in tackling Edna St. Vincent Malay's "Aria da Capo." It was hard to know what the play was about, with its harlequin characters speaking of, or engaging in, horrendous activities, like murder and suicide. It was quite something for a high school troop to attempt and probably over the heads of most of the county.

By the time our turn had come, the impending fright and terror of being on stage alone had replaced anything else that had been a bother earlier in the day. Arlene was excited but cool and in control. We talked about the non-kiss scene movements and how much fun it was going to be to pull this off.

The house lights dimmed, and I walked onto the darkened stage into my jail cell, outlined only by a projected simulacrum of bars. I knelt and started to slowly bang a spoon on the floor until finally throwing it down and yelling, "Hello out there," three times to no one in particular. As the lights came up, I was trying not to look at the audience as I spoke. But my busy brain was checking things out anyway.

It was very quiet, and I knew why; their attention was being focused on the stage and seeing a sole Negro, out of place from their everyday world. That had to be unsettling for some, which was a major factor in Miss McGreevy doing the play like this. She wanted to make some people uncomfortable and consider the inconsiderable for a few minutes. Still, it was a risk performing the play this way in Harford County, in 1969. Otherwise, nothing about the original play was changed; the only change was me, which changed everything.

After a bit, and with the appearance of the sheriff on stage, I started to feel comfortable enough to glance at some of the audience. I finally struck up a visual conversation with two nuns in habits on the left apron of the stage. They were watching my every movement intently, and I would check back with them ever so often, to make sure they were still with me. The contentious conversation with the sheriff ended with him yelling at me, saying he was trying to stop the lynch mob, but he was badly outnumbered. Right after that, the town girl, Arlene, in the character of a slightly slow, misaligned, sad young food delivery girl, came onto the stage. Her fair complexion and red hair stood in screaming contrast to my character in the cell, and it was not missed by the audience. I checked back with the nuns, and they had not skipped a beat.

Arlene and I traded a few halting lines before I saw my chance to con away the jail cell keys and save myself. It was very quiet, and we could feel the eyes of a couple of hundred people wondering what was getting ready to occur, as my voice found a comfortably tender spot to register with Arlene. There were a couple of times she and I had to swallow a little laugh or share a half wink at what we were doing and who we were doing it to. We just couldn't take it too far, as rewarding as that would be. It would be scary enough for some of them to contemplate the idea that two very different people would like, or need, each other, even for a short time.

The town girl came closer to the cell bars to bring the food as I started to tell her how pretty she was and how nice her hair looked. But I was still looking for the keys on her. Then I looked at her, and something changed in my attitude. I still wanted the keys, but there was an attraction to the girl that I had suddenly noticed. It was also noticed by the nuns and the audience. It was time.

At that point, Arlene and I were close, only separated by the shadows of the make-believe prison bars. We shared a final little private, "Are you ready look," delivered our last lines, and moved in. It was as quiet as I had ever heard in a packed room. We moved closer and closer until the light between our faces was almost extinguished. We nearly eliminated the small distance remaining, and then held motionless, suspended for two counts, before slowly pulling away, thinking about what had almost just happened. From the reaction of the audience, we had done exactly what we had planned, with the desired effect. You could feel the tension in the air of the room abate as we finished the scene, with Arlene leaving and me still keyless.

The final scene came, and I was shot dead in my cell, by Eddie Mays' over-the-top redneck, with a pistol character. And, the play was done. There was a post - festival evaluation by some guests and teachers. Their only complaint about our play was that the projected prison bars made it a little difficult for the audience to see what I was doing in the cell. Otherwise, we got outstanding reviews, and we were pleased that our work was appreciated by most people. We heard a little expected grumbling from one of the high schools about what we did and how we did it. But, Arlene and I had a good laugh about what we had pulled off in plain sight of the county, despite Banick.

CHAPTER 25

A Fine Colored School

By early April, I knew something was amiss and seriously funky with Miss Lampson, the Ole Miss, just like Bootsy had said. Learning that Lampson had told Bootsy not to tell me about the University of Delaware scholarship was followed by a rejection letter in the mail from the college itself, which bothered me greatly. No matter how I looked at it, it just didn't add up, and it smelled bad to boot. Why would Delaware take a random C+ average Black student, who hadn't shown any interest in their college, over me? I didn't think Delaware would, but I was sure the Ole Miss would have no problem doing it. Bootsy refused her offer because he wanted to go to a Black college, Morgan State. Lampson accepted Bootsy's desire to go to a Black college without trying to talk him out of it. She was just trying to get rid of the telltale papers from Delaware as soon as possible before I found out about them.

After Bootsy refused the offer, Mrs. Lampson continued down her short list of acceptable Black students still in her favor, and who she had decided did not need voluntary, self-re-segregation, like me. She found such a comfortable choice of student, and, obviously, she didn't care what I knew, or noticed, at that point. Lampson would have found somebody in special ed, the shop building, the restroom, or she would have put black face on a White student to make him pass and give the scholarship to him. I was beginning to think that I had pushed them too far by trying to ignore them and their slights. But they were nothing if not easily offended. I had truly gotten to them, and they were out for some retribution for my insolence, insubordination, and offensive Blackness.

When I got the second rejection letter from Bucknell College a week later, it was clear to me what was happening, and that I was going to need some help in fighting it. It seemed fairly obvious what Lampson and Banick had done. I was thinking—they wrote some nonsense in the letters of recommendation, that made me seem like someone I was not, but they deeply wished I was. There wasn't any rational complaint they could have come up with against me, but the possible irrational ones were limited only by their white consciences and Christian morality, which meant I was in deep trouble. Whatever they said was enough to have two good schools pass on me, and the scent of a few bad White adults at work was overwhelming in the deal. It strained the imagination to think it was all merely a series of monumental coincidences.

What had I done to them to warrant this; the answer to that was nothing, except being me. The problem was something deep in them and always had been. In almost five years at the High School, I had exchanged not even a monosyllable with Mr. Banick. Our communications consisted of him displaying to me his disapproving gelid stare down his nose, in the hall by his office. He would lock on to me for several seconds, tracking me down the corridor. I didn't spend much time wondering what was behind an unfriendly look like his, and perhaps I should have. I was good at ignoring the common slights in a school day that could come my way from either race.

My way of trying to keep control of the affairs in school was to make myself as academically big and untouchable as possible, from the standpoint of the teachers and the administration. But my grades and good school citizenship, in the end, didn't stop them from concocting some imaginary deficit that had nothing to do with academics. They must have made up fantastical things about grades 9 through 11. What they would deem to be my troublesome time, in the 12th grade, was not done to them, by me, until after the college transcripts were already out. Their initial irritation with me started long before my unplanned, accidental 12th grade coming-out party. These folks were serious, and not playing around. They had been at this game for a while, and the time to graduation was getting short.

It was eerie trying to put myself in the heads and minds of Banick and Lampson, attempting to understand how they could justify their decision to do what they had apparently done. I knew why they did it; I am offensively and suspiciously Black, which superseded everything else. That was reason enough. Lampson had said as much in our guidance meetings. It never mattered to her how many quarterly 4.0 GPAs a year I could produce because I belonged in a "fine colored school," for my own good and happiness, according to "The Ole Miss." My race nullified all I had done in four years at the school. It must have bothered both of them to see and sign all those superior achievement letters from the 11th grade, which should have counted significantly in their college evaluation letters, but evidently did not. I forced them to acknowledge my excellence. They had never found much to celebrate about me, but they never had anything negative to hang me with either. So, they invented it.

They must have been very creative in their letters to the colleges to explain away those colored 4.0s, or they could have simply lied about the "colored boy." Either way, it probably wouldn't cause them much loss of sleep. I tried to consider, under what circumstances could they have believed what they had done was moral, correct, or defensible? I had to turn things around on them…quickly. It is one thing to be aware of the history of the asymmetric power dynamic between Black people and White people in this country. But it is a different thing, entirely, when their white power, arrogance, penchant for inquity, and self-righteous misconceptions were pointed directly, and personally, at you; a 17 year old boy in their charge. If it was a few decades earlier, there was no telling what they would have felt at liberty to do, to assuage their considerable anxieties caused by my being around.

As long as I didn't know about what they did, it didn't matter to them. At times, it felt like they were either afraid of me or afraid of what I might become someday if they didn't do something about it now. It was their last chance to scuff up someone like me and make the world safer, for people like them. It made me wonder if this was occurring in other schools in the county. I didn't think it stopped at my school, and I was pretty sure some other Black students in the county had received similar treatment in their schools. It was still Harford County.

My popularity, with most of my classmates, must have been a source of constant wonderment and annoyance to them. I was pretty surprised, amazed, and thankful for the overwhelming support of my classmates, much to the dismay of the nonplussed office people. After all, my classmates had elected me vice president of the class of 1969, and President of the United States of America (in our class mock election) all in the first two months of school. Also, my classmates elected me and Penny, my former chemistry student from the summer, as "Best All Around" in the class of 1969. I didn't force them to do it. After being around me for four years, most of them knew who I was, and wasn't. Yes, my classmates seemed to like me just fine for the person they saw, and I liked them too. That did not go unnoticed by the powers in the school. Some in the administration had not a qualm, nor a second of hesitation, in using their substantial powers stealthily, to negatively affect the rest of my life, and get away with it.

Banick had probably thought numerous times, "Why can't Ford just be in the shop building with the other "normal colored boys," stay out of the chemistry lab and leave the rest of us alone?" Trying to imagine the darkness and decay residing in the heads of adults who could justify attacking a 17-year old boy in their charge, shook me in an unfamiliar and threatening way.

They weren't anything new. Banick and Lampson were merely the latest European travelers on the country's long racist strand that they hardly ever acknowledged. It had existed since the first White colonists saw their first free Indian, and were immediately afraid of independent heathens residing so close to their purity. They eventually decided their dominion over the Indian natives was part of their White God's given manifest destiny, for White Christians. The line connecting the recent and past travelers on the national race track was undeniable to most Black people, and probably Indians too. But, as a concept worthy of consideration, it was unknown to most White people, and therefore not real to them, or anyone else.

Mr. Banick, the principal, was the ringmaster in the show, and he had veto rights over what would happen. Since I had never had any communication with him, other than his glares in the hall, he was a very large unknown to me. I was going to have to use all my knowledge, and Colored School powers, to fight the kind of deep, comfortable evil at play here, determined to affect the rest of my life. I mulled over what to do for a day but couldn't come up with a foolproof plan yet. Since you only get one shot at the king, don't miss. Mom knew that something was bothering me, but I did not dare speak to her about it for fear of igniting World War III, with things completely out of control.

I was starting to feel like my character in the play we did a month ago, "Hello Out There." The nameless man in jail was lynched in the end, by the town's people. At least in the play, the mob owned up to their deed and did me in face to face. But my mob here, at the High School, was conducting my teenage academic lynching in the quiet, in the dark, beneath the roses. I'm sure the play didn't endear me to Banick, but it could not have affected what they wrote in the letters of recommendation, which were sent to the colleges six months earlier.

Their dislike for me had been simmering since the 8th grade and the early incident with the music teacher. My 9th grade yearlong encounter with Bissett, the science teacher, and purveyor of colored "C"s, as well as my forever tussles with the guidance counselor, further irritated them. But that was all during the time in school when I was almost invisible, except in the classroom. They didn't like the invisible me, and they despised my more fleshed-out version.

My personal Shakespearean senior year melodrama, with real villains, was moving with distressing pace into act 3, and I needed an appropriately dangerous, but smart and mean junkyard dog for some help, friendship, and protection until graduation.

Thinking about Shakespeare pointed me in the right direction to get some help with my college problem. I needed a person on my side whom I trusted, and who could get right in Banick's face and tell him she knew exactly what he was all about. There was only one candidate for the job, Mrs. Gladys Allison, my 11th grade English teacher. Any teacher that made sure all the students understood the more risqué parts of Shakespeare, and what Othello was all about, would probably be interested in my pressing dilemma.

Mrs. Allison was the daughter of a coal miner, from eastern Kentucky, and she still sounded like it. There was nothing that Banick could throw at her, concerning me, that she hadn't lived, seen, or heard in a room she was in. She knew right from wrong, and what some White people's nonsense and rationalizations sounded like when it came to race, even when it donned a nice suit, possessed a college degree, and spewed relaxed poison to perfection in the King's English.

After school the next day, I went down to the auditorium to sit alone in the dim, dusty light, to gather my thoughts before going to talk to Mrs. Allison. It took about 5 minutes to think about the detailed presentation I wanted to give, but which proved to be unnecessary. Mrs. Allison was observant, and way ahead of me in some ways. She had her point of view on things in the school that I hadn't considered.

I walked up the set of old stairs to the third floor, while the school was very quiet, with no students in the halls. Mrs. Allison's classroom door was slightly open, and she was alone. I froze in the hallway out of her view, but I still could see her arms to the elbows. They were on her desk, as she was shuffling through stacks of student papers. After a final deep breath, I rapped gently on her door to announce my presence. She looked up at me without her usual easy smile. She already had seen the unease on my face that alerted her to something important that was coming her way.

I said, "Hello, Mrs. Allison, I need to speak to you about something." She looked up at me with some concern and said, "Yes, Larry. Come in. I have been expecting you."

I was not all that surprised to hear my showing up at her door was not unexpected. She was a very perceptive person with a keen eye for people and their behavior, which included me. We talked for about half an hour. I told her about the University of Delaware scholarship and the questionable, underhanded actions of Mrs. Lampson, the guidance counselor. Mrs. Allison was visibly disturbed, as I told her of my 2-year battle with Lampson concerning my college choice. I desired to go to an integrated college, and not a "colored college," but I was strongly, curiously, and paternalistically rebuffed by her. I told Mrs. Allison that of all the strange things that had happened to me in this school, the interaction with Lampson was the strangest, most complicated, and the most insulting. It was like she wanted me to voluntarily re-segregate myself to make her feel better since there wasn't much in it for me.

Mrs. Allison listened intently as I relayed my suspicions that the rejections from Delaware and Bucknell were likely related to what the administration wrote in their letters to the colleges. I believed this because nothing else made sense. I had gotten brochures sent to me from many college admissions offices last summer, including Bucknell. They contacted me to apply and then rejected me. It didn't make any sense, until it did. She mostly listened, but she asked a few questions to fill in the details. She wanted to know if I had any applications that had not been returned. I told her no, but I had the application to Syracuse University that I had not sent in. Whatever they wrote had not been seen by Syracuse.

Mrs. Allison understood exactly what I was saying, and she got it in ways I could not. She surely had been in the room, more than once, when the true unbridled feelings about race cascaded from the mouths of comfortable White people, in a safe setting. What she had heard from me agitated her to the point that her neck and facial skin areas were pulsing vermilion, accenting the tension in her jaw muscles.

Her voice remained controlled as she began to give me the direction I had come for. She told me that she believed everything I had said. Without saying anything directly, she seemed to have prior knowledge of, or suspicions about, dubious academic machinations coming from the school office, and involving me. Mrs. Allison scribbled a few notes on a piece of paper and told me to come see her tomorrow after school and to stay as far away from Banick and Lampson as possible.

I felt much better after speaking with Mrs. Allison, and it was good having someone else in the school aware of what was going on, other than the perpetrators. She gladly accepted sharing my burden and giving me some help in how to deal with some fairly backward and sly people. It was important to get the school straight on this point, so it doesn't happen to another Black student. Personally, I wanted the administration to never again feel so comfortable doing their dirty deeds in dark back rooms. Mrs. Allison was as tough as the hills she came from, and she didn't mind confronting her people about the way she knew they were. She looked genuinely offended by the transparent, ten-cent, flimflam plot cooked up by the office people, to limit where I went to college.

Basically, she was pissed…really, really pissed. I was sorry I was not going to see the show when she cornered and jacked up Banick, right in his own office. He knew what he did had no defense, but he didn't think he was going to need one. Banick was going to have the biggest surprise of his day, when Miss Gladys showed up full frame in his face, looking like a very aggrieved, and pissed-off, junkyard dog. Like that old blues song about hunting goes, "Shooty, Shooty, Bang, Bang…. It ain't no fun when the rabbit got the gun." They don't like it when the prey fights back....... Bang!! I had one bullet, and I used it.

The next day ticked by slowly, as I mostly secreted myself with Mr. Hovermill in the chemistry lab, with the smart kids from the 10th grade. I was hopelessly distracted the entire day thinking about college, Mrs. Allison, and the folks in the office. My money and an important part of my life was riding on her, and her willingness to take on every misguided assumption that Banick represented, endorsed, or lived.

By the afternoon, I assumed whatever was going to happen in the office had already occurred. The bomb had gone off, I just hadn't heard it yet or felt the blast. When the final class bell rang, I took my time going to my locker, wanting to give Mrs. Allison time to finish her school business, before our talk. On arrival at her room at about 3:30, she was in a state of barely controlled agitation and annoyance. She was even more riled than she was the day before, and I figured the meeting with Banick must have been one contentious donnybrook for all time. But what was his defense going to be after getting caught red-handed?

Mrs. Allison didn't give a blow-by-blow description of her meeting, and I didn't expect one. She usually didn't say specifically who she had talked to, and she didn't have to. She would use the pronoun "they" like I do a lot. I didn't need her to name any names because the list of likely suspects was extremely short. She had the shaken look of someone who had engaged with something intentionally malevolent and toxic, in close word-to-word combat. In a soft drawl, she said that she had demanded to see the full college transcripts sent on me. She didn't say how much of a tussle with Beelzebub it was to get it, but she got them. She read every word they had communicated to the colleges about me. After reading it, she was neither happy nor surprised. I was, unfortunately, correct in my suspicions of what Banick and Lampson had engineered in the shade.

Mrs. Allison found the letters misleading and containing questionable information or just plain untrue misperceptions on their part. She told me more of her reaction to whomever she had conversed, "I told them, I know what they are trying to do to you and that I am here to keep them from doing it," she recounted as I sat silently on the desk chair. "I told them that they are to rewrite a factual, unprejudiced evaluation of you and your academics, and give it to me tomorrow for my approval before it goes back in your records." Mrs. Allison backed up her request with a promise; if they didn't do it her way, then what they did would be made public in every way available to her, and she would try to make the heavens fall upon their useless pates. She told them, "I will not let you do this to him, and if I have to, I'll make you wish you took my first request more seriously because you are wrong…and you know it."

I was impressed but not surprised at the grit and determination she showed against them. They were clearly in the wrong, and there was not anything reasonable, or believable, they could begin to utter to justify what they had done. They got caught with no plan B and were rolled in their own cynical game by a Kentucky girl, who knew their every thought. It did not immediately help my position, but it was wonderful to see them get checked in style, just the same. Mrs. Allison told me to put in the application to Syracuse and that she would make sure the truthful letter was sent to the college.

But she was not finished. When the exasperation of the news from her meeting died down, she looked straight into my face and told me this; "None of this had anything to do with your grades, which is pretty obvious. Larry, they don't like you but don't have a good reason for it that does not involve the color of your skin. The major problem with you is that you are Black, and they do not like who your friends are. They specifically told me that. Do you understand what they are talking about? You were born with a couple of strikes against you, which you already know. You cannot make people like them just disappear because they have been around forever. You have to be aware of their presence, perspective, and power. They do not like that White students like and respect you, especially the girls, and you should be careful about that as much as you can."

All that was distressing and disappointing, but hardly surprising news. I thanked Mrs. Allison for all she had done. However, I had no intention of defending who my few good friends were to anyone. Besides that, Mom liked my friends and was very happy I had found people I could comfortably be with and learn from; that's all that counted for her this year. So, the office people wanted to pick the college that I would go to and my friends too, and those two things were not unrelated in their minds. That was "mighty white" of them, as the old southern saying goes.

They don't like my friends. All of them, or just some of them? Which ones? …. This was all the more telling and ridiculous since I didn't have the worrisome friends Banick was referring to, until the start of the school year. Before that, I was too busy purging those 4 colored "C"s from 9th grade science, given by a teacher who should not have been teaching Black students anywhere. I was busy with other things and unaware of any enjoyable sides to school that I may have been missing. School was a job, and a series of encounters to survive. I was not aware that who your friends were was a graded subject, but it was, in my case.

I shared a deliciously dark, smug little smirk with myself, at the prospect that these White folks may think I am a dangerous, swarthy Svengali, or an even darker practitioner of black voodoo, entraining my helpless, young, gullible White classmates in my thrall and control. Cool, if they thought I had that kind of power over their children. They were afraid of me, they just could not decide how much, or explain why in a way that didn't expose their bare racist sinew.

Mrs. Allison told me that she needed to speak to some people first, and then get back together with me, to share some thoughts about my future. I was relieved to have some help and direction in getting out of my hole, even so late in the year.

Havre de Grace Senior High School

700 CONGRESS AVENUE • HAVRE DE GRACE • MARYLAND • 21078

OFFICE OF THE PRINCIPAL

Date MAR 10 1969

To the Parents of Larry Ford :

I am very pleased to inform you that in a recent report to me, Larry's teachers report that he/she is doing superior work in the subjects listed below:

Problems of Democracy

Biochemistry

I hope this fine progress will continue. Your help and cooperation are greatly appreciated.

Sincerely yours,

Robert J. Banick
Principal

RJB:hlb

ADM. 22
3-1-67

(Photo by L. J. Ford)

Havre de Grace Senior High School

700 CONGRESS AVENUE • HAVRE DE GRACE • MARYLAND • 21078
OFFICE OF THE PRINCIPAL

Date _____ JAN 2 1968

To the Parents of _____ *Larry Ford* 11-5 :

I am very pleased to inform you that in a recent report to me, *Larry's* teachers report that he/she is doing superior work in the subjects listed below:

U. S. History

Chemistry

Physical Education

I hope this fine progress will continue. Your help and cooperation are greatly appreciated.

Sincerely yours,

Robert J. Banick
Principal

RJB:hlb

ADM. 22
3-1-67

(Photo by L. J. Ford)

238

CHAPTER 26

Old Black Joe

Syracuse University sent my acceptance letter quickly, within two weeks, which took a lot of pressure off. However, it didn't do much to help my attitude about Havre de Grace High School and my unending war with the people inside. I thought I knew a lot about how things worked in the world between Black and White people, but seeing the adults up close in the school daily gave me a greater appreciation of the lengths they would go to make things happen and the methods they would use to get what they wanted. They were manipulative and determined to influence my life in opposition to my wishes. It was chilling to speculate on the question of why they felt compelled to do it and why do it like this? They were sending me a message that I could not completely decode at the moment.

The school had never dealt with a student like me, who made them so uncomfortable. So, they decided to try to put me in a future racial quarantine at a "fine colored college" and away from them, their kind, and their anxieties. Okay…but to what end? In their view of the world, what was their ultimate plan for me and my place in America? Did I have a place in their country? School was almost over, and Mrs. Allison and her junkyard dog alter ego had insulated me well enough that I didn't expect any other major problems from the office people. I wasn't having a good time in my last days of school; I was still at war.

As vice president of the class of 1969, I had one official duty left to perform and two other promises to fulfill for two classmates before graduation. Of the two unofficial events, one was fun, coaching the class girls in softball against the teachers. A couple of days before it was scheduled, Lynn, the same classmate who tossed me the football in the girl's Powderpuff Game last year, asked me to be the coach of their team. I couldn't say no to an opportunity to hang out with the class ladies once more on an athletic field. Also, I knew Rudolph would play for the teachers and would surely have something negative to send my way once again.

The girls' softball team didn't actually need a coach, which made the offer and opportunity more endearing to me. My classmates liked hanging out with me even if Rudolph, and a few others, couldn't understand why. The girls did their part playing on the field, and I tried to keep things light and entertaining in the dugout and to make myself the butt of as many jokes as possible. There was a close play at first base that resulted in our girl being called out, which she probably was. At that point, I channeled my inner Earl Weaver, the argumentative, mercurial, curmudgeonly gnome-like manager of the Baltimore Orioles. I pretended to be exercised over the bad call and was nearly apoplectic, with faux incredulity thrown in for a minute. The girls had fun watching their nerdy, usually quiet classmate going off the rails over a baseball play.

Of course, Robert Rudolph saw nothing funny in it or me. After the game, he had the complete shamelessness, and fortuitous shortness of memory, to inquire why I had ruined the softball game for everybody with my antics. At that point, I knew for sure he lived in a house and world without mirrors or other reflective surfaces. That was my last encounter with Rudolph. And overall, in our personal cold war, he lost, and he knew it. But to his credit, he always gave me the grade that I earned in his class, which was usually an "A."

The most intriguing request, late in the year, was from my classmate Jack, who headed a school social organization that was associated with the town's Rotary Club. Jack's club did community service around the town. I was never a member of his club, but he asked if I would come to a meeting with the Rotarians at the Bayou Restaurant. Given the long history of the soft segregation of many restaurants in Havre de Grace, it would be my first time going to a hometown eatery, ever. Most people that I knew didn't go to restaurants in town either because of feeling unwelcome or hearing of the experiences of other Black people. It wasn't something talked about often; it was just a fact about the town. I had always wanted to know what clubs like the Rotary, Elks, Oddfellows, and the Masons do. It all seemed so very White, secretive, and mysterious by design. I had heard the food was very good at the Bayou, which would add to my late school year adventure.

The Rotary Club met monthly, and we would be their guests. There were about eight high school classmates at the meeting with many important business owners of the town. I knew several of them by face, but most were strangers. They were ten, or twelve older White men who seemed to own everything around. They were bankers, realtors, manufacturers of various products, and generally the kind of people I would never meet on my own. We took our places at the tables in the dining room, as the restaurant staff prepared to serve our food. The head Rotarian an overweight, balding man with a droning monotone of a voice and not a particularly kind face, was in charge at the head table. He called the meeting to order, welcoming the members and the high school guests.

Then, as was apparently their custom, the leader led the group in singing the selected song to start the meeting, "Old Black Joe." I didn't know what to think about the song choice, but I didn't sing it. I sat listening and wondering why?

> Gone are the days when my heart was young and gay,
> Gone are the friends from the cotton fields away,
> Gone from the earth to a better land I know,
> I can hear the darkies singing, Old Black Joe

I had been asking myself the same question for 5 years: Are White adults that clueless, or they simply don't give much thought to the feelings and sensibilities of persons different than themselves? However, the answer to the question was less important than devising a way to survive living in a country populated with singers of songs like "Old Black Joe" without totally wasting my time and health. We never sang "Old Black Joe" at the Consolidated School, just like we didn't celebrate Slave Day. Like Mrs. Allison told me, these people are out there, and they aren't going away. I have to deal with them on my terms, as much as possible, but realize their ability to change is limited in the short run, and willingness to do so is negligible, always.

My remaining official duty item left on my plate was surviving Senior Day. On that day, late in the school year, the graduating senior class got to take over the school and a good part of the city government too. It was usually a fun day for everyone, and it was impossible to cut class that day. Some of the seniors went downtown to city hall or the police department, shadowing the movers, shakers, and jailers of the town. At the school, seniors would be teaching classes, assisting somewhere, or just plain old playing hooky.

The president of our class, Ralph, was to be the school principal for the day, and I was scheduled to be the vice principal by line of succession. As I was walking to school the morning of Senior Day, I had a lot to think about, like— how am I going to make it through the day, being in the office close to Banick? The same office where Mrs. Allison put the Bogart on him, right in his face. I still had never spoken a word to Banick, and I was hoping to keep that record intact, but it was not looking good. There may have been no way out of hearing his voice today.

When I got to school, I quickly learned that things were a lot worse than I could have imagined. Ralph loved drafting and engineering. So, he decided to teach the drafting class instead of being the school principal for the day. His abdication elevated me to be school principal, which I wanted no part of. I was hiding out in an empty classroom, looking for some inspiration or a simple, quick answer to my problem. It was nice playing Ralph's vice president because I didn't have to do anything. He was a study in efficiency. He had no idea what a potential ill wind he had left me by teaching drafting. I didn't have to ponder, scheme, or pray on it for too long.

My salvation, and deliverance, came walking down the hall in the person of a classmate, Cindy, who wasn't in the line of class succession. But she was in the Student Council, and she bore a needed gift for me. My classmate had decided she really wanted to be school principal for the day, and all she had to do was to convince me that the change would be in my interest too. Cindy had no idea that I wanted her to be the principal also, and, likely, I wanted it more than she did. We did a little Tom Sawyer fence whitewashing jig together before I gave her what we both wanted; for her to have a day in the principal's office with Robert J.

Banick. Cindy was very happy, and I was very relieved. There was nothing to be gained with any attempt at communication with the office people. I was sick of them and was looking forward to life minus their baggage.

It felt like I had avoided something that would have been agonizing, at the least, and unlikely to generate any good feelings for anyone. I am terrible at making small talk with people I detest and who feel the same about me. We understood each other and there was no reason to pretend there was a reason to exchange ideas on anything. Banick had already shown me exactly who he was. Free of the office of the principal for the day, I found the school's actual vice principal, Mr. Meade, who I was pretty sure was aware of my situation with Banick on some level. I thought Mr. Meade was a good man, and he might understand my not wanting to be around the office a lot on senior day or any other day.

For most of the time as vice principal, I walked around the school halls and stuck my head into a couple of classrooms where my friends were teaching, including Ralph's drafting class. But the safest place for me was across Congress Avenue, in the gym building. It was as far away from the office as you could be and still be on school grounds.

I found coach Marron in his office, and I bothered him for a while, talking about football, girls, school, and my future plans. He was a plain shooter and easy to talk to. I wanted to ask him about that pretty woman who showed up at football practice that day last summer. The one who parked her pink Mustang in front of the practice field, and everything stopped…. everything. Coach Marron just smiled at the memory as the bell rang for the change of class, and he never did answer my question about the Mustang lady. We both got a good laugh out of it, which was all that mattered.

When the final bell rang at the end of the day, I thought I had won, and my five-year record of never speaking a word to Banick was intact and solid as ever. Graduation was the following week, and it couldn't come soon enough.

Meanwhile, back at school, the class was trying to find an acceptable site to host our graduation party. Many people wanted the function to be held at the Elks club in town, where many of my White classmates had eaten. They raved about the food and atmosphere of the place. But we weren't able to get the Elks Club, and the party was held at the bowling alley, in Aberdeen, where we could all attend. I wondered what songs the Elks sang to open their meetings.

CHAPTER 27

A Warm Hug

By the time graduation day came, I was ready to pack up and make my getaway from the halls of the Havre de Grace High School, the erstwhile white school, and all the mess and commotion that came along senior year. My classmates were happy, too, about moving on to their future. Everyone knew where they were going to college, what service branch they were headed for, where they would start working. And a few even to marry. "Enter to learn, leave to serve" was the motto over the schoolhouse door.

I certainly did learn a lot. Much of it was from the books, and the rest was from what I had witnessed, engaged in, been affected by, and managed to survive. The non-book knowledge was painful priceless, and, I hoped, useful. There was no doubt that the knowledge gained would be called upon again and would be essential in my understanding of and future negotiations with my country.

It was only fitting that the buffeted, politically whipsawed Class of 1969 got to go out to some absolutely fabulous music. You could be cutting class, driving around town, or up Route 155, listening to "Light My Fire," "Ode to Billy Joe," or "Sergeant Pepper," Or you'd be groovin' down Route 40 to all 17 minutes of Iron Butterfly's "In a Gadda Da Vida" on your self-installed 8-track tape deck, with your best buddy riding shotgun, in your Chevy SS 396. You could be cruising downtown, in your Mama's Pontiac ride, or down to the park, digging on Junior

Walker's "What Does It Take," Marvin Gaye's "Heard It Through the Grapevine" or Sly and the Family Stone's "Dance to the Music."

And, of course, the class was regularly treated in school to Buddy's dancing in the hall and singing "It's Your Thing," with a little step to go with it. Buddy loved the Isley Brothers and even Jimi Hendrix, who I still didn't quite get. Bootsy loved music too, and his main thing was to over-animate "Expressway to Your Heart." Music seemed almost as important as breathing to many in the Class of 1969. We also had Bubble Gum music on the radio to balance out the acid rock, so the little guys would have something more wholesome to consume. Oh, yes. We had the music.

However, I was still picking through the wreckage of the last semester. I got to see how things worked and some of the people who were working it. But I wasn't supposed to see it and then recognize it for exactly what it was. Now, I was probably more dangerous than what they were afraid of, to begin with, thanks to them.

The perpetrators were very mad at Mrs. Allison and me. She backed them down but way short of the point of embarrassment or enlightenment. I was only hoping that some of the younger Black students had seen Karen and me on the Honor Society stage 2 years ago. I wanted them to know that doing well was possible, even with people like Lampson and Banick around. Lampson never did mention the University of Delaware scholarship to me, but she had to know I was aware of who she gave it to. I wondered if she told that student not to tell me about it also, like she had told Bootsy. But mainly, I was still mystified by how she could justify her actions when she was alone, all by herself. Or if she ever even thought about what she had done.

It seemed that at the end of the semester, hardly any seniors were in school in the afternoons, and nobody cared. They were enjoying the great tunes and weather in our last days of pre-adulthood. I went to all my classes because I didn't know what else to do. My head was somewhere else, though. I was sure that, except for Bootsy Jr., no one in my class had a clue as to what was going on with me and the office people. But my classmates had been unaware of what I, and other Black students, had been dealing with for the last five years, even when it was occurring in their sight and right under their noses, daily.

There were no more official class vice presidential duties for me to perform. As long as Ralph, the class president, stayed healthy enough to deliver his scheduled graduation address, things would remain that way. It was almost too righteous to think about, and it was unneeded fodder for my more inappropriate cerebral regions; if Ralph were indisposed, I would be in line to give the graduation speech as the class vice president. It would be unlikely that Mr. Banick would ever let that happen. At this point, he shouldn't have had any faith that I would conduct myself in a way that would make him proud or comfortable.

Watching me deliver the graduation speech may have sent him right over the edge. He would have found some excuse to stop it, by either a sleight of hand or with a more ham-fisted remedy. In my dream speech, I would not have been able to comport myself like I had learned all those years at the Colored School. It would be joyous letting loose a couple of well-directed verbal harpoons and an appropriately tart final bow shot, given in perfect Latin before they called the law. No, that wasn't going to happen, but it was satisfying seditious thought.

The next day, I saw Butch walking in the hall with Rita. He saw me and yelled out, "Hey Jake! Wait up!" Butch caught up with me and immediately started laughing to the point of near strangulation. "Jake" was the name that Bootsy and Butch had given to me over the last 2 years of school, and it stuck in our small circle. The handle "Jake" was always prefaced with "Shakin'."

Butch goes, "Man, I got something funny to tell you." It must have been funny because he could hardly get it out. "You know, Ford, my mom is old Italian, so she has her set ways." He was trying to compose himself, and not destroy the timing of the morsel he was delivering. He finally got it together enough to say, "My mother must have seen Lee driving you and Buddy in the park yesterday. So, she said to me, 'You Know, I saw Lee driving his car with those two classmates of yours. Doesn't Lee have anything better to do than drive those two colored boys around all day?'" — She was concerned that Lee may be wasting his time when he could be engaged in more gainful activities.

When I heard it, I let out a full belly laugh that bounced off the floor and walls of the hall and came back to me in an instant. It was easy to see why Butch had so much trouble getting it out in the first place. We were laughing so hard that we had to hold each other up as we rolled against the lockers. We both had tears in our eyes, knowing that the answer to his mom's question was this; No. Lee had nothing better to do than drive the two "colored boys" around that day because that was what Lee wanted to do.

We left it at that, knowing his mom would never quite get it. Butch and I knew it was the kind of laugh you could have only after knowing a person for some years and being sure we were laughing about the same thing. If Butch had a car, he would drive me around, too, if I needed it, and vice versa. It was a good, unexpected laugh to start the day. Some adults just couldn't grasp the fact that most of their children had no problem being friends with people who were not White...most of them.

A few days before graduation, Mrs. Allison told me to drive up to her home near Bel Air, to have a serious talk. I knew I had selected the right "Junkyard Dog," who also knew Shakespeare, but I didn't fully comprehend the bargain that had come my way. She was personally offended, but not surprised, by the deceitful shenanigans of the office people, and she was invested in undoing some of the evil they had sent my way.

She was even more capable and connected than I was aware. Mrs. Allison had been watching me closely, in her class and out, for two years. She had also been in meetings, the halls, and in the teacher's room to hear whatever information was being wafted about on a particular day. There was no telling what kind of things had been said about me at the school for several years, but not all bad. I didn't really care what they said since it was obvious that Banick and Lampson couldn't find anything about me to like, but a lot that they wanted to control or have a furtive, villainous hand in a particular outcome. And of course people like Mr. Rudolph didn't matter, except as tools of my social education and unintended deep cultural learning of how some White men just comfortably are when it comes to interacting with Black people when no one is listening.

I was fortunate to have Mrs. Allison there when I hit a scripted slick spot in school and was sent careening into a pre-arranged skid. I never asked for help from anyone for anything. But I knew I needed help at that most critical time in all my schooling. We talked in her living room for an hour, after which I finally had a much better vision of what my future could be.

She told me things I had never heard at the high school. She sincerely thought that I was very smart, to a degree that I would not dare entertain myself. My abilities had not been appreciated or were ignored by some at the school. But people knew I was not an average anything, and that was a scary problem for some. If it had been anyone else, another Black student not named Ford, the office probably wouldn't have been as dismissive and later hostile. After all, they did find an acceptable Black student to award the scholarship to the University of Delaware. I was not acceptable in their eyes, but acceptance by them was never expected or sought by me. I simply wanted to pass through them on the route planned by me.

Mrs. Allison thought that the study of the sciences would fit my personality. Or, I could do non-science-based study, too, if I wanted. She said not everyone was capable of doing both. She had thought about a college that would fit my abilities and desire for a fine education. Her choice was The Johns Hopkins University in Baltimore. I first thought she was kidding before remembering that she doesn't kid. I had looked at Johns Hopkins but never considered applying. The school was very small, with a class size of about 700. It was renowned for its expertise in science and medicine. It was a very serious, little, all-boys school, a fact that wasn't lost on Mrs. Allison. For her, it heightened the school's desirability, in my case. It didn't bother me, either. I mean, I didn't go to either prom in high school and didn't feel like I had missed anything.

I would go to Syracuse for a year, do very well, and then apply for a transfer to Johns Hopkins. She gave me some information about the school and told me to think about it because it would require some work and dedication on my part. She told me we should talk again in a week after graduation.

I drove back home with a new direction and a lot to think about. She was refreshingly serious and encouraging. And she was, without question, on my side. She was, in many ways, like Mrs. J.P. Turner, my 5th grade teacher from the Consolidated School.

The next two days in school went by without incident. The class walked, strolled, pimp-rolled, and laughed our way through graduation practice in the gymnasium. I assumed the partying went on after school hours too in anticipation of our ascent to adulthood and being a day closer to paying our own bills.

Mom was happy that I would be the second of her children to graduate with honors, a first for Black families at the Havre de Grace High School. Mom never outwardly emoted much over our academic achievements. Due to her guiding hand through the years, she expected her children to do well. She provided us with the awareness, direction, and attitude for us to make it. But basically, she knew what kind of brains she gave us, and the rest was up to us.

I had managed to hide from Mom most of the goings on of the tumultuous last three months of school, which was difficult. I eventually told her what happened during senior year when it was safe; about forty years later. She was not happy hearing about what happened even then. She was satisfied by the fact that I was able to figure out things for myself, knew when to get help, smacked some folks around a bit on my way out the door, and that I never let them see me sweat, not once.

I sincerely hoped that Karen and I made it easier for the young Black scholars in the auditorium watching on the day of our National Honor Society induction. I didn't want another Black student to have to conquer social and academic funambulism just to make it through high school. And equally, I didn't want the administration, counselors, or teachers to think they could easily get away with what they did one more time. I was lucky to have found out what they were up to in time to blunt some of their deviousness and treachery. The next Black student may not be so fortunate as to have a person like Mrs. Allison around, to even things out.

On graduation day, everybody was "Pomped," "Circumstanced," and ready to go. The evening was classic high school graduation fare, with School Board dignitaries, as well as school administrators and guests on the stage. Our class president, Ralph, gave a speech to the graduates and audience entitled "The Times They Are A Changing." It was timely, well received, and aptly named. I was staring at the people on the graduation stage, and a couple of them doubled as suspects in my eyes. It was a relief that this would be the last few minutes of my subjugation to their particular, and peculiar, views on education and society. Banick, the principal felt he had the right to negatively view me because of my acquaintances in the 12th grade, above all else. He felt comfortable saying it to Mrs. Allison, like it was a reasonable, rational take on things, instead of the reactionary racist reflex it truly was. She knew it was self-serving nonsense based solely on who I was and his reaction to people like me.

It seemed like I could always be under suspicion, or on trial, for something they ginned up or decided was lacking on my part. It took a lot of effort, and some guile, for me to get out of high school in one piece, and I was hoping the rest of my education wouldn't be full of all this extra weight. No doubt, this kind of double-dealing was a part of the system, which was available for the intended use by its devotees…no instructions needed. Many White people knew the not-so-secret game well, as well as the fallacies it was built on. I had gotten a little peek at the cogs inside the machine that had served them so well for so long.

I was trying to process the knowledge gained and square it with what I had suspected all along. I knew a few things for sure; the devotees of the system were self-righteous, happily delusional (when needed), and willing to exercise their alternative reality option frequently while getting the desired effects, generally. They had been at it for a while, and they were good, efficient, and blameless. But beneath all the bluster, power, intimidation, and gaslighting, there was a genuine, unaddressed, essential fear in them, of something…of anything…of everything different. It seemed they always needed to be afraid of something, which justified whatever they wanted to do next.

I would occasionally glance over at my family, sitting in the crowd. My little sisters were excited, as usual. My brother was observing and taking in everything in the gymnasium. Mom was looking confident and satisfied, knowing she would see her second child wearing a gold tassel, signifying academic excellence, and graduating with honors. She was as excited as Mom got.

I wasn't excited, just relieved and ready to break out of jail as soon as possible. The time to receive diplomas, had come. As it had occurred daily for almost five years, our names were called alphabetically once more, starting with Andrews and ending with Wooten. My final bit of grace came from the fact that Mr. Meade, the vice principal, was giving us our diplomas; so I didn't have to touch any part of Banick on the way out. Before my name was called I was able to make eye contact with Karen, my old friend from the 1st grade at Havre de Grace Consolidated School, C1. She also was adorned with the gold honors tassel of academic achievement in the class of 1969. She was quietly super intelligent, and

I was always happy to try to keep up with her in class. Everybody liked Karen, and nobody ever bothered her, despite her being so very smart. But she was a girl with brains like my sister, Pat.

The pace of the procession had picked up, and things were moving along nicely. I returned to my seat after getting my exit papers and casting a short parting glare Banick's way. If he had bothered to look, I wanted him to know what I was thinking and the contempt I held for him one final time. He was going to be glad I was gone, so he could stop worrying about me corrupting the nice, smart, popular, and otherwise exemplary White students at the school, which was delusional at best.

After Wooten received her diploma, the final remarks were given, and the Class of 1969 was free to retire to the cafeteria for our final meeting. The room was noisy and bustling with talking, laughing, and a bit of requisite wistfulness, mixed with a lot of "I am happy that it is finally over!"

I was saying goodbye to people around me, or I'll see you at the bowling alley, when I noticed across the cafeteria, Sandy, with the big blue eyes, from eighth grade Slave Day. She was one of my classmates who wasn't a close friend but I wanted to make it a point to say goodbye to her. She was a very nice and brave girl. I hugged her and said good luck. I got to talk a little with long leg Lee, Buddy, and Bootsy. I saw a few teacher including Miss McGreevy, the drama teacher, Mr. Johnson, and Mrs. Allison.

Some of the ex-Consolidated ladies, Barbara, Wanda, and KK, were standing together with Bootsy, Elroy, and Jeff Christy near the punch bowl table. They all looked delighted because we had made it through the White School and came out of the experience mostly okay.

While all the conversing and cavorting was playing out, one valiant teacher with a microphone was trying to read congratulatory messages sent from well-wishers to the class by Western Union telegram. The teacher was reading the names of the senders, some of whom she knew as former elementary school teachers of the class. Many of my classmates reacted positively to hearing the names, and the greetings, with clapping and vocal approval. To that point, I didn't know any of the names she had read, but the next name was unfamiliar to her, and she stumbled over it a bit.

"This is a message…I don't recognize the name…but it was sent from Indiana…. from a Miss Carry McWhite," said the teacher.

The room was in a low buzz, trying to figure out who Miss McWhite was and why she sent congratulations to the Class of 1969 of Havre de Grace High School. Bootsy, Karen, and Barbara heard the name too, and it was instantly recognized as an unexpected thrill for some of us. It felt like a warm, comfortable, long distance Consolidated hug from my 1st grade teacher that closed my educational circle, and it put things in a better perspective on my bitter-sweet graduation day.

I immediately straightened myself up, as if I was again in her classroom, and I thought to myself, "Well, I guess Miss McWhite forgave me for breaking her long, pretty fingernails while she was putting on my rubber boots on rainy days because I couldn't." She was my very first teacher at the Consolidated School. Hearing from her on graduation day, after all these years, put a smile on my face and gave a needed boost of determination to my foundation, so carefully built by our beloved teachers.

The principal and vice-principal with the officers of the Class of 69'. I was the first Black student elected as a class officer at Havre de Grace High School.

Images: Courtesy of Harford County Board of Education

My fellow officers and I standing on campus.

Images: Courtesy of Harford County Board of Education..

My summer chemistry student, Penny, and I were elected "Best All Around" for the Class of 1969.

Images: Courtesy of Harford County Board of Education

In the loving memory of my mother, Mrs. Mercides Robinson Griffin —
A Phenomenal Woman.
LJF/FORD/GRIFFIN COLLECTION!!!

Printed in the USA
CPSIA information can be obtained
at www.ICGtesting.com
LVHW041447141023
761111LV00001B/51

9 781647 498306